Computer Science Workbench

Editor: Tosiyasu L. Kunii

Computer Science Workbench

N. Magnenat Thalmann, D. Thalmann: Image Synthesis. Theory and Practice. XV, 400 pp., 223 figs., including 80 in color. 1987

B. A. Barsky: Computer Graphics and Geometric Modeling Using Beta-splines. IX, 156 pp., 85 figs., including 31 in color. 1987

H. Kitagawa, T. L. Kunii: The Unnormalized Relational Data Model. For Office Form Processor Design. XIII, 164 pp., 78 figs. 1989

N. Magnenat Thalmann, D. Thalmann: Computer Animation. Theory and Practice. Second Revised Edition. XIII, 245 pp., 156 figs., including 73 in color. 1990

N. Magnenat Thalmann, D. Thalmann: Synthetic Actors in Computer-Generated 3D Films. X, 129 pp., 133 figs., including 83 in color. 1990

Nadia Magnenat Thalmann
Daniel Thalmann

Computer Animation

Theory and Practice

Second Revised Edition

With 156 Figures, Including 73 in Color

Springer-Verlag Tokyo Berlin Heidelberg New York
London Paris Hong Kong Barcelona

Prof. NADIA MAGNENAT THALMANN
MIRALab, CUI
University of Geneva
12, rue du Lac
CH-1207 Geneva
Switzerland
Phone: 41-22-787-6581
Fax: 41-22-735-3905
Email: thalmann@uni2a.unige.ch

Prof. DANIEL THALMANN
Computer Graphics Lab.
Swiss Federal Institute of Technology
CH-1015 Lausanne
Switzerland
Phone: 41-21-693-5214
Fax: 41-21-693-3909
Email: thalmann@eldi.epfl.ch

Series Editor:
TOSIYASU L. KUNII
Professor and Chairman
Department of Information Science
Faculty of Science
The University of Tokyo
7-3-1 Hongo, Bunkyo-ku
Tokyo, 113 Japan

ISBN-13: 978-4-431-68107-6   e-ISBN-13: 978-4-431-68105-2
DOI: 10.1007/978-4-431-68105-2

Library of Congress Cataloging-in-Publication Data

Magnenat Thalmann, Nadia, 1946-
Computer animation: theory and practice/Nadia Magnenat Thalmann, Daniel
Thalmann, — 2nd rev. ed. p. cm. — (Computer science workbench) Includes bibliog-
raphical references and index. 1. Computer animation.
I. Thalmann, Daniel. II. Title. III. Series. TR897.5.M33 1990 006.6—dc20 90-46535

Typesetting: Asco Trade Typesetting Ltd., Hong Kong
Printing: Sanshodo Printing, Tokyo
Binding: Kubota Binding, Tokyo

Series Preface

Computer Science Workbench is a monograph series which will provide you with an in-depth working knowledge of current developments in computer technology. Every volume in this series will deal with a topic of importance in computer science and elaborate on how you yourself can build systems related to the main theme. You will be able to develop a variety of systems, including computer software tools, computer graphics, computer animation, database management systems, and computer-aided design and manufacturing systems. Computer Science Workbench represents an important new contribution in the field of practical computer technology.

Tosiyasu L. Kunii

Preface to the Second Edition

Computer graphics is growing very rapidly; only computer animation grows faster. The first edition of the book *Computer Animation: Theory and Practice* was released in 1985. Four years later, computer animation has exploded. Conferences on computer animation have appeared and the topic is recognized in well-known journals as a leading theme. Computer-generated film festivals now exist in each country and several thousands of films are produced each year. From a commercial point of view, the computer animation market has grown considerably. TV logos are computer-made and more and more simulations use the technique of computer animation. What is the most fascinating is certainly the development of computer animation from a research point-of-view. Until 1985, the theory of computer animation was rather poor. In 1989, the situation has really improved and excellent papers have been published. This second edition tries to take into account these new trends in computer animation.

This second edition brings major changes in various chapters. In particular, the discussion of organizations in the field of computer animation has been updated, and new teams in this area are mentioned. Three-dimensional (3D) computer animation is emphasized: in a new chapter, the basic techniques of geometric modeling are introduced, and another chapter covers important concepts in motion control like 3D shape interpolation, parametric keyframe animation, and algorithmic animation. The two chapters on rendering have been considerably improved and new techniques have been added: complex light sources, radiosity, and optimization techniques for ray-tracing and solid texturing. The chapter on human modeling and animation has been completely rewritten and now discusses body deformations and abstract muscles in facial animation. A completely new chapter on automatic motion control has been added; it introduces the impact of mechanics, robotics and artificial intelligence in computer animation. In particular, the following topics are presented: positional constraints, inverse kinematics, dynamics, adaptive motion control, trajectory planning, obstacle avoidance, deformation based on finite element theory, task planning, and behavioral animation. The last chapter explains the making of

Dream Flight, Rendez-vous à Montreal, Galaxy Sweetheart, and *Eglantine* directed by the authors.

The appendix provides an exhaustive list of computer-generated films from 1961 to 1989. Finally, a complete bibliography on computer animation is given at the end of the book.

N. MAGNENAT THALMANN
D. THALMANN

Acknowledgements

The authors are very grateful to Professor Tosiyasu L. Kunii who strongly encouraged the publication of this book. They would also like to thank all the individuals and organizations who provided illustrative material and/or comments and suggestions:

Norman Badler, University of Pennsylvania
Loren Carpenter, Pixar
Edwin Catmull, Pixar
Robert Cook, Light Source Computer Images
Franklin Crow, Xerox PARC
Charles Csuri, Ohio State University
Tom DeFanti, University of Illinois
William Fetter, SIROCO, Bellevue, Washington
Alain Fournier, University of British Columbia
Copper Giloth, Real Time Design Inc.
Donald Greenberg, Cornell University
Pat Hanrahan, Princeton University
Don Herbison Evans, University of Sidney
Pat Lehman, Community College of Denver
Nelson Max, Lawrence Livermore Laboratory
Xavier Nicolas, Ex Machina, France
Alan Norton, IBM
Frederic I. Parke, New York Institute of Technology
C. Sleichter, Computer Image Corp.
Jane Veeder, Real Time Design Inc.
Marceli Wein, National Research Council of Canada
David Zeltzer, MIT
Association for Computing Machinery
IEEE Computer Society

The authors are also indebted to the students and research assistants who have produced images with the MIRA system: Philippe Bergeron, Marie-Andreé Allaire, Dominique Boisvert, Benoit Lafleur, Richard Laperrière, François Marceau, Lucie Marchard and Ross Racine. They also would like to thank Ann Laporte who revised the English text.

The authors express their gratitude to the "Service de la Recherche des Hautes Etudes Commerciales de Montréal," which partly sponsored the production of the illustrations.

Finally, the authors are very thankful to Evelyn Kohl of the University of Geneva (Switzerland), who has produced the manuscript of this book.

Table of Contents

1. Introduction

In the beginning, computers were used to assist animators in conventional animation. As early as 1974, in Hungarian Peter Foldes won the *Prix du Jury* at the Cannes
Film Festival with his computer-aided film, *Hunger*. This film is based primarily on
the so-called "interpolation" technique which involves supplying the computer with
two drawings and asking it to compose a certain number of intermediate images.
The technique was a boon to animated-film makers, since the essence of animation
lies in producing a rapid series of drawings, each slightly different from its pre-
decessor, to create the impression of movement or change in shape.

From a technical point-of-view, we know from the theory of computer graphics
that two-dimensional and three dimensional (3D) graphical objects may be constructed using geometric modeling techniques. In a three-dimensional space, scenes
are viewed using synthetic or virtual cameras and they may be lighted by synthetic
light sources. These techniques are important because they allow any geometrical,
physical, or chemical situation to be visualized **at any given time**. However, the most
interesting aspect of many phenomena is their **evolution over time**; e.g., motion of
electromechanical devices (robots), chemical reactions, fluid motion, cloud motions,
or heat conduction. Experiments are often very expensive and sometimes impossible; e.g., crashes or explosions. It is generally easier and less expensive to produce
computer simulations of such phenomena.

This type of complex graphical simulation is also computer animation. But in
this case, it consists of making a three-dimensional scene evolve over time. Consider
for example a 3D scene; we may say that it is composed of three types of entities:
objects, cameras, and lights. Each entity has characteristics which may evolve over
time according to arbitrary complex laws:

1. **For objects:**
   location (e.g., car), orientation (e.g., robot arm), size (e.g., plant evolution), shape
   (e.g., cloud, human heart), color (e.g., fire, sunrise), transparency (e.g., fog simulation)
2. **For cameras:**
   viewer position (e.g., flight simulator), interest point (e.g., tracking), view angle
   (e.g., zoom in)
3. **For light sources:**
   intensity (e.g., nightclubs), location (e.g., car light simulation)

One of the main challenges for the next few years is the development of an integrated animation system for the creation and animation of three-dimensional scenes involving **human beings conscious of their environment**. Such a system should be based on an interdisciplinary approach, and integrate aspects and methods from animation, mechanics, robotics, physiology, psychology, and artificial intelligence (A.I.). The system should achieve the following objectives:

- automatically produce computer-generated human beings with natural behavior.
- improve the complexity and the realism of motion; realism of motion needs to be improved not only from the joint point-of-view as for robots, but also in relation to the deformations of bodies, hands, and faces during animation.
- reduce the complexity of motion description.

In future animation systems, based on synthetic actors, motion control will tend to be automatically performed using A.I. and robotics techniques. In particular, motion will be planned at a **task level** and computed using physical laws.

As computer animation evolves, the new generation of animators will direct synthetic actors like Marilyn and Humphrey in the film *Rendez-vous à Montréal*, using very simple commands in natural language. The question is now: should we continue to use the term "computer animation"?

At a behavioral level, we will have to take into account group level behavior as well as individual behavior. For example, in the task of walking, everybody walks more or less the same way, following more or less the same laws. This is the "more or less" which will be difficult to model. And also a person does not always walk the same way every day. If the person is tired, or happy, or just got some good news, the way of walking will appear slightly different. So in the future, another big challenge is open for the computer animation field: to model human behavior taking into account social differences and individualities. Finally, computer animation will have less and less to do with the techniques of traditional animation. A computer director will direct at the video screen synthetic actors, decors, lights, and cameras, using commands. If it is in real time, it will be like directing a real film but in a synthetic world. We will enter into the era of producing real computer-generated films, produced in a virtual world and directed by real human directors.

2. Conventional Animation

2.1 Basic Principles of Conventional Animation

Animation can be defined in different ways. For John Halas [1968], one of the world's most famous animators, "movement is the essence of animation." A similar approach defines animation as "art in movement." Some more precise definitions are given below:

1. Animation is a technique in which the illusion of movement is created by photographing a series of individual drawings on successive frames of film. The illusion is produced by projecting the film at a certain rate (typically 24 frames/second).
2. Animation refers to the process of dynamically generating a series of frames of a set of objects, in which each frame is an alteration of the previous frame.

Although these definitions describe the principle of animation as it was conceived 80 years ago, they are still valid today in many cases. Conventional animation is generally based on a frame-by-frame technique. Computer animation is often carried out using a similar strategy. However, in the case of real-time animation, the definitions (especially the first one) are inaccurate. For example, video games are quite different from the products of conventional animation. Moreover, it is quite limitative to state that animation is similar to movement, because animation can exist without movement, for example:

– In metamorphosis, where one object is transformed into another
– In color changes (e.g., the hero turns red with emotion)
– In changes of light intensity (e.g., the sun disappears behind the mountains)

Conventional animation is oriented mainly towards the production of two-dimensional cartoons. Every frame is a flat picture and is purely hand-drawn. These cartoons are complex to produce and may involve large teams like Walt Disney or Hannah-Barbera productions.

2.2 How Are Cartoon Animated Films Made?

Cartoon animated films are produced in studios, which differ in their production methodologies. However, a brief description of the major common steps can be given:

1. **The story**
   As in an ordinary film, the animated film generally tells a story. To describe this story, three "documents" are required, each refining of the previous one:
   - **The synopsis** is a summary of the story in a few lines (one page maximum).
   - **The scenario** is a detailed text that describes the complete story without any cinematographic references.
   - **The storyboard** is a film in outline form. It consists of a number of illustrations arranged in comic-strip fashion with appropriate captions. The number of individual illustrations within a storyboard will vary widely. What is important is that they represent the film's key moments. It is also important to note that a film is composed of **sequences** that define specific actions. Each sequence consists of a series of **scenes** that are generally defined by a certain location and set of characters. Scenes are divided into shots that are considered as picture units. Figure 2.1 shows the organization of a film.

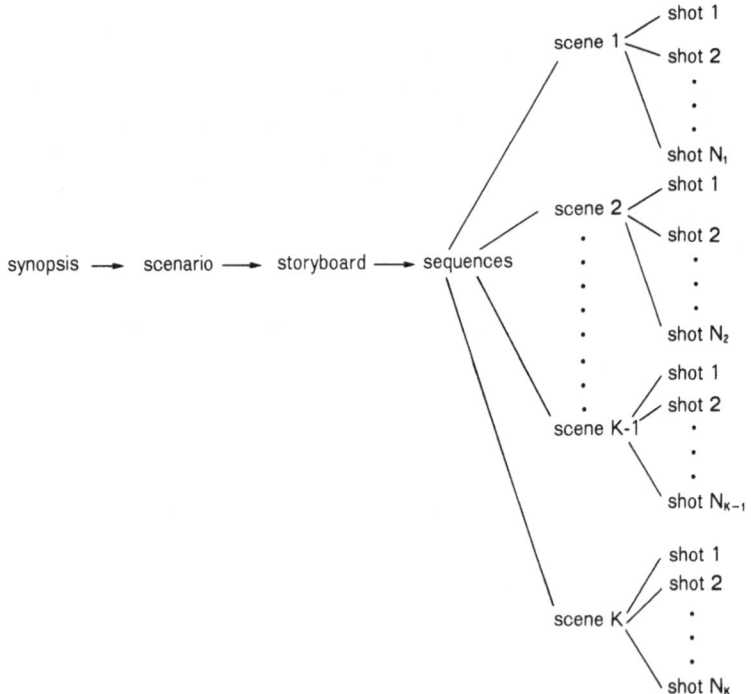

Fig. 2.1. Organization of a film

2. **Layout**

   This step consists mainly of the design of the characters to be animated and action plotting. Based on the storyboard, the relationship between shapes and forms in the background and foreground is decided.

   The layout department in an animation studio has to finish drawings of the settings and sketch background layouts. The artists must have knowledge of the physical characteristics of the camera that will be used to photograph the frames.

3. **Sound track**

   In conventional animation, sound track recording has to precede the animation process, since the motion must match the dialog and/or music.

4. **Animation**

   The animation process is carried out by animators who draw key frames. Often an animator is responsible for one specific character.

5. **In-betweening**

   "In-betweens" are defined as drawings which are placed between two key positions, or frames. Assistant animators draw some in-betweens and in-betweeners draw the remaining figures. The work of the assistant animators requires more artistry than that of in-betweeners, whose task is almost automatic.

6. **Xeroxing and inking**

   Sketches are usually drawn in pencil. They then have to be transferred to acetate cels, using modified Xerox cameras. Lines must be inked in by hand.

7. **Painting**

   As cartoon animated films are usually in color, they must go through a painting stage. This work requires patience and accuracy. Cels must have the right degree of opacity and static backgrounds also have to be painted.

8. **Checking**

   Animators need to check the action in their scenes before shooting.

9. **Cameras**

   The final photography of composite animation is usually done on color films or videotapes.

10. **Editing**

    This last step is considered part of the postproduction stage.

2.3 Multiplane and Shooting Phase

The shooting phase in film production is not a trivial operation. Movements can be simulated at this stage by moving certain cels in relation to others. To facilite this process, producers use complex machines called **multiplanes**. As shown in Fig. 2.2, a multiplane is a machine 3.50 meters high, with a camera at the top. The animation board has a plate glass base. A number of glass layers are placed beneath the camera lens at varying distances. Note that during simulated camera motion, the motion speed of the different decors must be inversely proportional to the distance between the decor and the camera.

Multiplanes allow the operator to produce special effects which we will define in the next section.

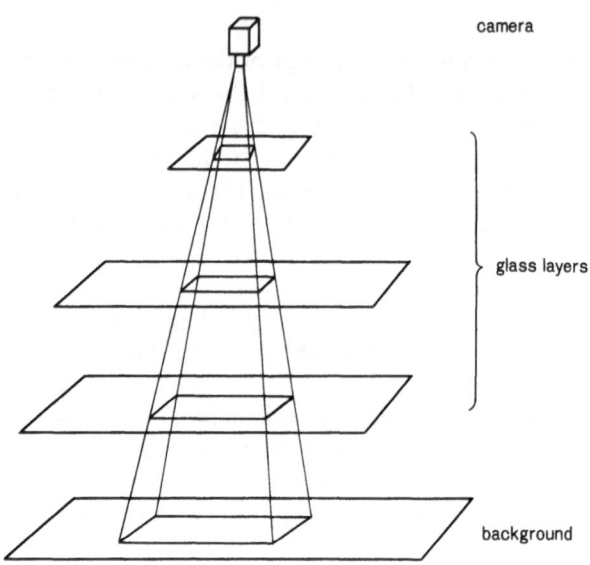

Fig. 2.2. Multiplane

2.4 Some Techniques and Special Camera Effects

Special camera effects are used in conventional animation, but they can be difficult
to produce and sometimes very expensive. As they can be easily simulated using a
computer, the most important techniques will be defined here.

Pan	A pan (contraction of panorama) is an effect in which the camera is moved horizontally from one point to another.
Tilt	A tilt is an effect in which the camera is moved vertically from one point to another.
Zoom	A zoom is an effect which makes a subject appear larger of smaller. In a two-dimensional cartoon, the effect can be obtained by moving the camera closer to or further away from the subject. This technique of moving the camera is quite impossible in three dimensions, because of the perspective effect; however, excellent zoom lenses can be used in the camera to get the three dimensional effect. A zoom can be continuous.
Spin	A spin is an effect produced by rotating the camera.
Fade-in	A fade-in is an effect used at the beginning of a scene: The scene gradually appears from black.
Fade-out	A fade-out is an effect used at the end of a scene: The scene gradually darkens to black.
Cross-dissolve	A cross-dissolve is an effect that is very often used for the transition between scenes. It corresponds to a fade-out of one scene and a fade-in of the next scene over the same length of film.

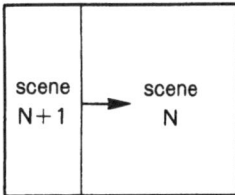 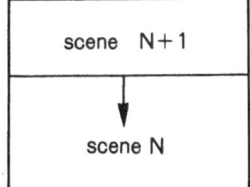 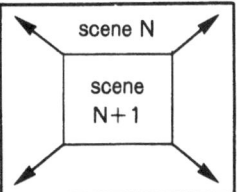

Fig. 2.3. Wipes

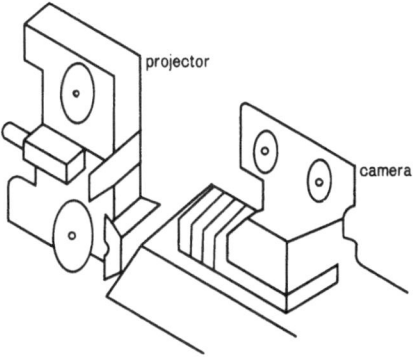

Fig. 2.4. Principle of a simple optical printer

Wipe   With the wipe effect, one scene appears to slide over the preceding scene. Figure 2.3 shows different possible forms for the dividing lines between the scenes.

For other special effects like superimpositions or multiple-image effects, an **optical printer** is essential to conventional animation. This is a movie camera which is focussed on the gate of a lensless movie projector to duplicate one piece of film onto another. Figure 2.4 shows the principle of a simple optical printer.

Optical printers can be used:

- To make positive and negative prints
- To convert from one format to another (16 mm, 35 mm)
- To modify the speed of an action
- To improve the quality of a film
- To reprint several cycles of a repeated motion
- To superimpose titles and logos
- To provide fade and wipe effects

2.5 Bar, Route, Model, and Exposure Sheets

A great volume of paper flows through an animation studio. In addition to storyboards, already discussed, four main kinds of information sheets are used:

1. **Bar sheets** carry a visual synopsis of the animation sequence; they serve as a guide in every phase of production because they indicate the number of frames allotted per action and the timing of the dialog, mouth actions and music.
2. **Route sheets** list the length, the location, the person responsible and various other statistics of every scene.
3. **Model sheets** show the original characters drawn in a number of representative poses.
4. **Exposure sheets** are the most detailed documents concerning a film. Each frame has a line on the exposure sheet. Camera movements, zooms, and the number of exposures are written here for each frame. An essential tool for the animator and for the cameraman, an exposure sheet is shown in Fig. 2.5.

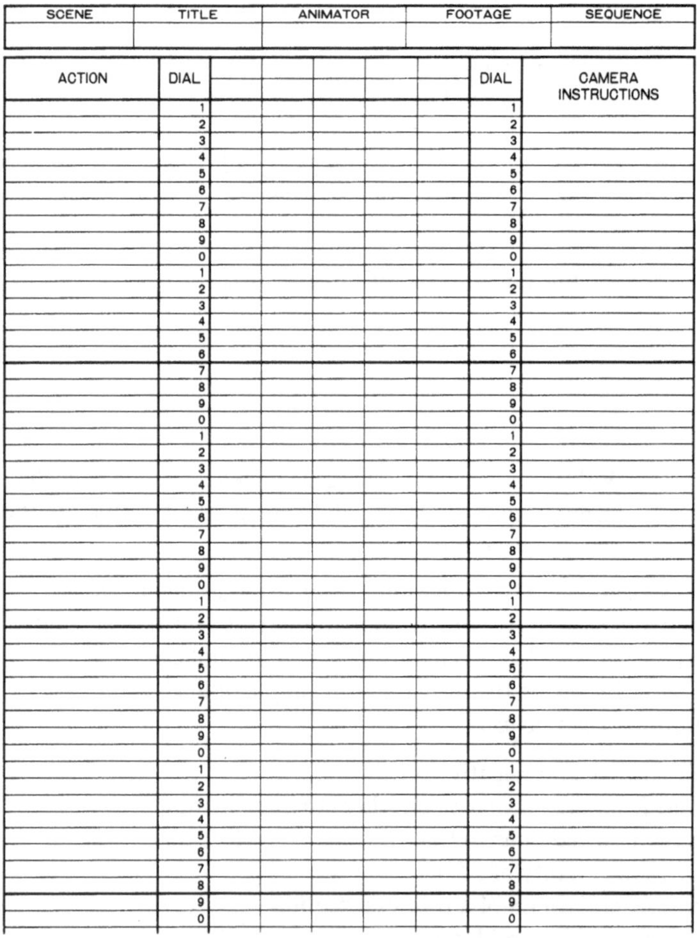

SCENE	TITLE	ANIMATOR	FOOTAGE	SEQUENCE

ACTION	DIAL						DIAL	CAMERA INSTRUCTIONS
	1						1	
	2						2	
	3						3	
	4						4	
	5						5	
	6						6	
	7						7	
	8						8	
	9						9	
	0						0	
	1						1	
	2						2	
	3						3	
	4						4	
	5						5	
	6						6	
	7						7	
	8						8	
	9						9	
	0						0	
	1						1	
	2						2	
	3						3	
	4						4	
	5						5	
	6						6	
	7						7	
	8						8	
	9						9	
	0						0	
	1						1	
	2						2	
	3						3	
	4						4	
	5						5	
	6						6	
	7						7	
	8						8	
	9						9	
	0						0	
	1						1	
	2						2	
	3						3	
	4						4	
	5						5	
	6						6	
	7						7	
	8						8	
	9						9	
	0						0	

Fig. 2.5. An exposure sheet

2.6 Postproduction

Under this term we include all the actions required to transform the shot film into a final product. This includes **processing** and **editing**.

Film processing involves a series of laboratory operations in which the images exposed on film are developed with chemical solutions. Films are made in cellulose acetate and as shown in Fig. 2.6, the standard format is 35 mm, although other formats are available. Table 2.1 lists those currently on the market.

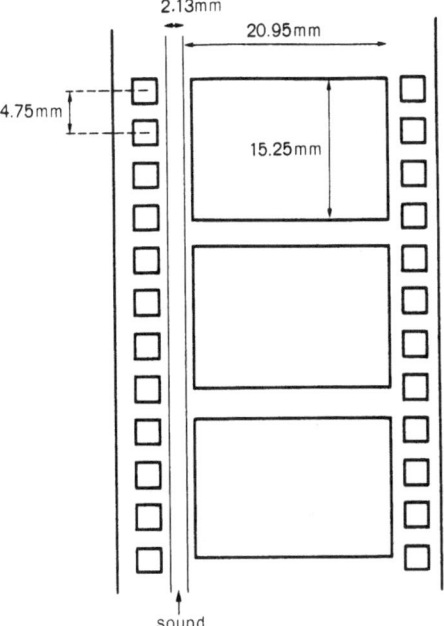

Fig. 2.6. 35 mm format

Table 2.1. Main film formats

Formats	Image size (height × width)	
70 mm	1 × 2, 1 × 2.33	
35 mm	1 × 2, 1 × 1.85	
17.5 mm	9.5 × 14.5	
16 mm	7.4 × 10.4	(without sound)
	7.16 × 9.6	(with sound)
9.5 mm	6.5 × 8.5	
super-8	5.36 × 4.01	
8 mm	3.7 × 5.2	

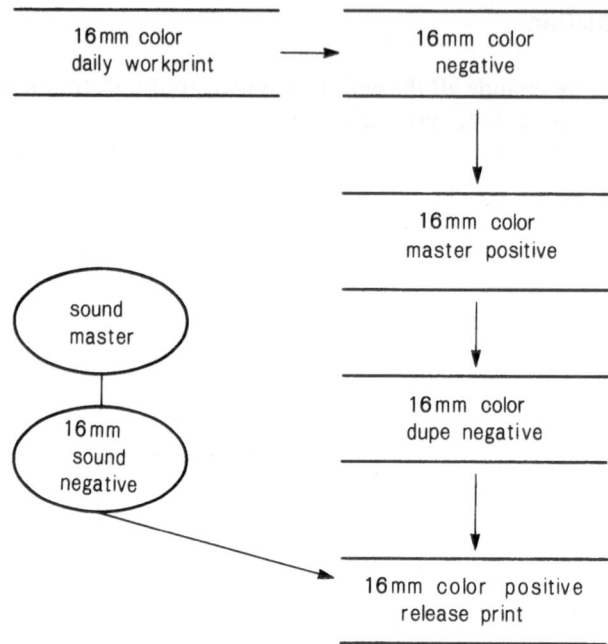

Fig. 2.7. Flowchart of the processing of a 16 mm sound film

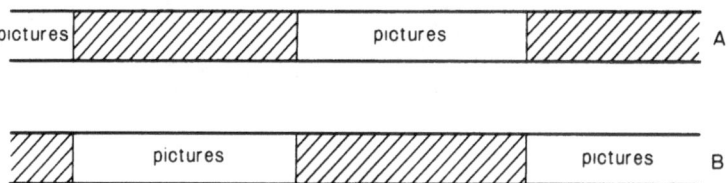

Fig. 2.8. A and B rolls

Because production failures can complicate the editing phase, postproduction can imply reshooting. But editing usually consists mainly of assembling, sorting and splicing the film. Sound synchronization also comes into play in postproduction. Figure 2.7 shows a simple flowchart of the processing of a 16-mm sound film.

Generally, odd-numbered scenes are cut together to form what is called the A roll and even-numbered scenes are similarly spliced into another the B roll. This strategy makes it easier to add superimposition and fade effects during the post-production phase. Figure 2.8 shows the A and B rolls.

2.7 Historical Background

Picture animation was invented in 1831 by a Frenchman named Joseph Antoine Plateau. He created the illusion of movement with a machine called a phenakistoscope, a device that consisted of a spinning disc that held a series of drawings and windows that framed the viewer's perception of the drawings.

Then, in 1834, the Englishman Horner extended the phenakistoscope idea and invented the zoetrope. A revolving drum with regularly spaced slits in its sides, the zoetrope held the drawings on its inner walls. When the drum revolved, the viewer could see the drawings through the slits. The zoetrope was refined by the Frenchman Emile Reynaud who developed the praxinoscope. The slits were replaced by mirrors that spun in the center of the drum.

In 1892, Reynaud created the first movie theater in Paris, the Theater Optique. The first animated film, however, was produced in 1906 by the American J. Steward Blackton. It was called *Humorous Phases of a Funny Face*. In 1908, the Frenchman Emile Cohl made black drawings on white paper and took pictures of them. He used the negative on the screen, thus producing the animation of white figures on a black background. One of his most important animated films was *Drame chez les Fantoches*. In 1909, the American Winsor McCay produced *Gertie the Trained Dinosaur*, which can be considered the first cartoon. Although the movie was short, McCay used about 10,000 drawings. During the years 1913–1917, various American cartoon series were produced, the most well-known of them *Felix the Cat*, by Pat Sullivan.

In 1915, the American Earl Hurd introduced the technique of **cel animation**, which took its name from the transparent sheets of celluloid that it used. But, of course, the father of commercial animation is certainly Walt Disney. In the ten years 1928–1938 he produced Mickey Mouse, Donald Duck and the Silly Symphony Series. His first Mickey Mouse short, in 1928, was the first film with fully synchronized sound. Then came the full-length commercial animated cartoon, *Snow White and the Seven Dwarfs*. Meanwhile, other pioneers were developing animated films in different countries; for example, Atamanov, Pashchenko and Ivanov in Russia, Trnka in Czechoslovakia and Bartosch in France. Two very well-known pioneers should be especially mentioned: John Halas in Britain and Norman McLaren in Canada.

2.8 Applications of Animation

There are several areas where animation can be extensively used. These areas can be arbitrarily divided into five categories:

1. **Television**
   A powerful motivator for the rapid development of animation, TV has used it for titles, logos and inserts. But its main uses are in cartoons for children and commercials for a general audience (Fig. 2.9).

2. **Cinema**
   Animation, as a cinematic technique, has always held an important role in this industry. Complete animation films are still produced by the cinema industry.

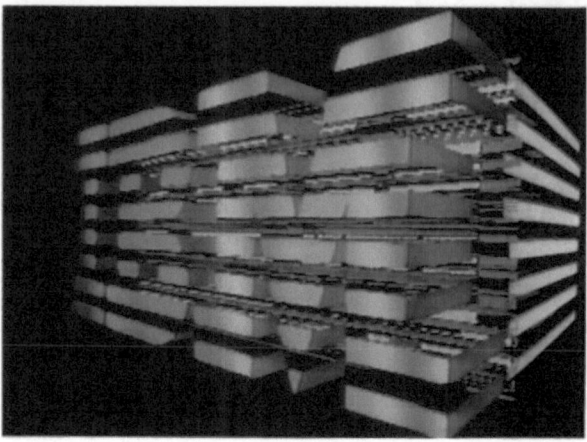

Fig. 2.9. "Journey" by Publicity, IBM Canada. This 10 seconds sequence produced by Computer Image Productions, Inc., Denver, CO USA for IBM Canada involves an intimate journey through the intricate facets of a chip (Producers: Paul Sutherland, Robert Hopp. Agency: Robert Hopp and Associates, Toronto, Canada. Production House: Computer Image Productions, Inc. Director: James Sibley. Animators: Vivian Zezula-Aragon, Brad Jorgensen, Rob Bekuhrs. Tech. Staff: David Cline, Steve Cosgrove, Mike Snyder. Art Director: John Wood, Cliff Erickson. Computers: CAESAR, SCANIMATE, SYSTEM IV)

But it is also a good way of making special effects, and is frequently used for titles and generics. [Crow 1978].

3. **Government**

   Animation is an excellent method of mass communication and governments are, of course, great consumer of such techniques for publicity.

4. **Education and research**

   Animation can be used extensively for educational purposes. Fundamental concepts are easily explained to students using visual effects involving motion. Finally, animation can be a great help to research teams, because it can simulate situations, e.g., in medicine [Thalmann et al. 1985] or science [Isaacs 1989; Papathomas and Julesz 1987].

5. **Business**

   The role of animation in business is very similar to its role in government. Animation is useful for marketing, personnel education, and public relations [Magnenat-Thalmann and Thalmann 1985e; Bolduc et al. 1987].

6. **Engineering**

   Engineers do not require the realistic images the entertainment field demands. It must be possible to identify unambiguously each separate part and the animation must be produced quickly [Noma and Kunii 1985; Muir 1985].

3. Computer Animation

3.1 The Role of the Computer in Animation

Although computer plays an ever-increasing role in animation, the term "computer animation" is imprecise and can sometimes be misleading. This is because the computer can play a variety of different roles:

1. **In the creation of drawings**
   i)   Key drawings can be digitized.
   ii) Key drawings can be created with an interactive graphics editor.
   iii) Complex objects can be produced by programming.
2. **In the creation of motion**
   In-betweens can be completely calculated or complex motions can be directly generated by the computer.
3. **In coloring**
   Drawings can be painted using an interactive computer system or complex and realistic images can be generated.
4. **In shooting**
   A physical camera can be controlled by computer, or virtual cameras can be completely programmed.
5. **At the postproduction stage**
   Editing and synchronization can be controlled by computer.

3.2 How to Classify Computer Animation Systems?

There are a number of different ways of classifying computer animation systems. First, we can define various levels of systems:

Level 1: used only to interactively create, paint, store, retrieve, and modify drawings. These do not take time into account. They are basically just graphics editors used only by designers.

Level 2: can compute in-betweens and move an object along a trajectory. These systems generally take time into account and are mainly intended to be used by or even replace in-betweeners.

Table 3.1. Functions of computer animation systems

	Computer-assisted animation	Modeled animation
Object creation	– character digitizing – use of a graphics editor	– 3D reconstruction programs – 3D graphics editor – 3D object modeling programs
Motion	– in-between calculation – movement along a path	– 3D motion programming – actor systems
Coloring	– painting systems	– 3D shading systems
Camera	– physical camera control	– virtual cameras
Postproduction	– editing systems – computer-assisted synchronization	– in theory, modeled systems could eliminate the postproduction phase by updating films automatically

Level 3: provide the animator with operations which can be applied to objects: for example, translation or rotation. These systems may also include virtual camera operations like zoom, pan or tilt.

Level 4: provide a means of defining actors; i.e., objects which possess their own animation. The motion of these objects may also be constrained.

Level 5: are extensible and can learn as they work. With each use, such a system becomes more powerful and "intelligent."

Another popular and simpler way of classifying computer animation systems is to distinguish between **computer-assisted** and **modeled** animation.

Computer-assisted animation, sometimes called keyframe animation, consists mainly of assisting conventional animation by computer. Keyframe animation systems are typically of level 2.

Modeled animation means the drawing and manipulation of more general representations which move about in three-dimensional space. This process is very complex without a computer. Modeled animation systems are generally of level 3 or 4. Systems of level 5 are not yet available.

The computer's role in animation is summarized in Table 3.1, which compares the functions of computer-assisted animation systems with those of modeled animation systems.

3.3 Real-time vs Frame-by-frame

In the preceding sections, we have classified animation systems on the basis of their role in the animation process. Another consideration is the mode of production. Is computer animation just a special case of animation defined as a succession of images, each differing from the one preceding it? In other words, is the computer used to produce each frame individually to be photographed? Or is the "film" produced directly on a terminal? This is a question of time.

To see this, the computer-generated sequences of the film *Tin Toy* can be compared with a video game like TETRIS. Both can be considered computer animation.

But in *Tin Toy*, the images are very complex and realistic. This means that several minutes are required to produce one frame. These frames must be recorded (photographed), and then projected at a rate of 24 frames/second. In a video game, on the other hand, animation is immediate; the objects move rapidly and there is complete interaction between the user and his images. This is "real-time" animation, because the moment at which the user makes a decision becomes the moment of materialization. Real-time animation does not require films to be recorded, because the results can be seen directly at a terminal.

Real-time computer animation is limited by the capabilities of the computer. A real-time image must be displayed in less than $\frac{1}{15}$ second, because the illusion of continuous movement breaks down at slower speeds. This is a severe limitation, because only relatively simple calculations can be made in this time. The constraints are imposed by the computer's cycle speed, storage capabilities, word length, instruction set, and graphics processing.

One sign of expanding possibilities for real-time computer animation is the development of special hardware like array processors and graphics processors. In the meantime, the following statements can be made:

1. Real-time animation is generally not possible on a multi-user system. TETRIS, for example, can run on a MacIntosh but not on a main-frame system with one hundred users.
2. Real-time, three-dimensional shaded animation with refraction, textures, and shadows is for tomorrow, not for today.
3. Real-time animation is possible on a microcomputer because it is a single-user machine, but its resolution is poor and its color range is limited.

We give an example: we move a car 100 meters along the x-axis in 5 seconds; the car is located at $\langle 5,0 \rangle$. We assume a sequence at 24 frames per second, which gives 120 frames for 5 seconds. The following program produces such an animated sequence:

in real time:

```
STEPX := 100/120;
create CAR;
place CAR (⟨5,0⟩);
draw CAR;
for IMAGE := 1 to 120
    wait;
    erase CAR;
    translate CAR (⟨PASX, 0⟩);
    draw CAR;
```

frame by frame:

```
STEPX := 100/120;
create CAR;
place CAR (⟨5,0⟩);
draw CAR;
for IMAGE := 1 to 120
```

record the frame;
wait;
erase CAR;
translate CAR ($\langle PASX, 0 \rangle$);
draw CAR;

In the near future, very complex animation will be produced in a very short time, due to the research in parallel processing and multiprocessors. Image synthesis algorithms like ray-tracing and scan-line may be easily distributed between several processors. Moreover, animation may be considered as a set of parallel processes with and without communications between them.

3.4 Frame Buffer Animation and Real-time Playback

The illusion of real-time animation can be created with a frame buffer, which can be viewed conceptually as a two-dimensional array of pixels. As shown by Booth and MacKay [1982], there are different techniques for limited frame buffer animation. As the time required to rescan all the pixels is too long for animation, only static images are considered. This means that the actual contents of the memory pixels never changes, but the way of interpreting the bits does, causing the illusion of animation.

Color Table Animation

The value of a pixel is generally an index in a look-up table of colors. Animation can be obtained by modifying the look-up table. The modification can be cyclic, alternated, or selective. Details of these techniques can be found in a paper by R. Shoup [1979].

Zoom-pan-scroll Animation

Pixel memory can be divided into different regions and the display can cycle through the different images. For example, a 512- × -512 frame buffer can be divided into four 256- × -256 images. By using zoom, pan, and scroll operations, the four images can be successively and rapidly displayed.

Crossbar Animation

The principle of crossbar animation consists of routing any of the bits from pixel memory to any of the input lines in look-up tables.

Real-time Playback

As shown, it is generally impossible to compile frames at the rates required for real-time presentation, especially when images must have a certain degree of realism. However, as it is very difficult to imagine the effects of animation in a frame-by-frame system, the alternative is to compile all the frames in advance at non-real-time rates and save the frames (or the display code) in mass storage. A real-time program then displays the frames. This technique is called **real-time playback**.

3.5 Systems vs Languages

Computer animation was first developed in the mid-sixties. The early films were produced using programming languages or interactive systems accessible only to computer scientists. Then user-friendly interactive systems were developed, allowing artists to make films without too much intervention by computer scientists. These interactive systems have the great advantage of being dedicated to artists, but they impose limits on the creativity of those who would like to exploit all the computer possibilities. Four arguments can be put forward for the development and use of a programming language for computer animation:

1. Such a language could exploit all the power of the computer.
2. It would permit the easy development of interactive computer animation systems that are compatible with the language, especially in terms of graphical data structures and temporal concepts.
3. Developments in the design of programming languages have led to concepts that are fundamental to the control of motion and temporal events. In particular, research in structured programming and data structures has allowed the design of high-level languages such as PASCAL and SIMULA-67. Work on data abstraction [Liskov and Zilles 1974; Guttag 1977] is the basis of abstract data type existing in a number of languages such as ALPHARD, CLU and ADA. Concepts of synchronization and message passing exist in SMALLTALK [Goldberg and Robson 1983], CONCURRENT PASCAL [Brinch Hansen 1975], MODULA-2 [Wirth 1983] and ADA. Research has also been done on actor systems like PLASMA [Hewitt and Smith 1975], which has important implications for computer animation.
4. Computer programming knowledge is no longer restricted to computer scientists.

In summary, animator-oriented systems are necessary, because they can attract artists who may be wary of all technology, and computer programming in particular. But computer animation languages must also be developed because they permit more impressive special effects. In addition, research must be done to provide animators with more powerful user-oriented animation systems by using artificial intelligence theory, for example.

4. The Development of Computer Animation in Various Organizations

4.1 The Early Systems: BEFLIX and EXPLOR

During the period 1963–1967, a dozen computer films were made at Bell Telephone Laboratories. Apart from Ken Knowlton [1964, 1965], the most important computer animators at Bell Labs were:

- E. Zajac [1966], who made the first computer-animated film *Two-gyro gravity-gradient attitude control system* in 1963.
- F. Sinden [1967], who made *Force, Mass and Motion*, a film that demonstrates Newton's laws of motion; the programming language was FORTRAN.
- Huggins and Weiner, who made *Harmonic Phasors*, a film concerning the composition of complicated periodic waveforms; the film was produced by programming in PMACRO [Alexander and Huggins 1967].

Four other animators should also be mentioned:

- McCumber, who made a film illustrating the Gunn oscillation effect in semi-conductors
- Julesz [1966] and Bosche [1967], for their experiments in human vision and perception
- Noll [1965, 1967], for his films on stereo viewing

(More details on films and animators can be found in the appendix.)

BEFLIX is a language that was created by Ken Knowlton [1964] on an IBM 7094. The language directly manipulates a matrix of 252 × 184 "pixels" of three bits, representing eight grey-levels. The primitives are:

- Read/write pixel
- Manipulation of filling areas bounded by previously drawn lines (copy, move, permutation, zoom, fill, scale, smooth)
- Perspective projection
- Motion primitives
- Grey-scale commands

For example, PAINT, A, B allows the user to fill up the rectangle defined by two vertices A and B. There are almost no mathematics in BEFLIX. Animation is completed by sending electronic signals (waves) to make image distortions: sinusoidal, horizontal/vertical deformations, etc.

Several films were produced with BEFLIX:

- A film on BEFLIX by Knowlton (17 min)
- A film on the list-processing language L6 (2 parts: 16 min and 32 min)
- "*Man and his World*", for EXPO 67 in Montreal (1 min)

As BEFLIX contains little mathematics, Ken Knowlton has combined this language with FORTRAN IV. This produced the FORTRAN IV BEFLIX animated-movie language which was quite powerful for its time.

EXPLOR [Knowlton 1970] is an acronym for EXplicitly Provided 2D patterns, Local neighbourhood Operations and Randomness. This language, intended for scientific and artistic applications, stores pictures in raster-scan format. The artist manipulates a grid of 240×320 cells. A number between 0 and 255 that represents color and intensity is associated with each cell and can be applied to the cells of a rectangle that the user has to specify. For example, in the FORTRAN-coded EXPLOR, CALL PUT(X, Y, W, H, %, N) means "PUT the Nth color in the rectangle of center $\langle X, Y \rangle$, height H and width W. Only a percentage of cells (%) of the rectangle will be randomly colored. Although this system was designed for mosaics and abstract motifs, artist Lilian Schwarz made a well-known 3-minute film *Olympiad* with the system. Over 20 films have been made with EXPLOR, including *Picture From a Gallery*, which involves the manipulation of a family photograph. In short, the originality of EXPLOR lies in the fact that decisions do not define exact patterns but merely the rules for building an image. The rest is filled in randomly.

4.2 Picture-driven Animation: GENESYS

GENESYS is a picture-driven animation system which was developed by Ronald Baecker [1969b] at MIT for his PhD thesis. The system requires that the information defining the image transformation be itself in graphical form. This is the source of the name "Picture-driven animation". Moreover, for Baecker, immediate visual feedback is fundamental.

The hardware consists of a computer, auxiliary mass storage, a locator device and a graphics display. The software has four parts:

- A language for the construction of static pictures
- A language for the specification of picture changes
- A set of programs to produce the sequence of frames
- A set of input/output programs and real-time playback.

The system is based on the following strategy:

1. The animator creates a new film by using the command FORMMOVIE $\langle$name$\rangle$.
2. The animator sketches the background using the command FORM-BACK-GROUND and his locator device.
3. The animator sketches cells and then constructs a coherent object composed of

different cells. For example, a woman can be built by the following sequences of commands:

    FORMCEL   1   IN CLASS HEAD
    FORMCEL   1   IN CLASS BODY
        ⋮
    BIND BODY, HEAD ...

4. The animator designs motion by sketching a path called a P-curve. Because of the command BIND, the command SKETCHPCURVE BODY creates a path of motion not only for the body but also for the parts to which it is bound.
5. The animator can use PLAYBACK to evaluate the animation sequence.
6. The animator can type a sequence of choices of different positions for any object by using the TYPESELECTION command.
7. The animator can add rhythm to the motion.

What is interesting and new in the GENESYS system is its representation of dynamic behavior. Three concepts are introduced to achieve this:

1. **The P-curves** that define the motion path (this concept will be further discussed in Chap. 5).
2. **The selection descriptions** that define choices of cells from a cell class.
3. **The rhythm descriptions** that consist of sequences of instants of display time or intervals between frames. They define temporal patterns marking events.

GENESYS is still considered a useful basic animation system. The concept of picture-driven animation has shown that dynamic information can be abstracted, modeled and generated in the same way as in animated pictures.

4.3 Analog Systems: SCANIMATE and CAESAR

SCANIMATE [Honey 1971] is an "analog animation system." that allows the animator to modify the signals produced by a video synthesizer. The system, shown in Fig. 4.1, was created by Computer Image Corporation.

The figure shows that the artist can control animation at two points. At point A, the artist can zoom, shrink, rotate, and crop the image. At point B, colors and intensity can be easily modified.

SCANIMATE was used for many commercials and films including *2001: A Space Odyssey* and *Yellow Submarine*.

CAESAR [Honey 1971] stands for Computer-Animated Episodes-using Single-Axis Rotation. Also an analog system, it is more sophisticated and powerful than SCANIMATE because it permits figurative, or cartoon animation. In particular, CAESAR allows the component parts of a cartoon figure to be derived into several sections, each to be shown on a separate portion of the TV display and separately controlled. The animator can store any frame when he is satisfied. CAESAR can also compute the in-betweens of two cartoon figures. CAESAR has been extensively used to produce logos for the TV networks ABC, NBC, and CBS. Several cartoons have been produced; the most well-known is probably *Coyote and the Skunk*.

Figures 4.2 to 4.4 show images produced with SCANIMATE and CAESAR.

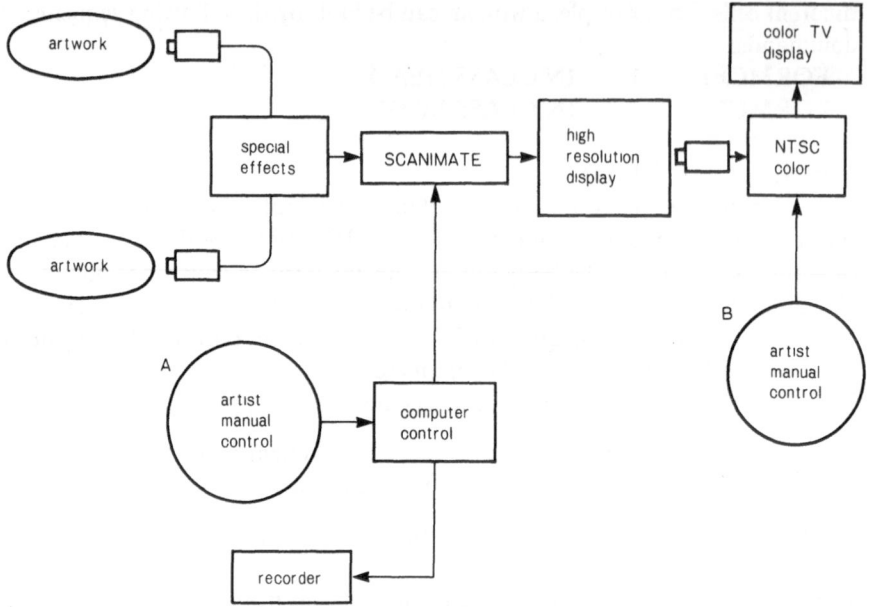

Fig. 4.1. The SCANIMATE system

4.4 ANIMATOR, ARTA, and MOP

ANIMATOR [Talbot et al. 1971] is a two-dimensional interactive film animation system that was developed at the University of Pennsylvania in 1971. As shown in Fig. 4.5, ANIMATOR comes with six modes of operation.

In the **picture definition mode,** the user creates a picture by associating a name to a sequence of picture primitives and previously defined pictures. The primitives are limited to points, lines, and circles.

The **motion definition mode** is the most interesting one, because it allows the animator to define parallel and/or sequential motions. These definitions are carried out by constructing operators based on motion, primitives such as translation, rotation, and zoom. Primitives can have an absolute or a relative effect. The **scene definition mode** is used to specify the pictures involved in a scene with their absolute starting positions and associated motion. The **movie segment definition mode** allows the animator to describe a movie with the relation between scenes. The **transmission mode** is used to enter actions and obtain specific results and the role of the **production mode** is self-evident. The ANIMATOR system is interesting because it is probably the first "modelled" system, although it was only in two-dimensions.

ARTA, also an interactive two-dimensional computer animation system, was created by L. Mezei and A. Zivian [1971] at the University of Toronto. Pictures are entered into the system on punched cards or using a light pen. Accurate work is done by using a grid, vector mode or by sketching freehand. In the vector mode,

Fig. 4.2. Three dimensional logo treatment produced off the CAESAR computer for Editel of Los Angeles (Designer/Directors: Susan Crouse-Kemp, Jim Johnson. Animator: Susan Crouse-Kemp. Tech. Staff.: Jim Johnson, David Cline. Computers: CAESAR, SCANIMATE. Production house: Computer Image Productions, Inc.)

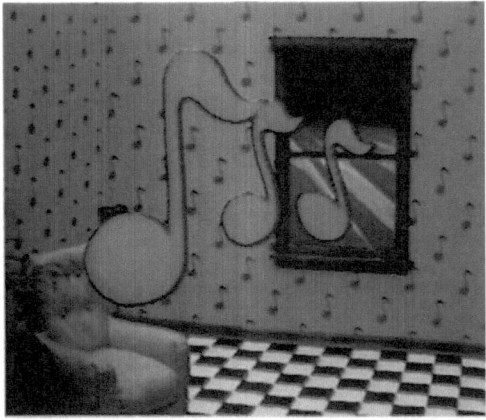

Fig. 4.3. *Music Room.* A unique blend of animation and model manipulation produced "*Music Room*", a generic: 25-second treatment (Producer: Brad Jorgensen. Production house: Computer Image Productions, Inc. Designer/Directors: Brad Jorgensen, Larry Cole, Jim Johnson. Animators: Susan Crouse-Kemp, Brad Jorgensen. Computers: CAESAR, SCANI-MATE)

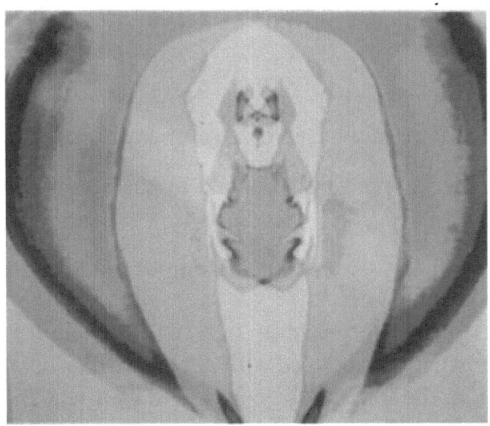

Fig. 4.4. *Video vitae.* Produced on SCANIMATE at Computer Image Corp. © Pat Lehman 1974

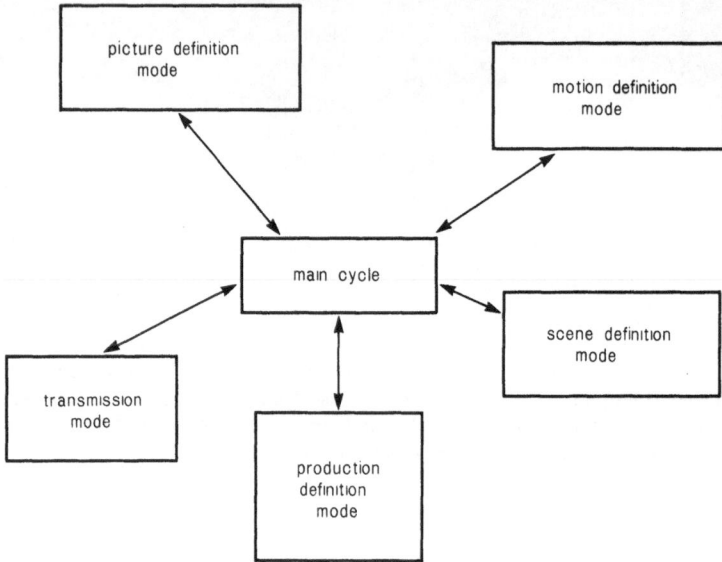

Fig. 4.5. The ANIMATOR modes

an interpolation routine could improve the curves by using the Akima algorithm [1970]. ARTA offers 80 menu-prompted commands. These are classified into:

Class A: operations that result in an output figure with the same number of points as an input figure:
rotation, translation, scaling.

Class B: operations that result in an output figure with a different number of points from the input figure:
interpolation, concatenation, texture, addition.

Class C: transformations of the input figure:
random movement, alteration of distances.

Input/output

Figure generators: circle, ellipse, polygon.

Miscellaneous

Animation features were mainly based on two operations:

− The motion of a figure along a path defined by the points of another figure
− In-betweening

Both operations, sitll basic operations of computer-assisted animation systems, will be further discussed in Chap. 5.

ARTA has been used in the production of a 10-minute film, *Art from Computers*. But the most well-known film produced with ARTA was *Sosoon*, by Georges Singer. Not a superproduction, the film can be considered as a real "painting in motion."

The film consists of the manipulation of simple geometric forms. Transformations are continuous, calm, and smooth.

MOP is a three-dimensional computer animation system that was developed by Edwin Catmull [1972] at the University of Utah and considered very advanced for its time. It removed hidden surfaces using the Watkins algorithm [1970] and performed smooth shading with the Gouraud method [1971]. (These concepts will be discussed in detail in Chap. 8.)

In MOP, objects are defined as a group of polygons; a hierarchical collection of objects is called a **body**. MOP is an acronym for MOtion Picture language, implying that some concept of motion forms the basis of the system. In fact, MOP can be considered an attempt at creating an actor system. The language MOP is designed to allow concurrency from the point of view of the user. The rate at which an object moves or changes can be given by a mathematical formulation or in a table of data. For example, a MOP statement can have the following form:

45,144 B ROTATE "WHEEL", 1,45

This statement means: "rotate the wheel around the axis 1 from an angle of 45° in 100 frames (45 to 144), using the table B." New accelerations can now be defined by modifying table B. Catmull made a movie of a hand to illustrate the MOP system. For a further discussion of that model, see Chap. 10.

4.5 Computer Animation at the National Research Council of Canada

Burtnyk and Wein of the National Research Council of Canada can be considered the pioneers of keyframe animation systems. In a famous paper [Burtnyk and Wein 1971a], they introduced the principles of in-between calculation by computer. Already, in 1967, the Tokyo Computer Technique Group had explored the possibilities of transforming one image into another. The most famous example of their work is *Running Cola is Africa*, which shows the transformation from a runner to a Coca-Cola bottle then to a map of Africa. Burtnyk and Wein integrated this concept into a working animation system called MSGEN [Burtnyk and Wein 1971b].

In the keyframe animation technique, the animator creates isolated frames at key intervals during a sequence. The in-between frames are computed by interpolation. (The complete technique will be presented in Chap. 5.) The first system produced by Burtnyk and Wein had a menu of commands. Some typical commands are listed:

Start sequence: stores the current picture as a reference start frame.
Interpolation: assigns an interpolation law to each individual cell in the current picture.
Store key: stores the current picture as a keyframe on disk.
Read key: brings in the next keyframe from disk.

Smooth and fluid movements are very difficult to achieve by linear interpolation. Moreover, the number of frames required is enormous. One way around this is to introduce a nonlinear path to control interpolation between the keyframes. However, the use of only one path is too restrictive. Burtnyk and Wein [1976] introduced a new technique for solving this problem: the use of skeleton-derived images. This technique (also discussed further in Chap. 5) is very simple: skeletons, or stick-figures, are used for computing new key images. The animator develops a complex motion sequence with only the skeleton of the image. Because of the simplicity of the skeleton, the degree of interaction can be very high.

The systems developed by Burtnyk and Wein were extensively used by the well-known artist Peter Foldes. A typical example is shown in Fig. 4.6. Foldes' films *Metadata, Hunger,* and *Visages* have achieved great recognition. In particular, *Hunger* received the Prix du Jury at Cannes in 1974, the Golden Hugo in Chicago and a special prize at the Barcelona Film Festival. The film was also nominated for an Academy award. As shown in Fig. 4.7, the interpolated images have the same artistic style as the first and last key frames.

More recently, Doris Kochanek introduced a popular algorithm for spline inter-polation [Kochanek and Bartels 1984], described in Sect. 7.7, and directed several computer-generated films including *"L'Anniversaire"*.

4.6 Computer Animation at Ohio State University

The Computer Graphics Research Group at Ohio State University is one of the most dynamic groups in computer animation research. Under the direction of Charles Csuri, another pioneer in the area, several computer animation systems have been developed:

1972– GRASS, a user-oriented real-time animation system [De Fanti 1976]
1975– ANIMA, a 3D real-time animation system [Csuri 1975]
1977– ANIMA II, a 3D color animation system [Hackathorn 1977]
1979– ANTTS, a very complex 3D animation system [Csuri et al. 1979]
1982– SAS, the Skeleton Animation System [Zeltzer 1982, 1982b] oriented towards human motion (Figs. 4.8, 4.9)
1984– TWIXT, a 3D Keyframe animation system [Gomez 1984]

By 1970, Csuri had already developed a real-time animation system on an IBM 1130 [Csuri 1970 and 1974]. Then a new system, called GRASS, was designed in 1972 [De Fanti 1976]. This system was particularly "habitable," i.e., the system could be used by a computer novice. Then, based on Csuri's language ANIMA, a new three dimensional real-time animation system was designed. The visual surface system was developed principally by Allan Myers. It provides clipping, perspective, and smooth shading of surfaces. The system also provides surface transparency, although not in real-time.

Hackathorn's ANIMA II, a 3D computer animation system which is not real-time, ran on a PDP-11/45 with a 64K memory and a 44-megaword moving head disk. The graphics terminal used was a 4096- × -4096 Vector General refresh CRT with a joystick, buttons and dials. All software was written in assembler.

ANIMA II provides the animator with 4 major functions:

1. **A real-time interactive geometric modeling program for creating complex objects.** Although the objects are modelled as surfaces composed of polygons, the user is only aware of positioning the objects and deciding their colors.
2. **A set of instructions for writing animation scripts.** Complex motions are broken down into simple changes through space and time. Parallelism is supported by

Fig. 4.6. *"Daphnis and Chloe"* renamed *"Portrait of a Man"* by Peter Foldes

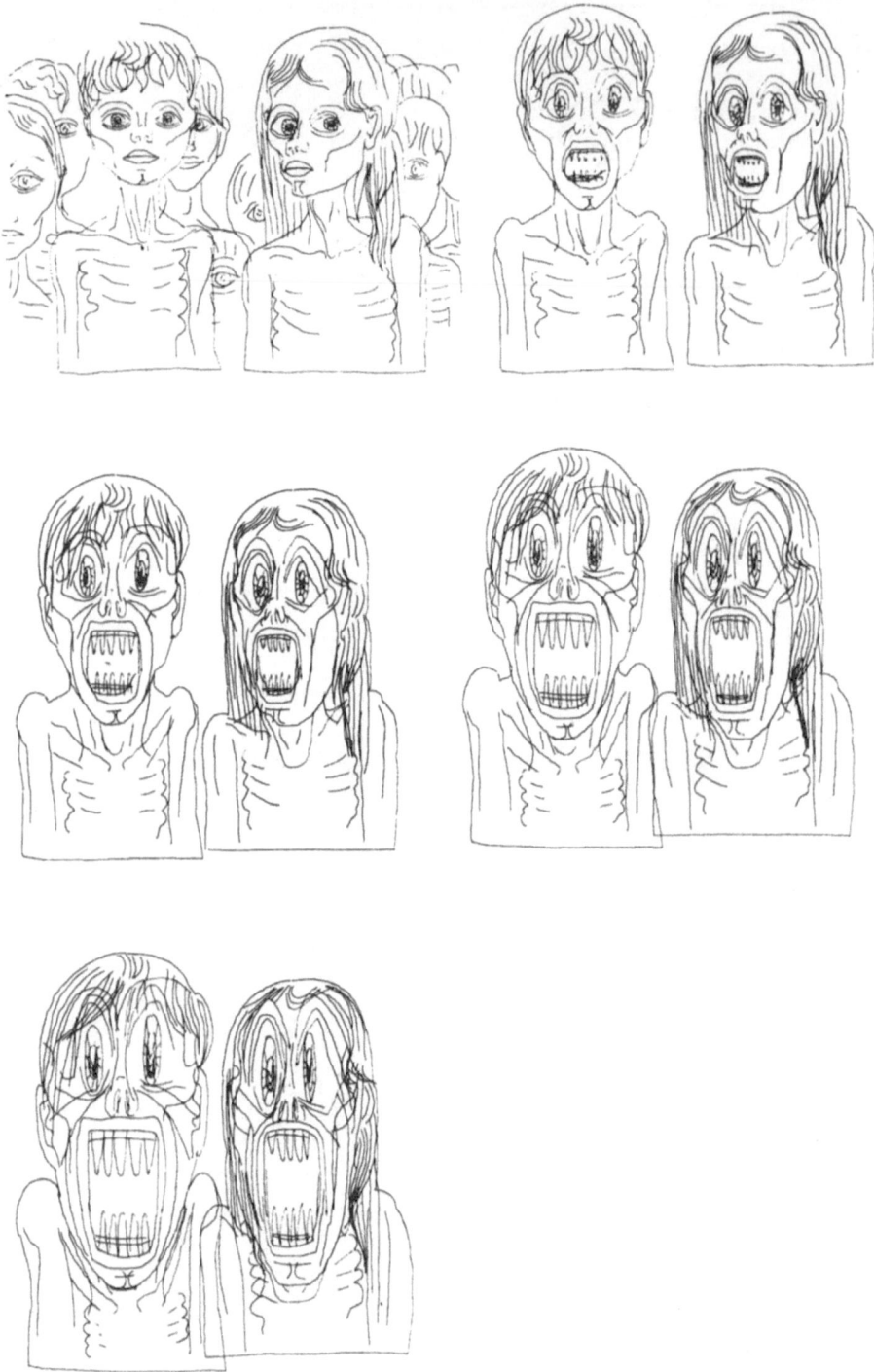

Fig. 4.7. "*Hunger*" by Peter Foldes (Production: National Film Board of Canada)

4.8

4.9

Figs. 4.8–9. Frames produced with the Skeleton Animation System (motion control software: David Zeltzer. Skeleton data generation: Donald Stredney)

language instructions that are scheduled to be active over a range of time during the animation process. A simple motion is completely controlled by **set** and **change** instructions. For example:

> set position ⟨name⟩ X, Y, Z at frame ⟨frame number⟩
> change position ⟨name⟩ to X, Y, Z from frame
> ⟨frame number⟩ to frame < frame number >

Instead of **position**, key words like **rotation, size, shape**, and **path** can be used to describe the different motions.

There is no need for loops or conditional statements. Parallel commands provide the ability to schedule language instructions. When the script is ready, it serves to control the whole scene.

3. **An animation language.** The script is analyzed by a preprocessor that builds a data structure for the complete animation sequence. In fact, the preprocessor handles in detail all the preparation of the scene and produces command blocks. The execution of the scene is driven by a scheduler that determines which command blocks must be processed for each frame. An interpreter then modifies the data structure according to the command blocks selected by the scheduler. A compilation routine calculates the color of each face, lighting and perspective and builds an animation file. This file can be displayed in real time on the Vector General terminal, but without color and lighting.

4. **A method of recording frames.** The Csuri group has developed a method of recording the animation files in NTSC format in real time.

The visible surface algorithm used in ANIMA II is a version of the Myers algorithm, already mentioned in the description of ANIMA. ANIMA II has several drawbacks: limited shading capabilities, no transparency, and aliasing problems.

For these reasons, a new system was designed: ANTTS (ANimated Things Through Space). The objectives were:

– To avoid the problems of ANIMA II
– To obtain good response time, but with no real-time requirement
– To allow editing of sequences
– To handle any type of drawing, including lines and 3D surfaces
– To generate textures and clouds

The most interesting aspect of the ANTTS system is the display algorithm, which processes data in a stream. It uses two large buffers: a run-length and a frame buffer. The algorithm processes data as follows:

1. Get a single triangle.
2. Apply image transformation to the triangle.
3. Determine the face color.
4. Compute perspective projection.
5. Orient the triangle projection with respect to its highest Y value.
6. Raster-scan the triangle into run lengths.
7. Pass the run lengths to the buffer by adding them to a list of run lengths at the same Y scan-line.

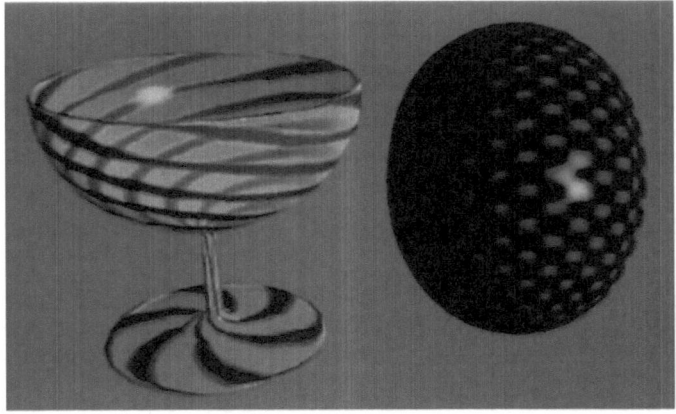

Fig. 4.10. Image produced by Frank Crow, Ohio State University

8. When the whole frame is processed, decompose the run-lengths into 3D pixels and compare them with the corresponding pixels in the frame buffer.

This display algorithm is quite efficient. Textured objects can also be produced by defining a three-dimensional perturbation of the object's surface.

ANTTS was implemented on a VAX 11/780 computer with different frame buffers [Csuri et al. 1979]. A subset was also implemented on a PDP-11/23 [Hackathorn et al. 1981].

TWIXT is a popular 3D keyframe system created by Julian Gomez [1984]. The system was used by the artist Susan Van Baerle [1986] to produce two excellent short computer-generated films: *Trash* and *Snoot and Muttly*.

The Computer Graphics Research Group at Ohio State University is still a leading group in computer animation (Fig. 4.10). Their demonstrations, as well as those of Cranston-Csuri Productions (Fig. 4.11 and 4.12) have been always well received at computer animation festivals.

4.7 From GRASS to ZGRASS

After his PhD from Ohio State University, Tom De Fanti expanded his system, called "the Graphics Symbiosis System," or GRASS [1976]. This three-dimensional real-time system was implemented by a team of 10 people. Written in assembler for a PDP-11/45 with a Vector General display, the GRASS language essentially has two types of primitives:

1. **Pictures**
   These are user-defined lists of 3D vectors. The pictures have names; up to 60 can be displayed concurrently.
2. **Commands**
   There are two kinds of commands:

Fig. 4.11. *"Wine Glasses on Mirror"* (Animator: Michael Collery, Cranston-Csuri Productions, Columbus, Ohio)

Fig. 4.12. *"Pencil City and Balls"* (Animators: Shaun Ho and Michael Collery, Cranston-Csuri Productions, Columbus, Ohio)

i) Commands that do not change the vector list; their functions are performed by the hardware. These include translation, rotations, scaling, etc. (There is also a command for changing intensity and one that moves a picture along a path similar to Baecker's P-curves.)
ii) Commands that change vector end-points like smoothing, perspective, chipping, windowing, and shading.

Users can also group pictures together and create a tree. Macros and conditional execution are also available in GRASS.

Several years after GRASS, Tom De Fanti developed the high-level graphics language ZGRASS [Dietrich 1983]. This was implemented on a low-cost micrographics system, the Datamax UV-1. With 16 2-bit frame-buffers, that system can generate standard NTSC signals. The artist-oriented language offers three different methods of animating an image in real time:

1. **Colormap animation,** as described in Sect. 3.4
2. **Bitmap animation,** with:
   i) **Additive animation** that consists of adding graphics elements to previous ones
   ii) **Snap animation** that basically creates a memorized image (a snapshot) and continuously displays it along a path. 2D 1/2 effects can be easily created with this type of animation.
3. **Framemap animation**
   Full-screen animation can be produced by taking advantage of the hardware. By cycling through a series of previously designed images, the 16 frame buffers can be used. This arrangement is fully programmable.

Several artists have produced numerous works using ZGRASS. The most well-known are Copper Giloth (Fig. 4.13) and Jane Veeder (Fig. 4.14).

Fig. 4.13. *"LIS31"* by Copper Giloth

Fig. 4.14. From "*MONTANA*" by Jane Veeder

4.8 New York Institute of Technology, Lucasfilm, and Pixar

NYIT (New York Institute of Technology) and Pixar are two well-known institutions that produce spectacular computer-animated images. Two of the most well-known specialists in computer animation, Edwin Catmull and Alvy Ray Smith, moved from NYIT to Lucasfilm, before creating Pixar.

NYIT has produced several computer animation systems in two and three dimensions.

Catmull designed the Computer-Assisted Animation System (CAAS) used at NYIT's Computer Graphics Laboratory. The hardware consists of animation stations, and frame-buffers controlled by several computers including a VAX 11/780 and PDP-11s. Three software packages were developed for assisting conventional animation.

1. TWEEN [Catmull 1979] is a program that provides a means of generating and manipulating digital forms of character images. The main objective of the system is the production of in-betweens. At any time, the artist can review the in-betweens and modify them with an electronic pen; the computer recalculates the other in-betweens.
2. PAINT [Smith 1978] one of the most well-known "paint systems," allows an artist to paint by using the pen and tablet and watching the color monitor. (PAINT will be further discussed in Sect. 5.9.)
3. SOFTCEL [Stern 1979] is a system that uses frame buffers to replace the conventional operations of hand copying pencil drawings onto cels and painting them. SOFTCEL handles filling operations and painted antialiasing characters that can be merged with a background image. Each frame can be stored on three frame buffers, one for each of the primary colors.

Figure 4.15 shows an example of the use of the computer in cartoons.

Fig. 4.15. Cartoon by Edwin Catmull

An ambitious project has been under development at NYIT for several years now: a wholly computer-generated feature film, *The Works*. This film, which has not been completed, was produced using BBOP [Stern 1983], a program that interactively animates hierarchically articulated three-dimensional figures.

BBOP is, in fact, a system for three-dimensional keyframe figure animation. There are three major data structures in BBOP: articulated tree-structured models based on polygons or quadric surfaces, a ring of virtual cameras, and a list of all the trees and rings of each frame. BBOP is implemented on an Evans and Sutherland Picture System with a VAX 750 as a host processor. Image rendering is performed by a shell program provided by the UNIX operating system. Hidden surface removal is performed by z-buffering (see Chap. 8); anti-aliasing techniques, lighting models, and texture mapping are also included.

Another area of expertise at the NYIT Computer Graphics Lab is human face modelling. This research has been carried out under the leadership of F.I. Parke and is described in Sect. 10.8.

Lucasfilm is a commercial film production house. However, the special effects in films like *Star Trek II* and *Return of the Jedi* [Duff 1983] are demonstrations of the state of the art in computer animation. As well as Catmull and Smith, Bill Reeves and T. Duff have also contributed greatly to the development of computer animation. Reeves [1983] has produced a method for modelling fuzzy objects such as fire, clouds, and water. The technique, called **Particle Systems** was used in the Genesis Demo sequence from the movie *Star Trek II* and for the explosion caused by the destruction of the Death Star's power generator in *Return of the Jedi*. (Particle systems will be further discussed in Sect. 9.7.) Software developed at Lucasfilm used the C language; Figures 4.16 and 4.17 show images produced there.

In 1986, members of the Lucasfilm Computer Graphics Division created a new company, Pixar. The company develops hardware and software for image synthesis, computer animation [Ostby 1989; Reeves et al. 1990], and medical imagery. Four excellent computer-generated films were produced under the direction of the traditional animator John Lasseter [1987]: *Luxo Jr.* (1986), *Red Dreams* (1987), *Tin Toy* (1988, Academic Award winner), and *Knickknack* (1989).

Fig. 4.16. "*SIGGRAPH Watch*" by Rob Cook, Lucasfilm and Stuart Sechrest, Cornell University

Fig. 4.17. "*Road to Point Reyes*" directed by Rob Cook, Lucasfilm Ltd. This landscape was defined using patches, fractals, particle systems, and a variety of procedural models. The various elements were rendered separately and later composited. Rob Cook designed the picture and did the texturing and shading, including the road, hills, fence, rainbow, shadows and reflections. Loren Carpenter used fractals for the mountains, rock and lake, and a special atmosphere program for the sky and haze. Tom Porter provided the procedurally drawn texture for the hills and wrote the compositing software. Bill Reeves used his particle systems for the grass and wrote the modelling software. David Salesin put the ripples in the puddles. Alvy Ray Smith rendered the forsythia plants using a procedural model. The visible surface software was written by Loren Carpenter and the anti-aliasing software by Rob Cook. The picture was rendered using an Ikonas graphics processor and frame buffers, and was scanned on a COLOR FIRE 240, courtesy of MacDonald Dettwiler and Associates Ltd. The resolution is 4K × 4K, 24 bits/pixel

4.9 MAGI/Synthavision, Robert Abel, Triple I, and Digital Effects

These four former companies produced computer-generated imagery for the film *TRON*, done at Disney Studios.

MAGI (Mathematical Applications Group Inc.) has been deeply involved in the animation and entertainment fields since 1966. Their application package, called Syntha Vision, converts models of quadric surfaces, polygons, and other geometric forms into three-dimensional images. These can be shaded and textured. A "Director's Language" allows the animator to assign motions to objects, cameras, and light. These techniques are, of course, highlighted in the work done on *TRON*.

Robert Abel and Associates was a commercial production house from Los Angeles. Some of their best computer-generated work includes numerous logos for TV programs such as the CBS Evening News. Since 1978, they have used an Evans and Sutherland Picture System II. Their animation software was developed by a team under the direction of Bill Kovacs. The film *TRON* incorporated their vector computer effects.

Information International Inc., (Triple I) also played a large past in the production of computer-animated images for *TRON*. The company has produced some of the best computer-generated images. In 1976, for example, they created a 40-second sequence film for "Futureworld" in which a clone of Peter Fonda was created. However, management decided to stop work on computer animation at the end of 1982.

The software Triple I used was very powerful, especially ASAS, the Actor/Scriptor Animation System developed by Craig Reynolds [1982]. This programming language, described further in Section 11.5, is a programming language extension of LISP. It allows the technical director to animate objects, colors, shading parameters, light sources, and the camera. Figure 4.18 shows an image produced by Information International Inc.

Fig. 4.18. *"The Juggler"* by Omnibus/Triple I 3D simulation

Digital Effects was another production house that worked on *TRON*. They used a laser-scanning system to digitize, store, and reproduce images. Judson Rosebush, former president of Digital Effects, was the primary designer of APL VISION and FORTRAN VISION, two computer animation packages. Numerous commercials have been produced by Digital Effects. The images from Times Square, produced in 1979, are especially spectacular.

4.10 And the Others?

This chapter has discussed the most important computer animation systems and languages since the development of this art. However, numerous computer animators and organizations have been omitted and we would like to briefly mention some of these. Information about movies can be also found in the appendix and of course readers are invited to explore the numerous references at the end of the book.

Among the earliest computer animation systems, three important systems have not been described:

- CAMP [Citron and Whitney 1968] is a language for computer-assisted production of animated film sequences based on mathematical curves.
- CAFE [Nolan and Yarbrough 1969] is a conversational system for describing geometrical forms and the sequence of such forms.
- ANTICS [Kitching 1973] is a keyframe animation system.

For more recent productions, the traditional SIGGRAPH film festival is certainly the place where the most comprehensive list of computer animation teams can be found. We would like to single out the work of a few individuals and organizations:

- James Blinn of the Jet Propulsion Laboratory—specialist in space travel simulation.

Fig. 4.19. *"Carla's Island"* by Nelson Max, Lawrence Livermore National Laboratory and Department of Energy

4.20

4.21

4.22

Figs. 4.20–22. Frames from *"Four Seasons of Japan"* (Director: Mayumi Yoshinari. Art Director: Tatsuo Shimamura. Technical Director: Junnosuke Kutsuzawa. © NHK)

Fig. 4.23. Synthesized watch by Sogitec Audiovisuel, Paris

- Nelson Max of the Lawrence Livermore Laboratory, who produced several films on molecules. Figure 4.19 shows a frame of his film *Carla's Island.*
- NHK, the Japanese television network, which produced an excellent film, *Four Seasons*, under the direction of Mayumi Yoshinari. Figures 4.20–4.22 show frames from this film.
- Pacific Data Images [Chuang and Entis 1983] a Californian company.
- Sogitec, a French company. Figure 4.23 shows an image in industrial design. The company merged in 1989 with TDI to form a new company, Ex Machina.
- Symbolics where Craig W. Reynolds introduced distributed behavioral animation (see Sect. 12.6) into the film *Stanley and Stella: Breaking the ice.*
- Successive companies created by John Whitney Jr.: Digital Productions, Whitney-Demos, Optomystic.
- New companies, especially for commercial spots, have appeared all over the world: The Fantastic Animation Machine (USA), Digital Pictures (UK), Post Effects (USA), Toyo Links (Japan), Japan Computer Graphics Lab (Japan), Animatica (Spain), Fantôme (France), Mental Images (Germany).

In the academic community, mention should be made of advanced research in Computer Animation in several universities including:

- University of Karlsruhe (Germany) who produced the film in ray-tracing *Occursus cum Novo* [Leister et al. 1988; Stösser et al. 1988]
- University of Calgary (Canada) where Brian Wyvill et al. [1986, 1989] produced the film *Soft II* and *Great Train Robbery*
- University of Pennsylvania (USA) where Norman Badler is an expert in human motion (see Sect. 10.3, 12.2 and 12.5).
- The Computer Animation Group at Massachusetts Institute of Technology (MIT) directed by David Zeltzer [1985, 1987, 1989].

Finally, we must mention our own work at MIRALab, University of Montreal since 1978, then at the University of Geneva and the Swiss Federal Institute of Technology in Lausanne since 1988.

5. Keyframe and Painting Systems

5.1 Computer-assisted Animation

We showed in Chap. 3 that numerous steps in conventional animation can be assisted or improved by computer. In particular, the computer can be used:

1. To input drawings
2. To produce in-betweens
3. To specify the motion of an object along a path
4. To color the drawings and create a background
5. To synchronize motion with sound
6. To initiate the recording of a sequence on film

These different aspects will be studied in detail.

5.2 The Input of Drawings

In conventional animation, it has long been a general practice to draw the different objects or parts of objects involved in a scene on separate celluloid transparencies (**cels**). Frames are produced by photographing a stack of cels.

With computers, the process of creating drawings can be improved by using a graphics editor. Although the graphics editor is less used in computer-assisted animation than in modelled animation, it allows the designer to create drawings, save, retrieve, modify, and delete them.

Typically, animators use free-hand drawings in cartoons; however, these can be combined with more regular drawings which can easily be created with a graphics editor. Moreover, graphics editors sometimes offer operations to improve drawings. This was the case of the graphics editor GRAFEDIT [Magnenat-Thalmann et al. 1982], which provided the user with an IMPROVE command based on local interpolation fit [Akima 1970] and Bezier curves [Bezier 1972]. Figure 5.1 shows an example of the use of the IMPROVE command of GRAFEDIT with the final results given in Fig. 5.2.

Although the process of making input drawings can be helped by computer, the major advantage is in the production of in-betweens, after two keyframes have been created.

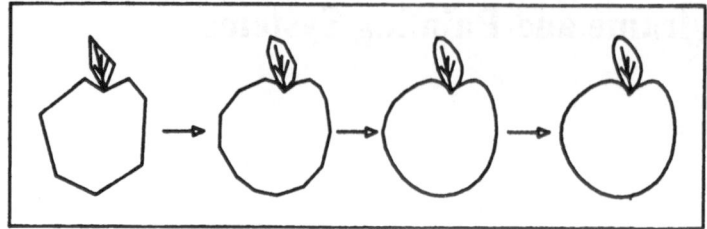

Fig. 5.1. The IMPROVE command in GRAFEDIT (Akima interpolation)

Fig. 5.2. Final results of an Akima interpolation

5.3 In-between Calculations

Basically, the "in-between" technique works as follows: the animator specifies two key drawings and the computer calculates additional drawings between them by computing linear distances between two corresponding points, as shown in Fig. 5.3. However, the process cannot work properly if the correspondence between both key drawings is not well defined. As key drawings do not generally have the same number of lines, this means that each drawing must be broken down into small line segments.

The process is explained more formally below based on the original ideas of Burtnyk and Wein [1971].

Key drawings are decomposed into cels and in-betweens are calculated by interpolation between cels. Each cel is itself composed of strokes that are defined as sequences of visible line segments. To perform an interpolation from a cel C1 with N1 strokes to a cel C2 with N2 strokes, the following algorithm must be applied:

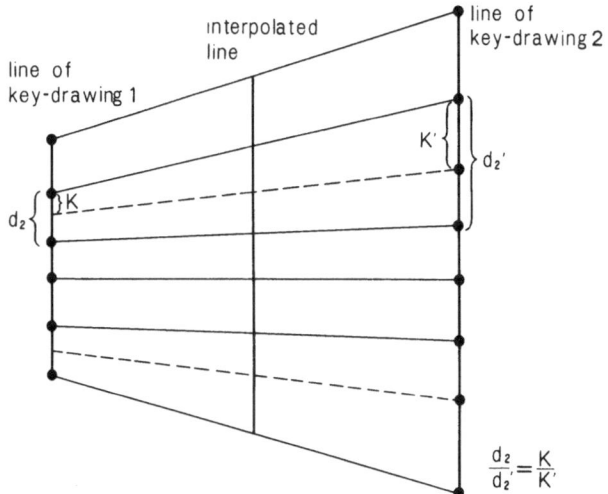

Fig. 5.3. The "in-between" technique

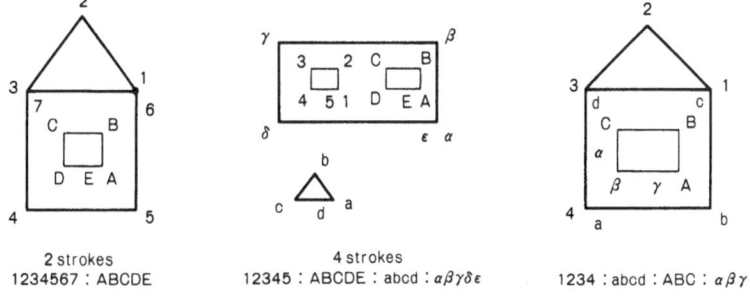

Fig. 5.4. Preprocessing of cels for in-betweening

If the numbers of strokes of both cels are the same (N1 = N2) and the number of points of the corresponding strokes also match, in-betweens can be calculated. Otherwise a preprocessing step is required. This preprocessing step can be separated into two parts:

1. **Preprocessing for cels with a different number of strokes**
   if N1 > N2
   (for N2 > N1, the algorithm is the same with N1 and N2 interchanged)
   then, N1 − N2 strokes must be added to C2. These sections are added as follows:
   i) N1 *modulo* N2 strokes of C2 are broken into N1 *div* N2 + 1 strokes
   ii) The other strokes of C2 are broken into N1 *div* N2 strokes. Figure 5.4 shows an example with N1 = 4 and N2 = 2.

2. **Preprocessing for two corresponding strokes with a different number of points**
   If both the cels to be preprocessed have the same number of strokes, all corresponding strokes must have the same number of points (NP1 = NP2). If this is not the case, for example:
   if NP1 > NP2
   then the following numbers are computed:

$$RT := (NP1 - 1)\,div(NP2 - 1)$$

$$RS := (NP1 - 1)\,mod(NP2 - 1)$$

RT points are added to the first RS line segments of the stroke of the second cel and RT − 1 to the others.

Figure 5.5 shows an example where NP1 = 12 and NP2 = 5. Two points are added to the three first segments and 1 to the last.
When preprocessing is finished, the interpolation process begins.

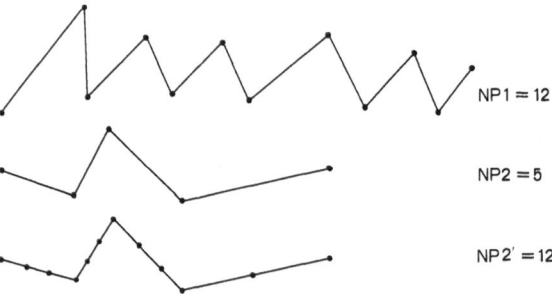

NP1 = 12

NP2 = 5

NP2' = 12

Fig. 5.5. Preprocessing of strokes for in-betweening

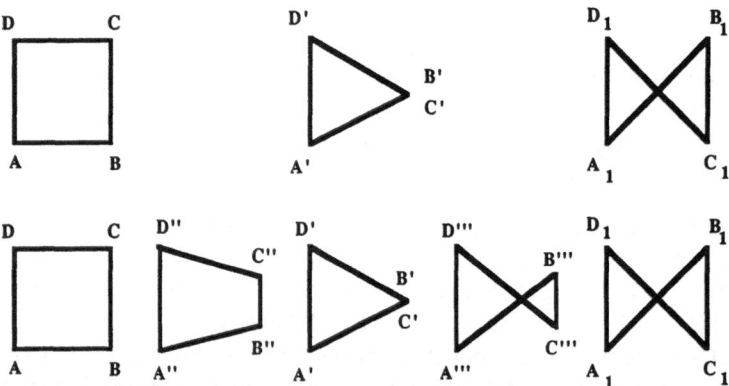

Fig. 5.6. Linear interpolation

```
program INTERPOLATION;
const
   NBINBETWEEN = 17; (* number of inbetweens +1 *)
   LAWX        =  4; (* linear interpolation in x *)
   LAWY        =  4; (* linear interpolation in y *)
var
   FILEC:FIGFILE;     (* file containing both cels *)
   FIRSTCEL,          (* cel 1 *)
   LASTCEL,           (* cel 2 *)
   RESULT:FIG;        (* result of the interpolation *)
   CURRENT:INTEGER;   (* current inbetween number *)
   FRACTION:REAL;     (* phase fraction of the interpolation *)
begin
   WINDOW(ORIGIN, << 719,359 >>);
   VIEWPORT(ORIGIN, << 1,0.5 >>);
   RESET(FILEC);
   READBINFIG(FILEC,FIRSTCEL);
   READBINFIG(FILEC,LASTCEL);

   PREPROCESSING(FIRSTCEL,LASTCEL);

   for CURRENT:=0 to NBINBETWEEN do
   begin
      FRACTION := CURRENT / NBINBETWEEN;
      RESULT:= INBETWEEN(FIRSTCEL,LASTCEL,FRACTION,LAWX,LAWY);
      draw RESULT;
      TAKEPICTURE;
      erase RESULT
   end
end.
```

Fig. 5.7. Program that draws in-betweens

Interpolation

To compute an in-between, an intermediary point is calculated by interpolating between two corresponding drawings. Figure 5.6 shows an example that explains the technique. Interpolation is linear: this means that the distance between two corresponding points is always regularly divided. Other divisions are possible by using other interpolation laws.

Figure 5.7 shows a program that computes and draws in-betweens. This program first reads two cels (FIRSTCEL and LASTCEL) and then performs the preprocess-

ing phase. It then computes and draws the in-betweens by using the function
INBETWEEN. The parameter law can be 0, 1, 2 or 3, corresponding to the different
possible interpolation functions described in the next section.

5.4 The Laws of Animation

Four fundamental laws have been used in interpolation; they allow motion between
two keyframes to occur at a constant speed, to accelerate, decelerate, or to accelerate
then decelerate. Figure 5.8 shows a PASCAL function called LAW (OP, MAXVAL,

```
function LAW(OP:INTEGER; MAXVAL,FRACT:REAL):REAL;

begin
   case OP of
      1: (* constant velocity *)
         LAW := MAXVAL*FRACT;

      2: (* acceleration *)
         LAW := MAXVAL*(1-COS(PI*FRACT/2));
      3: (* deceleration *)
         LAW := MAXVAL*SIN(PI*FRACT/2);
      4: (* acceleration then deceleration *)
         LAW := MAXVAL*(1-COS(PI*FRACT))/2
   end
end.
```

Fig. 5.8. The animation laws

```
create OBJECT(...);
for IMAGE := 1 to NBFRAMES do
begin
   FRACTION := IMAGE/NBFRAMES;
   VAL := LAW(OPERATION,MAXVAL,FRACTION);

   .. transformation using VAL to modify OBJECT into OBJ2 ..

   draw OBJ2;
   TAKEPICTURE;
   PAGEGRAPH
end;
```

Fig. 5.9. An animation program (excerpts)

FRACT) that gives a real value corresponding to a fraction (FRACT) of the total time expressed in number of images. OP is the operation (1 = CONSTANT, 2 = ACCELERATION, 3 = DECELERATION, 4 = ACCELERATION then DECELERATION). The value must vary in the range 0 to MAXVAL. Figure 5.9 shows how such a function is used in an animation program.

5.5 Skeleton Techniques

There are problems with the technique of in-betweening presented above. The first is that the motion of each point in the image is along a straight line and the same law is applied to each point. The second is that motion design requires several key-frames and there is discontinuity at these frames. Various techniques can be used to overcome these problems.

The idea behind the skeleton technique [Burtnyk and Wein 1976] is that "skeletons" of the figures, rather than the figures themselves, can be used as a basis for in-betweening. A skeleton, or stick figure, is a simple image composed of only a few points, describing only the form of movement required. This allows the animator to create many keyframes consisting only of skeletons. The computer can create much better in-betweens because the keyframes are much more similar; details can be added to the skeletons by computer according to a single model. In fact, this approach corresponds to how manual in-betweeners mentally use keyframes as guides without using all the detailed information contained in them.

The best way of defining a skeleton is to use a network of 4-sided polygons. Relative coordinates can be associated with each vertex. Suppose that any progression in a direction from one vertex to the next corresponds to a change of one unit, as shown in Fig. 5.10.

Relative coordinates of a point P (L and W) are defined as the fractional distance along each axis which is occupied by a line passing through P intersecting the two opposing edges of the polygon at this fractional distance. Consider Fig. 5.11, with

$$P_1 = \langle\langle X_1, Y_1 \rangle\rangle \qquad P_2 = \langle\langle X_2, Y_2 \rangle\rangle$$
$$P_3 = \langle\langle X_3, Y_3 \rangle\rangle$$

and

$$P_4 = \langle\langle X_4, Y_4 \rangle\rangle \quad \text{and} \quad P = \langle\langle X, Y \rangle\rangle$$

We have

$$P^1 = P_1 + L(P_2 - P_1) \qquad (5.1) \text{ with } P^1 = \langle\langle X^1, Y^1 \rangle\rangle$$

and

$$P^{11} = P_3 + L(P_4 - P_3) \qquad (5.2) \text{ with } P^{11} = \langle\langle X^{11}, Y^{11} \rangle\rangle$$

As the line $P^1 P^{11}$ passes through P, the following equation holds:

$$\frac{X - X^{11}}{Y - Y^{11}} = \frac{X - X^1}{Y - Y^1} \qquad (5.3)$$

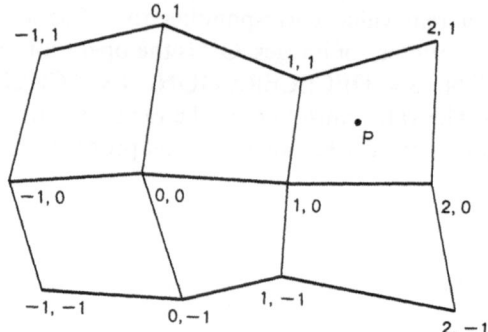

Fig. 5.10. Skeleton

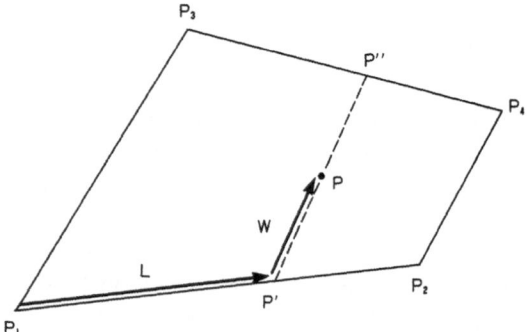

Fig. 5.11. Relative coordinates

By eliminating X^1, X^{11}, Y^1, Y^{11} from Eqs. 5.1 to 5.3, we obtain the relative coordinate W.

$$W = \frac{X - X_1 - L(X_2 - X_1)}{(X_3 - X_1) - L(X_2 - X_1 - X_4 + X_3)} \tag{5.4}$$

Generally, the axes are chosen in such a way that there are only two units in the W direction. This restricts the transverse distance and allows better control. Figure 5.12 shows examples of skeleton-derived images.

5.6 The Path of Motion and P-curves

Linear interpolation techniques are very convenient to transform the shape of an object; they can produce good in-betweens when the initial and final key frames are given. This method is the basis of the excellent film *Hunger* by Peter Foldes. However, because of the problems of continuity discussed in Sect. 5.4, linear inter-

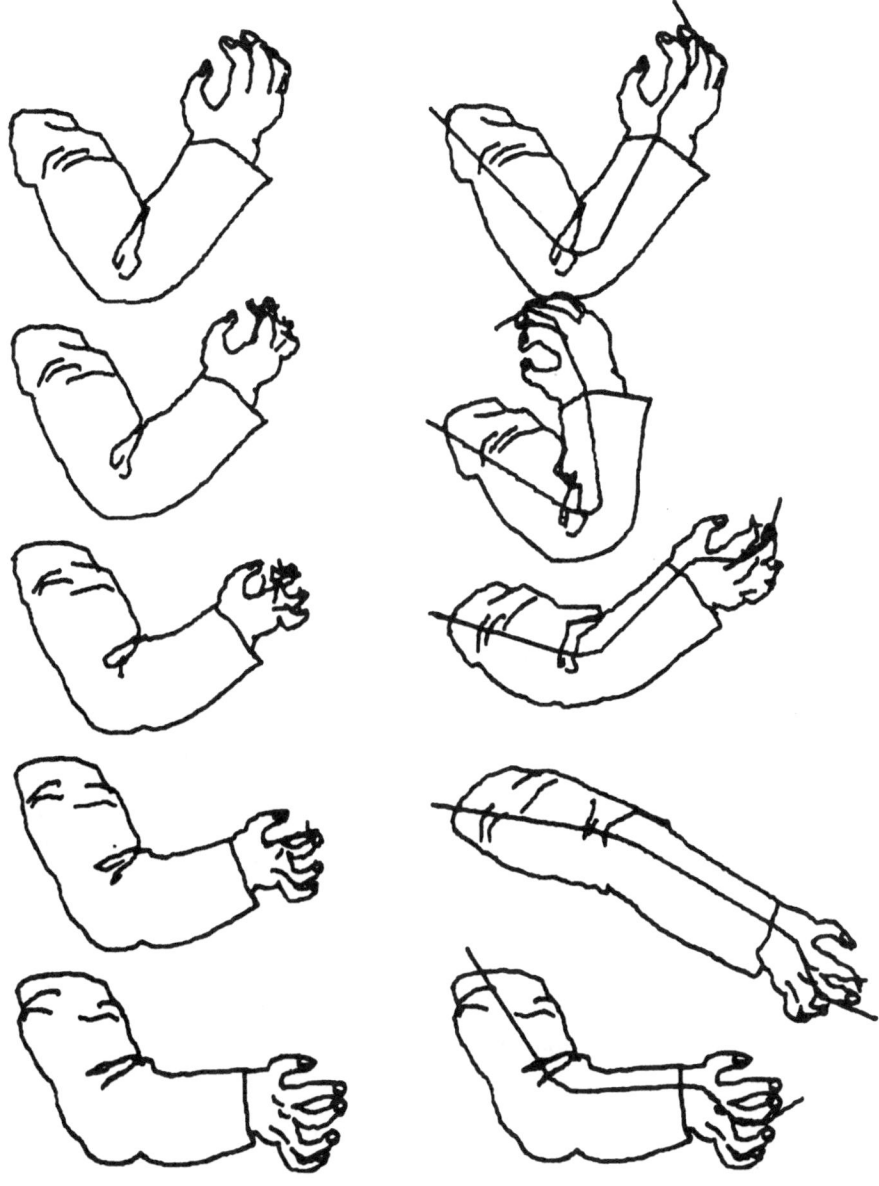

Fig. 5.12. Skeleton Technique Animation System by M. Wein and N. Burtnyk, National Research Council of Canada

polation is not suitable for producing classical movements involving a modification of location. This problem can be solved by programming all physical laws that drive this movement. However, this approach requires thorough knowledge of both physics and computer science. Moreover, physical equations for many motions are quite difficult to express.

An interesting technique that can be combined with interpolation, as shown in Sect. 5.7, involves the use of path descriptions and P-curves, as first introduced by R. Baecker [1969] in his GENESYS system.

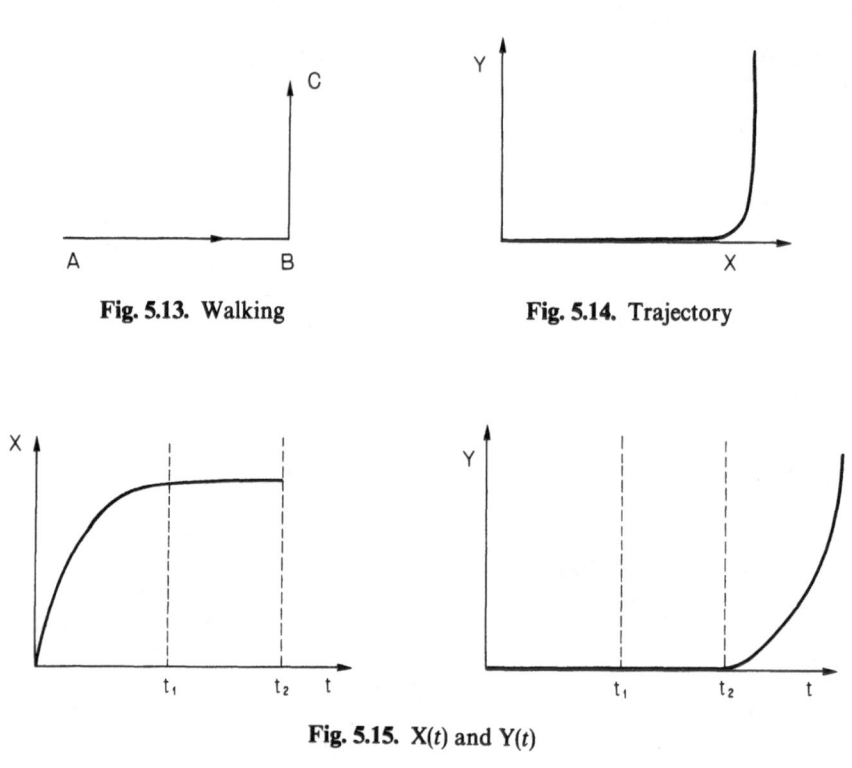

Fig. 5.13. Walking   **Fig. 5.14.** Trajectory

Fig. 5.15. X(t) and Y(t)

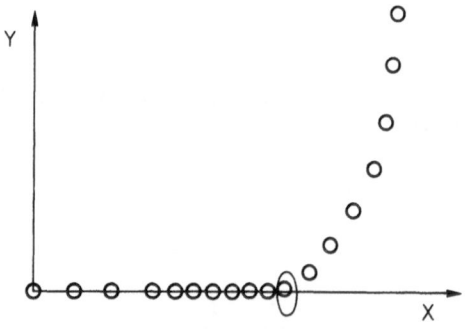

Fig. 5.16. P-curve

A dynamic picture is obtained by the continuous altering of a static picture. These alterations are obtained by specifying the temporal behavior of a parameter. For example, the temporal behavior of the position of a point can easily be represented by a P-curve.

A P-curve defines both the trajectory of the point and its location in time. In an example suggested by Baecker [1969], a person goes from one corner A of a square room to the diagonally opposite corner C by walking along two adjacent walls. Figure 5.13 shows the situation and the trajectory, $Y = f(X)$, is shown in Fig. 5.14. However, no indication of time is given here.

It is also possible to represent the two curves corresponding to the variation of X and Y with time $X(t)$ and $Y(t)$, as shown in Fig. 5.15.

We observe that there is almost no motion between t_1 and t_2; that is not shown on Fig. 5.14. A P-curve allows the animator to express the information contained in Fig. 5.14 and Fig. 5.15 on a unique graph. In our example, the P-curve has the shape of the trajectory, but a trail of symbols is used instead of a continuous line to depict the path. The symbols are spaced equally in time. This means that the dynamics are represented by the local density of the symbols, as shown in Fig. 5.16.

5.7 In-betweening Using Moving Point Constraints

As discussed, in-betweening often provides bad results, because of the use of linear interpolation. Even if a nonlinear law is used, this is a nonlinear variation in time only and not in space. In fact it is not sufficient to specify the speed of interpolation; it is also desirable to specify a nonlinear path. Reeves [1981] has proposed a method of in-betweening using moving point constraints. This method is meant to allow the specification of multiple paths and speeds of interpolation and to reduce motion discontinuities at key frames.

The principle of the technique is to associate a curve varying in space and time with some points of the animated object. This curve is called a moving point and it controls the trajectory and the dynamics of the point similarly to P-curves.

Figure 5.17 shows an example with three keyframes (K1, K2, and K3) and three moving points (M1, M2, and M3). The shape of the curves specifies the path of interpolation; for example, A1 is transformed into A2 using the moving point M1. B1 is transformed into B2 and then into B3 using the moving point M2. C1 is transformed into C2 and then into C3 using the moving point M3. Symbols along the curves indicate timing. Each symbol represents an equal length of time.

With such a strategy, only the moving points need to be defined; the curves in the keyframes do not have to be numbered and counted.

Several different in-betweening algorithms can be applied in the Reeves technique: the Miura algorithm [Miura et al., 1967], the Coons algorithm [1974] and the cubic metric space in-between algorithm [Reeves, 1980].

The three algorithms must operate on complete path networks. Figure 5.18 shows such a network corresponding to Fig. 5.17. Reeves [1980] has tested several simple algorithms for completing the networks.

In Fig. 5.19 we consider one patch, defined by four curves, involving parts of two keyframes (e.g., K1 and K2) and two moving points (e.g., M1 and M2).

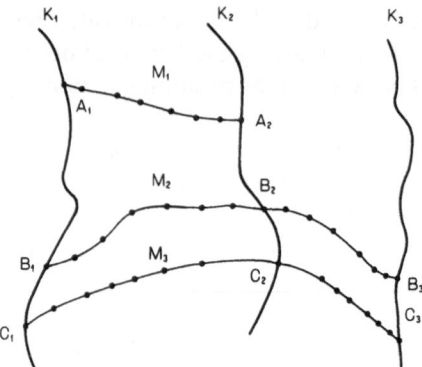

Fig. 5.17. In-betweening using moving point contraints

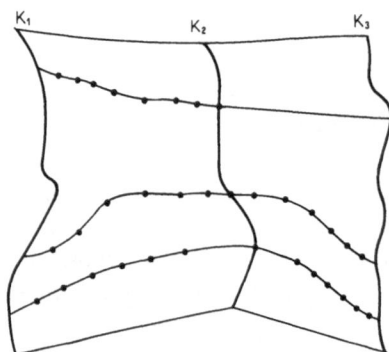

Fig. 5.18. Patch network

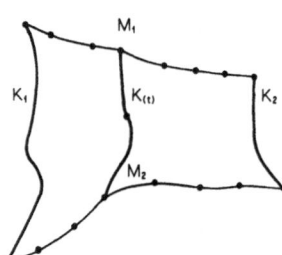

Fig. 5.19. One patch

The in-betweening problem is to find the curve $K(t)$ that represents the in-between part corresponding to K1 to K2 at time t.

The Miura algorithm consists of the following steps:

1. Approximate the curves K1 and K2 by two segment lines L1 and L2 with the same extremities as K1 and K2.
2. Find the transformation T_1 that transforms L1 into $L(t)$ where $L(t)$ is the approximation of $K(t)$ with the same extremities.
3. Find the transformation T_2 that transforms L2 into $L(t)$.

The transformations T_1 and T_2 are composed of translation, rotation, and a scaling. In parametric notation, the curve $K(t)$ can now be expressed as:

$$(1 - t)T_1 + tT_2 \qquad (5.5)$$

The Coons algorithm is based on the Coons representation for three-dimensional objects used in computer-aided design. It defines each patch by its four boundaries and normal derivative functions at these boundaries. Interpolation is performed by

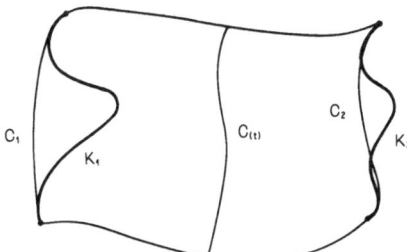

Fig. 5.20. Parametric curves

calculating a surface which will satisfy the boundary conditions. This means that adjoining patches will be curvature continuous across their common boundary.

The cubic metric space in-betweening algorithm is similar to the Miura algorithm but it produces much better continuity along boundaries between patches. Instead of using segment lines $L_1, L_2, L(t)$, Reeves uses cubic curves $C_1, C_2, C(t)$. As shown in Fig. 5.20, the parametric curves C_1 and C_2 match the positions of the key frames K_1 and K_2 at their two end points, but they also match the first derivatives. $C(t)$ is also a parametric cubic curve defined in such a way that the endpoints are the positions of the moving points at time t and its endpoint slopes are the time-weighted average of the slopes at the corresponding endpoints of K_1 and K_2.

The in-between shape $K(t)$ is obtained by applying to K_1 and K_2 the transformation that transforms C_1 into $C(t)$ and C_2 into $C(t)$ with the conditions that $K(t)$ much match $C(t)$'s position and slope at its end points.

5.8 Coloring Techniques

The use of color in cartoons is very important. When the number of cels that have to be colored is considered, it can be seen that the computer can play an important role relieving the tedium and expense of hand coloring. The principle is very simple: the artist points to an area on the color display by using a locator device, and the area is colored. The color has, of course, to be chosen beforehand by the artist. Generally, that it also accomplished by pointing to a selection in a menu of colors, called the **palette**. This operation of area filling or coloring is one operation of more general interactive systems called **paint systems**. These systems will be discussed in detail in the next section. The coloring operation is also often implemented in graphics editors. Figure 5.21 shows an example made with the graphics editor GRAFEDIT [N. Magnenat-Thalmann et al. 1982]. There are two kinds of coloring algorithms:

1. **Region-filling algorithms**, which are used to fill regions defined by pixel values in a frame buffer
2. **Polygon-filling algorithms**, which are used to fill polygons defined by their vertices

Fig. 5.21. An example produced with GRAFEDIT. © N. Magnenat-Thalmann and D. Thalmann

Region-filling algorithms are much faster because they work directly with pixels. However, they cannot be easily used in systems that manipulate objects by complex transformations. This means that region-filling algorithms are very suitable for coloring backgrounds, but they are not very adequate for coloring any cel.

A region-filling algorithm has to solve the following problem: given a connected set of pixels of color C1 bounded by pixels of different colors (all different from C1), change these and only these pixels from color C1 to a different color, C2. We consider that pixels are 4-connected, meaning that any pixel can be reached from another one by a sequence of any of the four one-pixel moves: up, down, left, right. A simple algorithm consists of first determining whether the pixel at $\langle X, Y \rangle$ is still of color C1. If so, the value is changed to C2 and the four neighboring pixels are then examined. The process is typically recursive.

Alvy Ray Smith [1979] has developed a more efficient algorithm (tint-filling) that is based on the same basic principle. However, instead of recursion, the algorithm works with runs. A run is defined as a horizontal group of adjacent pixels within the region. In this method, the contiguous horizontal run containing the starting pixel is colored with C2. Then by examining the row above the just-filled run from left to right, the right-most pixel of each run is found and stacked. The same process is applied to the row below the just-filled run. After processing a run, the next run is given by the pixel address at the top of the stack. The algorithm is finished when the stack is empty.

A typical polygon-filling algorithm is based on a scan-line method. The polygon is scanned by horizontal (scan) lines. For each scan-line, there are three steps:

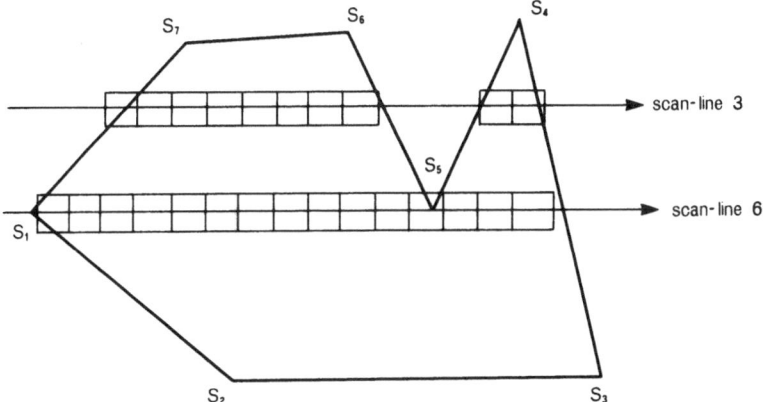

Fig. 5.22. Scan-line algorithm

1. Find the intersection of the scan-line with the edges of the polygon.
2. Sort the intersections by increasing x-coordinates.
3. Color all pixels that remain within pairs of intersections.

Figure 5.22 shows an example: at scan-line 6, there is a problem with the pixel at the vertex S_5; it must be counted twice.

The calculations of intersections can take a great deal of time. It should be noted that for each scan-line there are only a few edges of the polygon which may have an intersection with the scan-line. We may also assume that an edge which has an intersection with a scan-line has a high probability of intersecting the next scan-line. Moreover, it is possible to compute the x-coordinate (x_{i+1}) of the intersection point of an edge with the scan-line $i + 1$ using the x-coordinate (x_i) of the intersection point computed with the scan-line i:

$$x_{i+1} = x_i + \frac{1}{m} \tag{5.6}$$

where m is the slope of the edge.

These properties are taken into account in the scan-line color-filling algorithm. For each scan-line, only edges which have an intersection are considered; these edges are stored in the **table of active edges** (TAE). At each new scan-line, new intersections are computed using Eq. 5.6 and the TAE is updated. Edges in the TAE are sorted in increasing order of their x-coordinates in order to decide which pixels to color.

TAE may be more easily updated when another table is created: the **table of edges** (TE), including all edges of the polygon sorted in increasing order of their maximum y-coordinate. Each entry of the TE includes the smallest y-coordinate of the edge (used to eliminate the edge of the TAE), the x-coordinate of the edge bound which has the largest y-coordinate, and the value of $1/m$.

5.9 Paint Systems

A paint system is much more than an interactive system with area filling or coloring facilities. It simulates the normal tools of a painter. Typically, a paint system is a menu-driven program for handpainting two-dimensional images. The painter uses a stylus, or pen. First, he chooses a color from a palette, i.e., a color menu. Then, the artist selects a "brush" that can have any 2-dimensional shape. Painting is accomplished by moving the stylus. A stroke is drawn as a succession of copies of the brush.

One of the most well-known paint systems is PAINT [Smith 1978] which was developed at the New York Institute of Technology. The system offers several menus and many commands. In particular, the following is included in PAINT:

- Different modes of painting: simple, rubber stamping, smearing, filtered, anti-aliased
- Automatic filling (with the tint-fill algorithm)
- Brush creation and storage
- Palette creation and storage
- Picture storage
- A way of recording actions
- An input scanner
- Drafting aids like smoothing

Several other existing paint systems are described in the journal *Computer Graphics World* [CGW, 1982]. Recently, paint systems have been developed for microcomputers, e.g., MacPaint, PixelPaint, and SuperPaint. Algorithms for brush movements are proposed by Fishkin and Barsky [1985]. The Paint problem is further discussed by Giloth and Veeder [1985].

5.10 Color Simulation and Dithering

Coloring and painting systems can theoretically be implemented for any color raster terminal. However, very realistic images can only be produced using expensive devices. It is difficult to produce good images with a low-resolution screen, such as those currently available on popular home computer systems. But with a fairly reasonable resolution, say 512×512 pixels, it is possible to produce good images in two dimensions if colors, intensity, and so on are not too restricted.

For example, Magnenat-Thalmann et al. [1984a] developed a simulation of colors for a terminal with a resolution of 420×640 pixels. It had a choice of 64 different colors but only 8 could be displayed at the same time. However, the terminal had 120 patterns that could be programmed. These patterns had 8×14 pixels and allowed the user to control colors at the pixel level. N colors were provided to a procedure along with their weights and intensity in the mixture. This procedure produced then an $N \times M$ matrix of colors, which were then used to fill polygons.

To record the colors in the $N \times M$ matrix, we consider this matrix as a width tape of $N \times M$ "cells". Each "cell" has a color number. The tape is followed by putting in a color number every X "cells" according to the distribution of the color

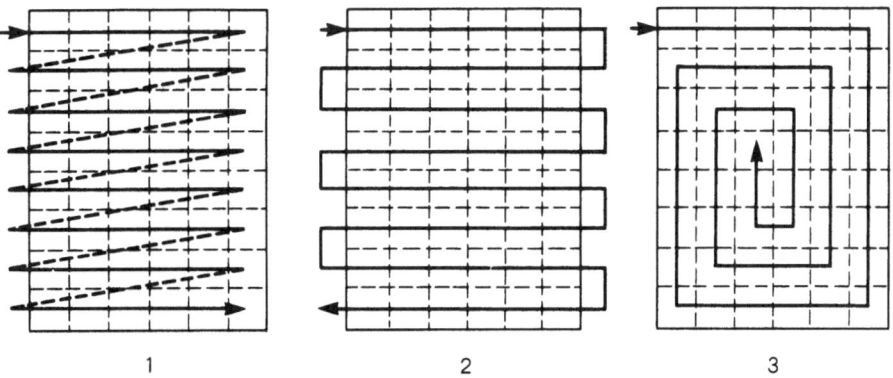

Fig. 5.23. Three methods of color distribution

in the mixture. This distribution is a function of the relative weights and density of the mixture and is calculated as follows:

- Add all the color weights.
- Compute the relative weights of each color, depending on the density.
- Compute the distribution step, a correction, and a correction frequency. The last two values are only used when there are collisions in the color distribution process.

Once distribution steps for each color have been computed, they must be used in the distribution process. But how is the pattern followed? How does the imaginary tape advance through the pattern? Three methods were studied, as shown in Fig. 5.23. The third method (spiral) was choosen because it produces the most homogeneity.

During the distribution process, collisions are possible; this means that a color number is assigned to a "cell" that is already occupied. We proceed as follows:

if the "cell" is occupied (collision)
then if we may go back *then begin* go back;
                        if the cell is free
                        then put in the color number
                        else go forward to the next free cell
                        end
              else go forward to the next free cell

Another way of simulating colors by pattern can be based on techniques used for halftone images like the **ordered dither technique**, which is used to display an *m-x-m* image on an *m-x-m* bi-level display (Judice et al. 1974). In this method, a pixel (x, y) is the desired intensity at the point (x, y) and D_{ij} is an element of the *n-x-n* dither matrix D. The indices i and j are calculated by the equations:

$$i = x \ modulo \ n \quad and \quad j = y \ modulo \ n$$

The dither matrices, calculated by Judice et al. (1974), are matrices where each of the integers 0 to $n^2 - 1$ appear once in each matrix. More recently, Hild and Pins [1989] introduced a 3D error diffusion dither algorithm for half-tone animation on bitmap screens.

5.11 Gradation Techniques

To produce realistic images in two dimensions, one of the best methods is the use of gradation. Many pictures can be represented by using gradations to simulate special effects such as shading, light effects, reflections, and so on. Typical examples of drawings with gradation include sunsets, sea, landscapes, trees, and mountains.

Gradation techniques start from an initial figure and "converge" to another, for example a line segment or a point. The gradation is obtained by coloring intermediate figures. At each step, the color is lighter or darker, depending on the parameters.

Three algorithms may be described:

1. **Gradation to a point P**
   The gradation is obtained by the following steps:
   i)   The initial figure is filled with the mixture defined by the array of colors and the initial intensity.
   ii) A ratio R of homothesis is computed based on the number of steps.
   iii) Intermediate figures are computed by homothesis with ratio R and center P, and are then filled with the mixture defined by the array of colors. The intensity is calculated by using the chosen rule.
   Figure 5.24 shows an example.

Fig. 5.24. An example of gradation to a point: "a candle" (Designer: N. Chourot. © N. Magnenat-Thalmann and D. Thalmann)

2. **Gradation to a line segment S_1S_2**

This method uses the two-figure interpolation technique introduced by Burtnyk and Wein [1971] and presented in Sect. 5.3. It requires that the initial and the final figures have control points that allow a correspondence between them. In the gradation example presented (Fig. 5.25), we have to add two control points to the initial figure F. These points correspond to the two intersections between F and the line passing through the segment S_1S_2, as shown. We also build a circular segment C that includes S_1 and S_2 as control points. Then the interpolation process starts between the figures F and C. All intermediate figures calcu-

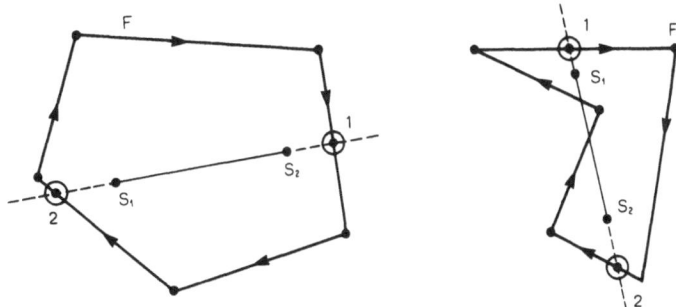

Fig. 5.25. Gradation to a line segment

Fig. 5.26. An example of gradation to a segment: "spheres in the sky" (Designer: N. Chourot. © N. Magnenat-Thalmann and D. Thalmann)

lated by the interpolation process are displayed and filled with the mixture obtained by using the array of colors and the intensity calculated with the chosen rule. Figure 5.26 shows an example.

3. **Gradation to another Figure F2**

   This method uses the same interpolation technique between the two figures. To suit both figures to the interpolation process, the following algorithm is applied:

   i) *look for* the left-most point P_{L2} of F2

       if P_{L2} is on the left of the highest point of F1

       and on the left of the lowest point of F1

       then look for the point P_{L1} of F1 that is the nearest to

       P_{L2} *else* look for the left-most point P_{L1} of F1

   ii) add P_{L1} as control point of F1

       add P_{L2} as control point of F2

When this algorithm has been applied, the interpolation and color process is the same as in the previous gradation method.

6. Object Modeling in 3D Animation

6.1 What is 3D Animation?

While computer-assisted animation is a highly valuable and interesting process, computer-modeled animation is even more fascinating. Here the computer becomes more than a support, playing a basic role in the creation of a three-dimensional world. Man, in fact, has always found it difficult to represent three-dimensional space in drawings; few people can draw in true perspective. Furthermore, it is simply impossible to produce all the tens of thousands of drawings needed for an animated film by hand. In this sense, the computer is not replacing man, since it does jobs which simply cannot be performed manually. Modeled animation has been used in television advertisements [Crow 1978] and for special effects in films like *2001: A Space Odyssey*, *Return of the Jedi* and especially *TRON*. Three-dimensional computer animation involves three main activities:

1. **Object modeling:** this consists of describing or constructing three-dimensional objects.
2. **Motion specification and synchronization:** to animate an object is to make it move, or to change its shape or position over a period of time. Not only must the movements be created for all the actors involved in each scene, but all these movements must be synchronized. When making an ordinary video film, movements can be filmed of course, but the camera itself can also be moved. The same principle applies to three-dimensional computer animation, although instead of wielding a real camera, a dummy, or "virtual," camera is simulated. The location of the camera, its positioning, and even focus are programmed. Furthermore, all these parameters can be varied or combined so that any camera motion can be simulated (pan, tilt, zoom). [Magnenat-Thalmann and Thalmann 1986b].
3. **Image rendering:** this is the process of producing a realistic image by removing hidden surfaces and adding effects like shading, shadows, transparency, and texture. These techniques will be discussed in detail in Chaps. 8 and 9.

6.2 Object Representation

Typically, object representations may be classified into three levels:

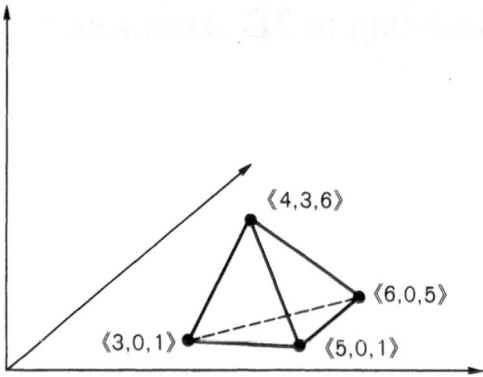

Fig. 6.1. A tetrahedron

- Wire-frame representations
- Surface representations
- Volume representations

In a **wire-frame representation**, objects are merely represented by a set of segment lines, typically by vertices and edges, with no data on the surfaces and volumes. Such a representation is frequently too simple and cannot be used to achieve a high degree of realism. Consider the tetrahedron shown in Fig. 6.1. This can be represented by:

moveabs ⟨3,0,1⟩
lineabs ⟨5,0,1⟩, ⟨6,0,5⟩, ⟨3,0,1⟩, ⟨4,3,6⟩, ⟨6,0,5⟩
moveabs ⟨5,0,1⟩
lineabs ⟨4,3,6⟩

where "moveabs P" moves to the location P and "lineabs P1, P2...PN" draws a line from the current location to the new locations P1 to PN.

In a **surface representation**, objects are represented by a set of primitive surfaces. Typically, three categories of description are used, depending on the object shape:

- Description by a set of polygons
- Description by the equation of an algebraic surface
- Description by patches

In a **solid representation**, objects are essentially considered as a set of primitive volumes or as a bounded portion of the 3D space.

When a user builds an object, certain things have to be known about the model used to represent the object. This model, which requires some knowledge about the object, is called an **external model**. A high level external model is a **procedural model**, which is in fact a model based on data abstraction. In a procedural model, the object is not defined explicitly but is represented by a piece of code (a procedure or a high-level graphic type) to which parameters are passed. For example, a procedural model for a box (parallelepiped) may only require four vertices. Then, the object is encoded according to an **internal model**. In our example, the cube may be defined:

- As a wire-frame: 12 segment lines (edges) defined by vertex coordinates
- As a surface: six polygonal facets defined by vertex coordinates
- As a volume: a solid defined by its boundary representation, a space subdivision, or as a volume primitive

Moreover, an object may be converted from a **geometric internal model** to a **display internal model**. For example, a parametric surface may be defined by a few coefficients, but converted into a polygonal planar facet internal model for the display step. Image-synthesis systems often convert all external models into a unique internal representation, because this facilitates the manipulation and transformation of objects. For example, the same deformation primitive cannot be easily applied to a cube and a sphere if the first is represented by planar facets and the second as a solid primitive. Ideally, internal models should be hidden from the user. However, most existing image-synthesis systems and languages require the user to have considerable knowledge of the internal models used.

6.3 Surface Modeling

The most well-known technique involves describing a surface by a **collection of polygons**. Lists of points and polygons are specified, where each polygon is defined by its vertices, identified by their rank in the list of points. For example, the tetrahedron of Fig. 6.1 can be defined as:

```
POINT      ⟨⟨3, 0, 1⟩⟩
POINT      ⟨⟨5, 0, 1⟩⟩
POINT      ⟨⟨6, 0, 5⟩⟩
POINT      ⟨⟨4, 3, 6⟩⟩
POLYGON    1, 2, 4
POLYGON    2, 3, 4
POLYGON    1, 3, 4
POLYGON    1, 2, 3
```

Polygons can model any object. However, if the object is curved, a large number of polygons may be required. For this reason, algebraic surfaces and patches are often used.

Algebraic surfaces are curved surfaces described mathematically by an equation. The most popular include the quadric surfaces like spheres (Fig. 6.2), cones, cylinders, and ellipsoids (Fig. 6.3). A new and powerful family of parametric shapes had recently extended these basic quadric surfaces: the superquadrics [Barr 1981]. These generalize the basic quadric surfaces by producing a continuum of useful forms with rounded edges and filleted faces. Angle-preserving transformations operate on a predefined surface or space curve, bending and twisting the object into a new form.

For representing car bodies or airplane surfaces, a good procedure is to use bivariate surface **patches**. Surfaces are constructed piecewise, sewing the patches

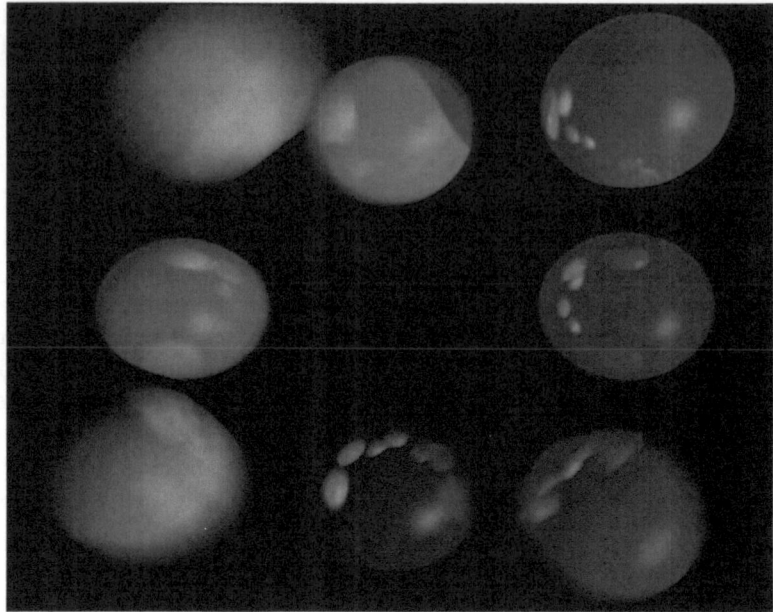

Fig. 6.2. Balls in motion by Tom Porter and Rob Cook

Fig. 6.3. Caterpillar by Don Herbison-Evans, Univ. Sydney

together with specified continuity conditions. The two most well-known surface patches are the work of Coons and Bezier.

In the technique introduced by Coons [1964], a surface patch is determined by four boundary curves, P(U, 0), P(U, 1), P(0, V), P(1, V) where U and V are in the range 0,1 and by a linear interpolation between these four curves:

$$Q(U, V) = P(U, 0)F_{00}(V) + P(U, 1)F_{01}(V) + P(0, V)F_{00}(U)$$
$$+ P(1, V)F_{01}(U) - P(0, 0)F_{00}(U)F_{00}(V)$$
$$- P(0, 1)F_{00}(U)F_{01}(V)$$
$$- P(1, 0)F_{01}(U)F_{00}(V) - P(1, 1)F_{01}(U)F_{01}(V) \qquad (6.1)$$

where the functions $F_{ij}(U)$ serve to blend the boundary conditions to form a surface.

In the method introduced by Bezier [1972], a surface is calculated from N curves given by M points. These points P_{ij} are called control points and the surface is calculated as:

$$Q(U, V) = \sum_{i=0}^{N} \sum_{j=0}^{M} P_{ij} B_{iN}(U) B_{jM}(V) \qquad (6.2)$$

where U and V are in the range $[0; 1]$.

$$B_{iN}(U) = \frac{N!}{i!(N - i)!} U^i (1 - U)^{N-i} \qquad (6.3)$$

$$B_{jM}(V) = \frac{M!}{j!(M - j)!} V^j (1 - V)^{M-j} \qquad (6.4)$$

Figure 6.4 shows an example of a Bezier surface in a line drawing.

Bézier surfaces do not pass through the control vertices. It is also essential to note that Bézier surfaces do not have **local control**. This means that while control points have greatest impact closest to them, they also have an influence anywhere on the surface. The movement of a single vertex affects the entire surface. The most important drawback of Bézier surfaces is their dependence on the number of control vertices. A series of N × M control points generates a Bézier surface of degree N + M − 2.

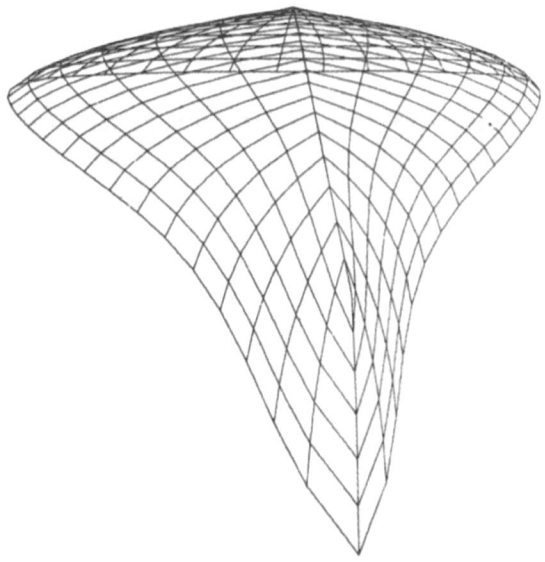

Fig. 6.4. A Bezier surface

B-spline surfaces provide partial solutions to two problems with Bézier surfaces: nonlocalness and the fact that the degree is dependent on the number of control points. Their formulation is not very different from that of Bézier surfaces. Consider a grid of $(N + 1) \times (M + 1)$ control points P_{ij} with corresponding knots t_i. A B-spline surface is defined by the following tensor product:

$$S_{k,l}(u, v) = \sum_{i=0}^{N} \sum_{j=0}^{M} P_{ij} N_{i,k}(u) N_{j,l}(v) \tag{6.5}$$

where k and l are the B-spline surface orders.

$N_{i,k}$ are **basis B-spline functions of order k**; they are recursively defined as:

$$N_{i,1}(t) = 1 \quad \text{if } t_i \leq t \leq t_{i+1} \\ \phantom{N_{i,1}(t) =} 0 \quad \text{otherwise} \tag{6.6}$$

$$N_{i,k}(t) = \frac{(t - t_i) N_{i,k-1}(t)}{t_{i+k-1} - t_i} + \frac{(t_{i+k} - t) N_{i+1,k-1}(t)}{t_{i+k} - t_{i+1}} \tag{6.7}$$

The basis function $N_{i,k}(t)$ is a polynomial of degree $k - 1$ which guarantees C^{k-2} continuity for the whole curve. In other terms, a B-spline of order k may be mathematically defined as a piecewise polynomial of degree $k - 1$ that guarantees continuity of the first $k - 2$ derivatives. A B-spline of order k for a span i may also be considered as weighted average of the B-splines of order $k - 1$ on the spans i and $i + 1$. As shown in Eq. 6.7, each weight is obtained by ratio of the distance between the parameter t and the end knot, to the length of the $k - 1$ spans. It is important to note that the calculation of $N_{i,k}(t)$ only involves knots t_i to t_{i+k}. This means that local control is possible; the modification of a single control point does not change the whole curve but only a limited portion. This feature is quite interesting for the development of interactive graphics systems. The order of continuity of a B-spline surface is controlled by the orders k and l. This order is independent of the number of control vertices. Unfortunately, when k or l is increased, calculations become much more complex. Moreover, as k and l are orders, they are integers and continuous variation, which may be required in animation, is quite impossible.

β-spline surfaces [Barsky 1984] are also produced from control points, but they have the great advantage of being based on geometric considerations. A β-spline surface is defined by the following tensor product:

$$S_{i,j}(u, v) = \sum_{r=-2}^{1} \sum_{s=-2}^{1} P_{i+r,j+s} b_r(\beta_1, \beta_2, u) b_s(\beta_1, \beta_2, v) \tag{6.8}$$

where $0 \leq u \leq 1$ and $0 \leq v \leq 1$, $i = 2$ to $m - 1$ and $j = 2$ to $n - 1$.

In the basis β-spline functions of Eq. 6.8, β_1 and β_2 are two parameters called **bias** and **tension**. The bias β_1 provides control over the symmetry of the surface generated from the control points, and the tension β_2 controls the degree of adherence of the surface to the control points. When β_1 is increased, the curve begins to skew to one side and approach the control polygon in an asymptotic fashion. When β_2 is increased, the curve flattens and uniformly approaches the control polygon.

β-spline surfaces may be easily used in an interactive environment because they are flexible and based on geometric relations. The method for transforming these surfaces is more natural than other methods based on algebraic considerations. The shape parameters may vary continuously since they are real numbers. As the degree 6 of β-spline surfaces is constant, the CPU time is the same for any value of the shape parameters. The main drawback of β-spline curves and surfaces is that they do not pass through any of the control vertices, not even the first and the last. This means that two fictitious control points may, if necessary, have to be added to circumvent the problem. Figures 6.5 and 6.6 show examples of bivariate surface patches.

It is important to note that an object is often build up as a combination of simpler objects that can be modeled in different ways. Figure 6.7 shows a wire-frame giraffe that is modeled as follows:

head ....box
neck ....series of circular cones
thigh ....truncated clliptic cone
knee-cap .... sphere
foreleg ....cylinder
hoof ....two bodies of revolution
tail ....cylinder and truncated cone

6.4 Object Creation

Whatever the external or internal model, graphic data must be entered into the computer by the user. Several practical methods are available and have been surveyed by Smith [1983] and Greenberg et al. [1982]. The simplest, but most inconvenient way is by numerical input from a keyboard. Although this is probably the most accurate method, it is also the most time-consuming. Graphic input methods are more popular and more widely accepted. Various approaches are possible:

– Direct 3D digitizing
– 2D Digitizing and 3D reconstruction methods
– Using object modeling systems
– Methods based on procedural models

3D Digitizing

The most direct 3D digitizing technique is simply to enter the 3D coordinates using a 3D digitizer. Three types of such devices are now available:

– Devices based on three orthogonal magnetic fields transmitted to a wand: the strengths of the fields are used to determine where the wand is located and establish a data point on the object's surface
– Devices based on three sound captors: the user digitizes 3D points, emitting a sound which is measured by the captors
– Devices based on laser light distance from the device to the object as determined by the laser

Fig. 6.5. Logo produced using B-splines (Designers: André Pavanello and Xavier Pintado. © N. Magnenat-Thalmann and D. Thalmann)

Fig. 6.6. Bézier surfaces (Designers: André Pavanello and Xavier Pintado. © N. Magnenat-Thalmann and D. Thalmann)

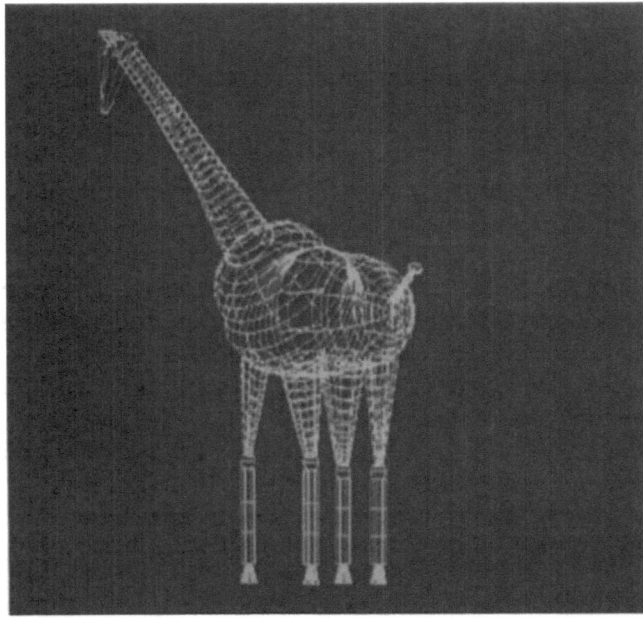

Fig. 6.7. A giraffe

3D Reconstruction from 2D Information

A more common way of creating 3D objects is by 3D reconstruction from 2D information. For example, the reconstruction may be based on photographs. In this case, the process is as follows:

1. Interesting points or grids are drawn onto the object.
2. Several pictures (e.g., four orthogonal pictures) are taken of the object. It is important to maximize the distance between the object and the camera and to use a telephoto lens. The error caused by perspective is therefore partially corrected. In fact, the object is generally situated on a turntable that allows the angle of the object to be changed depending on the orientation of the camera.
3. An appropriate coordinates system is drawn for each picture.
4. Each point is identified by a number. Points have to be identified in at least two pictures to compute the x-, y-, and z-coordinates of each point.
5. After placing the pictures on the digitizer, the user marks points that determine the boundaries of the pictures and those that identify the coordinate systems.
6. For each point, two different positions are successively marked.
7. Connections between the points are identified by numbers: this defines the strokes of points in wire-frame models and grids in facet-based models.

Object Modeling Systems

The purpose of an interactive object modeling system is to create three-dimensional objects, to modify them by geometrical transformations, and to assemble them to obtain a more complex object. Any object can be stored on a file; later, it can be retrieved for further modifications. The user communicates with the system by a set of simple commands and menus, guided by various messages and other feedback.

Procedural Models

Procedural models [Newell 1975; Clark 1976] represent objects procedurally in an attempt to retain the essential information concerning the global coherence of the objects. Typically, a procedurally modeled object is entirely represented by its procedure and its parameters, and so a procedural model is changed by changing its parameters. For example, a sphere can be modeled as a call to a *sphere* procedure, with its radius and center parameters. A *tree* procedural model is defined by parameters such as height, width, and number of branches. Procedural models also allow the implementation of geometric models to be hidden using the principle of data abstraction [Liskov and Zilles 1974]. In particular, abstract graphic data types were first introduced by Thalmann and Magnenat-Thalmann [1979].

Time-dependent procedural models can also simulate behavior. Several kinds of such models have been proposed:

– Actor and camera data types [Magnenat-Thalmann and Thalmann 1983b; Thalmann and Magnenat-Thalmann 1983]
– Procedural models based on data flow [Hedelman 1984]
– Subactor data types [Magnenat-Thalmann and Thalmann 1985c,d]
– Procedural models for natural phenomena [Green and Sun 1988]
– Time-based models [Chmilar and Wyvill 1989]

7. Motion Control in 3D Animation

7.1 A Classification of 3D Computer Animation Methods

Most authors [Magnenat-Thalmann and Thalmann 1985b] distinguish between two types of three-dimensional computer animation: keyframe animation and algorithmic animation.

Keyframe Animation

As already discussed in Chap. 5, keyframe animation consists of the automatic generation of intermediate frames, called in-betweens, based on a set of keyframes supplied by the animator. There are two fundamental approaches to keyframe animation:

1. The in-betweens are obtained by interpolating the keyframe images themselves. This technique is called **image-based keyframe animation** by Steketee and Badler [1985] and **shape interpolation** by Zeltzer [1985]. This is an old technique, introduced by Burtnyk and Wein [1971] and already discussed in Sect. 5.3 for 2D line drawings. A linear interpolation algorithm produces undesirable effects such as lack of smoothness in motion, discontinuities in the speed of motion, and distortions in rotations. Alternate methods have been proposed by Baecker [1969], Burtnyk and Wein [1976], Reeves [1981], and Kochanek and Bartels [1984]. According to Stekettee and Badler [1985], there is no totally satisfactory solution to the deviations between the interpolated image and the object being modeled.
2. A way of producing better images is to interpolate parameters of the model of the object itself. This technique is called **parametric keyframe animation** by Parke [1982] and Steketee and Badler [1985] and **key-transformation animation** by Zeltzer [1985]. In a parameter model, the animator creates keyframes by specifying the appropriate set of parameter values, parameters are then interpolated, and images are finally individually constructed from the interpolated parameters.

Algorithmic Animation

In this kind of animation, called **algorithmic animation** by Zeltzer [1985], **modeled animation** by Lansdown [1982] and Magnenat-Thalmann and Thalmann [1985a], or **procedural animation** by Isaacs and Cohen [1987], motion is algorithmically described. Physical laws are applied to parameters (e.g., joint angles). Control of these laws may be given by programming as in ASAS [Reynolds 1982] and MIRA [Magnenat-Thalmann and Thalmann 1983c] or using an interactive director-oriented approach as in the MIRANIM [Magnenat-Thalmann et al. 1985] system. With such an approach, any kind of law may be applied to the parameters. For example, the variation of a joint angle may be controlled by kinematic laws as well as dynamic laws. This latter approach has been recently introduced by several authors [Badler 1986; Armstrong and Green 1985a,b; Wilhelms and Barsky 1985; Girard and Maciejewski 1985] and will be further described in Chap. 12.

7.2 A Unified View

The three types of animation may be described in a more general and unified way. An animated object (actor) is characterized by a set of state variables that drive the motion of the actors. The evolution of the state variables is defined by an evolution law. The three types of animation may be redefined using the following terminology:

1. **Image-based keyframe animation**: actors are characterized by their vertices; motion is specified by giving keyframes. Each keyframe consists of a series of values corresponding to the vertices for that keyframe. In-betweens are calculated by applying an interpolation law for each corresponding vertex in the two keyframes. The interpolation law may be a linear law, a cubic law, or a spline interpolation law.
   state variables: vertices
   evolution law: interpolation law (e.g., linear interpolation, Reeves interpolation)
2. **Parametric keyframe animation**: actors are characterized by parameters; motion is specified by giving key values for each parameter. In-between values are calculated using an interpolation law such as a cubic law or a spline interpolation law.
   state variables: parameters
   evolution law: interpolation law (e.g., linear law, spline interpolation)
3. **Algorithmic animation**: actors are objects with a motion defined by a list of transformations (rotations, translations, etc...). Each transformation is defined by parameters (e.g., an angle in a rotation). These parameters may change during the animation according to any physical law.
   state variables: parameters of the transformations
   evolution laws: any physical law.

7.3 A Comparison of Methods

The various methods have advantages and disadvantages and may be compared using several criteria as shown in Table 7.1. From this table, it is clear that no one model is superior to all the others. In particular, methods which are efficient (low CPU time) do not provide very realistic animation except when human intervention is very important (e.g., shape interpolation with many keyframes). Several

Table 7.1. A comparative table of animation methods

	Animation quality	CPU time	Human intervention	Versatility	Source of difficulty
Shape interpolation	Depends on the number of key-frames	Depends on the number of points and the type of interpolation law	Very long; lack of creativity	Very bad	Often unrealistic except with many key-frames or a complex interpolation law
Parametric interpolation	Depends on the number of key-values	Depends on the number of parameters	Shorter, more creative	Better	To find the best parameters
Kinematic algorithmic animation	Depends on the laws, but often unrealistic	Depends on the laws, but not very expensive	May be difficult; depends on the human interface	Very good	Realistic laws are not so easy to find
Dynamic algorithmic animation	Very realistic	Very expensive	May be limited	Good	Complete dynamics-based models are too expensive for large sequences

authors have attempted to span the various approaches to animation [Hanrahan and Sturman 1985; Forest et al. 1986a,b; Schlag, 1986].

7.4 Three-dimensional Shape Interpolation

In this section, we describe a general shape interpolation algorithm [Hong et al. 1988] for facet-based objects. The shape interpolation technique may be defined as follows: two keyframes are given in advance in 3D; the method consists of producing a series of in-between images in such a way that the degree of the transformation is controlled by a real parameter varying from 0 to 1, as shown in Fig. 7.1.

The major problem is not to find the interpolation function, but the correspondence between the two given three-dimensional objects. The problem is much more complex than interpolation between line drawings (see Sect. 5.3), because the two facet-based objects generally have a different total number of vertices, a different total number of facets, and corresponding facets have a different number of vertices.

We call figure $\mathscr{F}$, a finite set of right-oriented polygonal facets: $\mathscr{F} = \{\langle p_i, N_i\rangle; i = 1, m\}$. Each facet p_i is defined as $p_i = \{S_{ij}; j = 1, n_i\}$ where S_{ij} are the vertices; N_i is the normal to the facet p_i.

Consider two figures $\mathscr{F}_S$ with N_S facets and $\mathscr{F}_D$ with N_D facets for which we wish to generate an in-between figure $\mathscr{F}_I$ with a degree of transformation controlled by the real parameter $\lambda \in [0, 1]$. The problem firstly consists of establishing a logical correspondence $p_{Dj} = f(p_{Si})$ between the facets p_{Si} of $\mathscr{F}_S$ and the facets p_{Dj} of $\mathscr{F}_D$; secondly, a correspondence must be found between vertices $D_{jk} = \phi(S_{ih})$ derived from facets p_{Si} and p_{Dj}, and finally the in-between figure $\mathscr{F}_I$ has to be constructed.

As both figures do not generally have the same number of facets and/or vertices, a "logical correspondence" must be found. By denoting these facets (or vertices) by $\{X_i; i = 1, m\}$ for $\mathscr{F}_S$ and $\{Y_j; i = 1, n\}$ for $\mathscr{F}_D$ and assuming $m \geq n$, we define as a "logical correspondence" a technique which:

- Selects the n most representative elements X'_1, X'_2, ... X'_n of the m elements of $\{X_i\}$ to be transformed into $Y_j; j = 1, n$, when $\lambda \to 1$. The n elements $\{X_{i'}\}$ which are transformed into n elements $\{Y_j\}$ are called the **main elements**
- Makes the $(m - n)$ remaining elements of $\{X_i\}$ gradually disappear as $\lambda \to 1$. These $(m - n)$ remaining elements are called **extra-elements**.

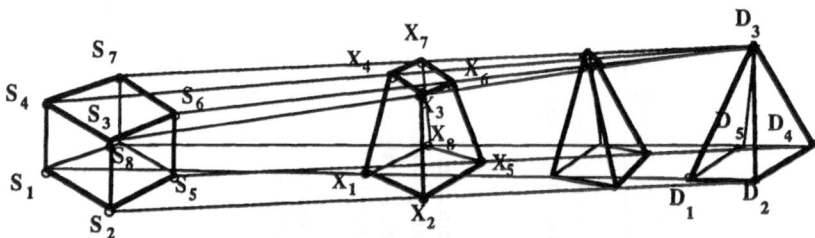

Fig. 7.1. An interpolation

If we assume that $N_S \geq N_D$, the algorithm works as follows:

Step 1: Perform a correspondence between facets

1.1 **Normalize** the two sets of centroids $\{C_{Si}\}$ and $\{C_{Dj}\}$.

1.2 Find the N_D most representative points of the N_S elements of $\{C_{Si}\}$ and make them correspond with the points of $\{C_{Dj}\}$ using a technique of **dynamic minimization** of distance. This means finding a subset $\{C'_{S1},...\} \subset \{C_{Si}\}$ and a bijective function f_1 such that:

$$f_1: \{C'_{S1}\} \rightarrow \{C_{Dj}\} \quad i, j = 1, n$$
$$C'_{S1} \rightarrow f_1(C'_{Si})$$

1.3 Find a mapping between the N_S-N_D remaining elements of $\{C_{Si}\}$ and those of $\{C_{Dj}\}$ using a technique of **image by neighborhood**. This means finding a mapping f_2 such that:

$$f_2: (\{C_{Si}\}\{C'_{Si}\} \rightarrow \{C_{Dj}\}$$
$$C_{Sk} \rightarrow f_2(C_{Sk})$$

1.4 Establish the facet correspondence as follows:

$$f: (\{C_{Si}\} \rightarrow \{C_{Dj}\}$$
$$C_{Si} \rightarrow f(C_{Si}) = f_1(C_{Si}) \text{ if } C_{Si} \in \{C'_{Si}\}$$
$$f_2(C_{Sk}) \text{ if } C_{Si} \in \{C'_{Si}\} - \{C'_{Si}\}$$

Step 2: Make a correspondence between vertices

First case: $C_{Si} \rightarrow f(C_{Si})$ where C_{Si} is a main facet:

2.1 Arrange all vertices of the facet j of $\mathscr{F}_D$ to **lie in the plane** of facet i of $\mathscr{F}_S$.

2.2 **Normalize** the set of vertices $\{S_{ik}\}$, $\{D_{jk}\}$, $S_{ik} \in P_{Si}$ and $D_{jk} \in P_{Dj}$.

2.3 Find the N_{Dj} most representative elements of the N_{Si} elements of $\{S_{ik}\}$ and make them correspond with those of $\{D_{jk}\}$.

2.4 Find a mapping between the $(N_{Si} - N_{Dj})$ remaining elements and those of $\{D_{jk}\}$.

2.5 Obtain a correspondence between vertices.

Second case: $f(C_{Si}) = C_{Dj}$ where C_{Si} is an extra-facet:

2.1b Consider $\{S_{ik}\}$ the set of vertices of the i-th main facet of $\mathscr{F}_S$, corresponding to $\{D_{jk}\}$ the set of vertices of the j-th facet of $\mathscr{F}_D$.

If there are more vertices in the i-th main facet of $\mathscr{F}_S$ than in the j-th facet of $\mathscr{F}_D$ then

find the neighborhoods $\{S_{ik}\}$ for $\{S_{hk}\}$ and then find $\phi_{hj}(S_{hk}) = \phi_{ij}(S_{ik})$. else

Solve the problem by temporarily replacing D_{jk} by $D_{jk} + \mu(\phi_{ji}(D_{jk}) - D_{jk})$

$$\mu \in [0, 1].$$

Step 3: Build in-between facets p_{li} of $\mathscr{F}_I$

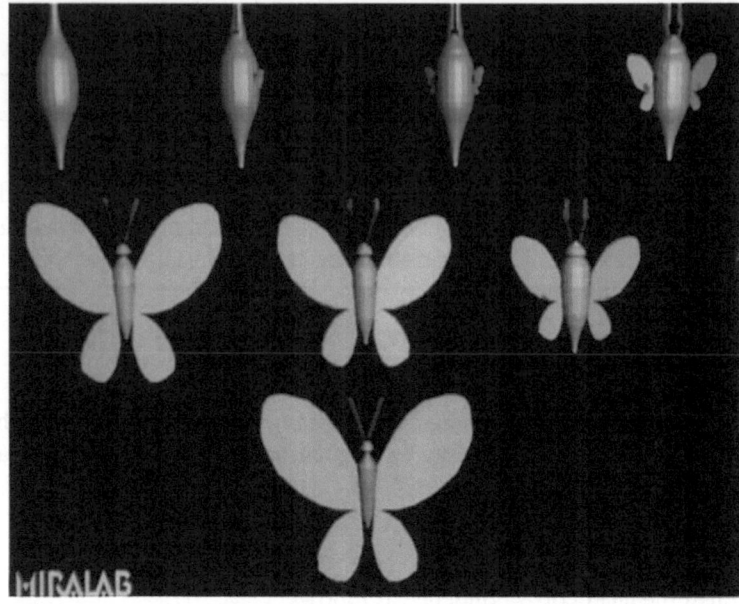

Fig. 7.2. Example of 3D shape interpolation (© Nadia Magnenat-Thalmann and Daniel Thalmann 1988)

Fig. 7.3. In this example, linear interpolation produces undesirable reduction of the arm length

The vertices of $\mathscr{F}_I$ are computed as follows:

$B_{ik} = S_{ik} + \lambda(\phi_{ij}(S_{ik}) - S_{ik}))$ if the interpolation is carried out between the facet i of $\mathscr{F}_S$ and the facet j of $\mathscr{F}_D$

Figure 7.2 shows an example of 3D shape interpolation using the above algorithm. Wesley Bethel and Uselton [1989] also propose an algorithm to solve this shape transformation.

With shape interpolation, it is theoretically possible to perform any motion. However, as shown in Fig. 7.3, this may produce undesirable distortions, especially for rotations. Consequently, for such motions, others methods should be used.

7.5 A Case Study: The Multiple Track Animator System

MUTAN [Fortin et al. 1983] is an interactive system for independently animating three-dimensional graphical objects (or parts of graphical objects), as in a scene. Its main purpose is to define, by key positions, the best motions for a graphical object. For example, MUTAN can synchronize motion with sound, light, or smell. Suppose, for example, that an animator would like to produce a film sequence in which two little girls are skating to music. There are two problems: the motion must be synchronized with the music and the two girls must be synchronized with each other.

To synchronize the motion with the music, marks are associated with appropriate frame numbers. These marks indicate that at this moment in time, the character is performing exactly a specific motion. As the intermediate frames are produced, it is not necessary to start again if the synchronization is found to be inadequate. The marks merely have to be moved.

An animator might also wish to adjust the motion of one individual without modifying the motion of the others. To solve this problem, we introduced the concept of a TRACK (as in sound reproduction). All animation constraints of a graphical object are recorded on each track.

The name MUTAN stands for "MUltiple Track ANimator," which means that the system can handle several tracks. It also provides a visual image that allows the animator to see exactly what is being done.

During an interactive session with MUTAN, the screen is divided into three areas:

1. **The chronogram/visual area**
   This displays either a schema of the tracks with the marks (chronogram mode) or a specific frame (visual mode), depending on the command.
2. **The animator-computer dialog area**
   Here the user may enter commands and receive error messages.
3. **The information area**
   This contains information about the tracks or about the current frame when it is displayed.

There are presently 19 commands in the MUTAN system, as shown in Table 7.2. Almost all commands have similar parameters:

- A track or a set of tracks
- A mark or a set of marks
- A frame number

CREATE ⟨track⟩, as the name implies, allows the animator to create a new track. This track of course has no marks. The command DELETE ⟨track⟩ is similarly self-explanatory.

If a film consists of a little girl MELANIE playing with a dog, the animator will use the commands CREATE MELANIE and CREATE DOG. These commands will initialize the tracks. To display them, the command TRACKS MELANIE DOG must be entered. Following this command, two red lines are displayed in the chronogram area. Each line identifies a track.

Now the marks must be placed on the tracks to define animation constraints. The command MARK ⟨frame number⟩⟨track⟩ allows the animator to create or modify a mark on a track and to define the frame number where the mark is placed.

Table 7.2. The MUTAN commands

ADD	– adds a certain number of frames
BACKWARD	– moves backward along the film
CREATE	– creates a track
CHRONOGRAM	– displays a part of film in the chronogram area
CUT	– cuts frames on one or several tracks
DELETE	– deletes a track
END	– ends the session
ERASE	– erases a mark
FILM	– produces the frames on a file
FORWARD	– moves forward along the film
GET	– memorizes a mark
IDENTIFY	– selects invisible marks
LOOK	– looks at any frame in the visual area
MARK	– creates or modifies a mark on a track
MENU	– displays a file indicated by an index
PUT	– replaces a mark on a track
READ	– reads mark information
TRACKS	– displays tracks in the chronogram area
WRITE	– writes mark information

For example, suppose the dog hears a whistle, stops running and then starts again. Two marks would be used.

MARK 15 DOG

MARK 18 DOG

For each MARK command, the animator receives the following message in the dialog area: "ENTER THE NAME OF THE FRAME"; he/she then types respectively "DOG STOPS", "DOG STARTS".

The MARK command can also be used without parameters. In this case the animator enters the mark on the red line representing the track. The principle is valid for other commands.

When the MARK command is used, the animator has to enter in the dialog area the name of a key position which identifies an image. The key positions can be created with a graphics editor, a graphical programming language, or by digitizing. The different key positions can be grouped into indices. The command MENU ⟨index⟩ shows the animator which key positions are available on the file indicated by the index. A mark can be erased with an appropriate command, while the command GET memorizes a mark before erasing it and PUT replaces it on the track.

The animator can move a window along the film by using the command CHRONOGRAM. This command has different forms. For example, CHRONOGRAM 50 75 MELANIE DOG, displays the frames 50 to 75 for the tracks MELANIE and DOG. At the same time, information about the different marks on this part of the film are displayed in the information area. If there are too many marks to display, only some of them are visible; others can be seen by using the command IDENTIFY.

As the work of an animator is essentially sequential, two commands have been added to move forwards and backwards along the film. FORWARD or BACK-WARD performs a shift to the right or left, moving the same number of frames as that presently displayed in the chronogram area.

The animator can cut one or several frames on one or several tracks by using the command CUT ⟨set of frames⟩⟨set of tracks⟩. All marks will be shifted to the left. Conversely, the command ADD ⟨frame number⟩⟨set of tracks⟩ adds a certain number of new frames to the right of the frame specified and on the chosen tracks. The number of frames added has to be entered by the animator in the dialog area.

The LOOK command allows the animator to look at any frame of the film in the visual area. For the frames where no marks exist, an interpolation is performed. It is also possible to select only one or several tracks: in this case, only a part of the frame is displayed. The command FILM produces the frames on a file to be recorded on a videorecorder or to be displayed for a camera. There are also commands to read and write MARK information on a file.

7.6 Parametric Keyframe Animation

Parametric keyframe animation is based on the following principle: an entity (object, camera, light) is characterized by parameters, the animator creates keyframes by specifying the appropriate set of parameter values at given time, parameters are then interpolated, and images are finally individually constructed from the interpolated parameters.

We now give an example: the joint of a robotic arm is characterized by an angle α varying during time t; the following values have been selected:

$$t = 0 \qquad \alpha = 10$$
$$t = 2 \qquad \alpha = 20$$
$$t = 5 \qquad \alpha = 45$$
$$t = 8 \qquad \alpha = 100$$

The value of the angle every $\frac{1}{30}$ second may be calculated by linear interpolation:

e.g., for $t = \frac{1}{30}$, we have $\alpha = 10 + \frac{20 - 10}{2 \cdot 30} = 10.1666\ldots$

However, as shown in Fig. 7.4, there is a first-derivative continuity problem: values of the angle for time $t = 2 - \frac{1}{30}$, $t = 2$ and $t = 2 + \frac{1}{30}$ are respectively:

$\alpha = 20 - \frac{20 - 10}{2 \cdot 30} = 19.81333$; $\alpha = 20$, $\alpha = 20 + \frac{45 - 20}{3 \cdot 30} = 20.2777\ldots$ We observe a discontinuity around the value 2. In summary, linear interpolation causes first-derivative discontinuities, causing discontinuities in speed and consequently jerky animation. The use of high-level interpolation such as cubic interpolation or spline interpolation is preferable, as shown in Fig. 7.5.

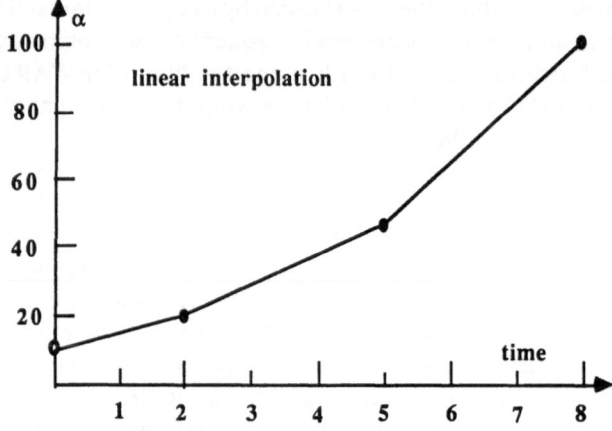

Fig. 7.4. Linear interpolation of the angle

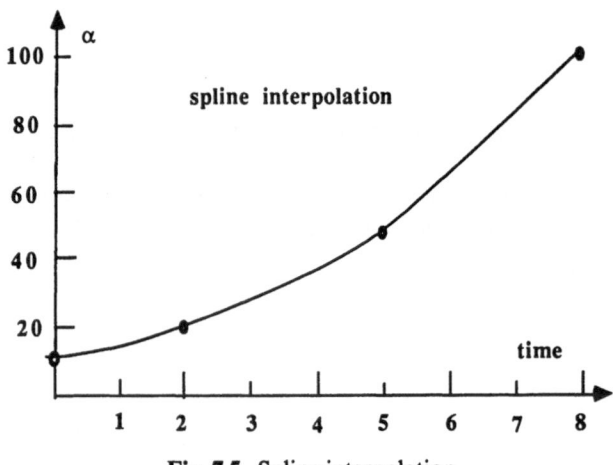

Fig. 7.5. Spline interpolation

7.7 The Use of Splines in Keyframe Animation

The problem of interpolation may be summarized as follows: given $N + 1$ data points, P_i, $i = 0$ to N, find a curve $Q(t)$ passing through these points. We assume that the value of the parameter t is given by the knots t_i of $Q(t)$. Two extreme cases are possible:

1. Join independently the pairs of points $\{P_i, P_{i+1}\}$

2. Find a unique curve passing through all the P_i by finding a polynomial $Q(t)$ of degree N. Since the degree of these functions is directly related to the number of points P_i, the interpolating curve tends to oscillate with large values of N. Moreover, it could be computationally very expensive.

Between the two extreme cases, there is a better approach—piecewise continuous interpolation of the curve. The interpolating curve must be continuous at the knots only up to a certain order m of its derivatives, i.e., it should be C^m continuous. For example, a piecewise third-degree polynomial can be constructed to achieve C^2 continuity (second derivative continuity) at the knots.

The term **spline** comes from a familiar drafting tool used in several industries. It is a thin and elastic lath used to draw a smooth curve though a set of given points as in interpolation. Splines can be described mathematically as piecewise approximations of cubic polynomial functions. Two kinds of splines are very popular: interpolating splines with C^1 continuity at knots, and approximating splines with C^2 continuity at knots. Approximative spline surfaces have been already described in Sect. 6.3. For animation, the most interesting splines are the interpolating splines: cardinal splines, Catmull-Rom splines, and Kochanek-Bartels splines.

Cardinal and Catmull-Rom Spline Interpolation

Consider again a list of points P_i and the parameter t along the spline. A new point V is obtained from each value of t from the four nearest given points along the curve (two behind, two ahead) by:

$$V = \mathcal{T} \mathcal{M} \mathcal{P}^T \tag{7.1}$$

where $\mathcal{T}$ is the matrix $[t^3\, t^2\, t\, 1]$, $\mathcal{M}$ is the spline matrix, and $\mathcal{P}$ is the matrix $[P_{k-1}, P_k, P_{k+1}, P_{k+2}]$.

With this approach, the spline matrix $\mathcal{M}$ is used to generate, for each four consecutive points P_{k-1}, P_k, P_{k+1} and P_{k+2}, the portion of the spline curve between the two middle points P_k, P_{k+1}. A popular spline matrix is the **cardinal spline** matrix:

$$\mathcal{M}_{CA} = \begin{bmatrix} -A & 2-A & A-2 & A \\ 2A & A-3 & 3-2A & -A \\ -A & 0 & A & 0 \\ 0 & 1 & 0 & 0 \end{bmatrix} \tag{7.2}$$

The parameter A, called the **tension**, causes the spline to bend more sharply; it increases the magnitude of the tangent vector at the knots. The special case A = 0.5 is known as the **Catmull-Rom spline**.

Kochanek-Bartels Spline Interpolation

Kochanek and Bartels [1984] propose a method of interpolating splines with three parameters for local control—tension, continuity, and bias. Consider again a list of points P_i and the parameter t along the spline to be determined. What is new is that a point V is obtained from each value of t from only the two nearest given points along the curve (one behind, P_i and one ahead, P_{i+1}). But, the tangent vectors D_i and D_{i+1} at these two points are also necessary. This means that we have:

$$V = \mathcal{T}\mathcal{H}\mathcal{C}^T \tag{7.3}$$

where $\mathcal{T}$ is the matrix $[t^3\, t^2\, t\, 1]$, $\mathcal{H}$ is the Hermite matrix, and $\mathcal{C}$ is the matrix $[P_i, P_{i+1}, D_i, D_{i+1}]$. The Hermite matrix is given by:

$$\mathcal{H} = \begin{bmatrix} 2 & -2 & 1 & 1 \\ -3 & 3 & -2 & -1 \\ 0 & 0 & 1 & 0 \\ 1 & 0 & 0 & 0 \end{bmatrix} \tag{7.4}$$

Kochanek and Bartels formulate the cardinal spline using Eq. 7.3 by defining the tangent vector D_i at P_i by:

$$D_i = a\,(P_{i+1} - P_{i-1}) \tag{7.5}$$

The Catmull-Rom spline is then obtained for $a = 0.5$:

$$D_i = 0.5\,(P_{i+1} - P_{i-1}) = 0.5\,[(P_{i+1} - P_i) + (P_i - P_{i-1})] \tag{7.6}$$

This equation shows that the tangent vector is the average of the source chord $P_i - P_{i-1}$ and the destination chord $P_{i+1} - P_i$. Similarly, the source derivative (tangent vector) DS_i and the destination derivative (tangent vector) DD_i may be considered at any point P_i.

Using these derivatives, Kochanek and Bartels propose the use of three parameters to control the splines—**tension, continuity**, and **bias**.

The tension parameter t controls how sharply the curve bends at a point P_i. As shown in Fig. 7.6, in certain cases a wider, more exaggerated curve may be desired, while in other cases the desired path may be much tighter.

The continuity c of the spline at a point P_i is controlled by the parameter c. Continuity in the direction and speed of motion is not always desirable. Animating a bouncing ball, for example, requires the introduction of a discontinuity in the motion of the point of impact, as shown in Fig. 7.7.

The direction of the path as it passes through a point P_i is controlled by the bias parameter b. This feature allows the animator to have a trajectory anticipate or overshoot a key position by a certain amount, as shown in Fig. 7.8.

Equations combining the three parameters may be obtained:

$$DS_i = 0.5[(1 - t)(1 + c)(1 - b)(P_{i+1} - P_i) + (1 - t)(1 - c)(1 + b)(P_i - P_{i-1})] \tag{7.7}$$

$$DD_i = 0.5[(1 - t)(1 - c)(1 - b)(P_{i+1} - P_i) + (1 - t)(1 + c)(1 + b)(P_i - P_{i-1})] \tag{7.8}$$

A spline is then generated using Eq. 7.3 with DD_i and DS_{i+1} instead of D_i and D_{i+1}.

Advanced Splines and Quaternions

Skeketee and Badler [1985] propose a new interpolation system which incorporates second-derivative continuity (acceleration), local control, convenient kinetic control, and joining and phrasing of successive motions. They use cubic splines to define a motion path parametrically. They then use another cubic spline function to relate the parameter to time, and thus obtain detailed control of the motion along the

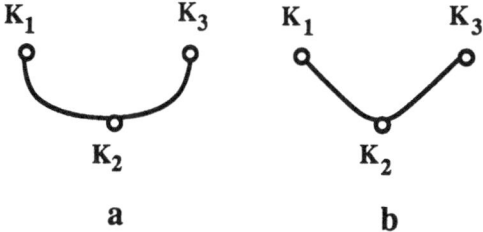

Fig. 7.6a, b. Variation of tension: the interpolation in **b** is more tense than the interpolation in **a**

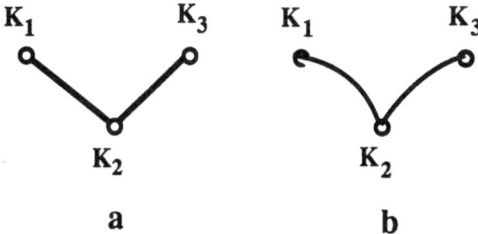

Fig. 7.7a, b. Variation of continuity: the interpolation in **b** is more discontinuous than the interpolation in **a**

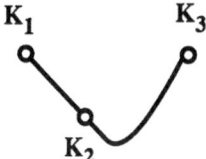

Fig. 7.8. A biased interpolation at K_2

path. To solve the same problem, Spencer-Smith and Wyvill [1989] introduce a four-dimensional spline. Pintado and Fiume [1988] introduce dynamic splines which mimic the kinematic behaviour of a particle moving in a field. Harada and Nakamae [1988, 1989] propose a method to improve the spacing of sampling points. The direct application of the method is for locating objects for computer animation. The technique consists of two parts: (1) obtaining the relative position of the sample points, and (2) mapping the sampling points on the cubic spline interpolant based on the relative position sequence obtained in (1).

Shoemake [1985] proposes a new kind of spline curve, created on a sphere, suitable for smoothly in-betweening sequences of arbitrary rotations. The method is based on the concept of **quaternion**, invented by Sir William R. Hamilton [1844]. Quaternions are an extension of the complex numbers to four-space, and are represented as four-vectors (w, x, y, z). To perform quaternion arithmetic, the four components are grouped into a real part (scalar) and an imaginary part (vector). Addition is easy: add scalar to scalar and vector to vector. Quaternions of unit length can represent orientation. When rotating an object, one can observe that one line of points remains fixed, the rotation axis. The unit quaternion which represents the rotation about an axis (x, y, z) of an angle 2β is as follows:

$$Q = (w, x, y, z) = (\cos \beta, x \sin \beta, y \sin \beta, z \sin \beta) \qquad (7.9)$$

Shoemake [1985] shows that there is a great deal of analogy between quaternions and rotation matrices. For example, vectors may be rotated by a quaternion Q as follows:

$$v' = Q^{-1}vQ \qquad (7.10)$$

Recently several publications have appeared promoting quaternions for rotation in graphics [Pletincks 1989], animation [Shoemake 1985; Pletincks 1988], and robotics [Brady 1986; Heise and MacDonald 1989].

7.8 Principles of Algorithmic Animation

In this kind of animation, called algorithmic animation, modeled animation, or procedural animation, motion is algorithmically described by a list of transformations (rotations, translations, etc.). Each transformation is defined by parameters (e.g., an angle in a rotation). These parameters may change during the animation according to any physical law [Magnenat-Thalmann and Thalmann 1985a]. These laws may be defined using an analytical form or using a complex process such as the solution of differential equations [Magnenat-Thalmann and Thalmann 1985b].

As an example of algorithmic animation, consider the case of a clock based on the pendulum law:

$$\alpha = A \sin (\omega t + \phi)$$

A typical animation sequence may be produced using a program such as:

```
create CLOCK (...);
for FRAME := 1 to NB_FRAMES
    TIME := TIME + 1/24;
    ANGLE := A *SIN (OMEGA *TIME + PHI);
    MODIFY (CLOCK, ANGLE);
    draw CLOCK;
    record CLOCK
    erase CLOCK
```

Instead of programming, an interactive system may be used like the director-oriented system MIRANIM [Magnenat-Thalmann et al. 1985], described in Sect. 11.2.

Finally, there should be a place for the use of the traditional principles of animation in 3D computer animation as suggested by Van Baerle [1986], Lasseter [1987], and John and Willis [1989a,b].

7.9 Motion Specification with Synchronization

One of the most difficult problems in three-dimensional computer animation is specifying motion with synchronization and parallelism. For us, the term "motion" may mean several different kinds of animation events:

1. Physical motions like rotations or translations of object
2. Physical transformations like alterations of the shape, size, or color of an object
3. Virtual camera motion

First, these motions must be expressed precisely. For example, to move a car a distance of 300 meters in 5 seconds along the x axis, 120 frames are required (we assume 24 frames/second). If car speed is constant, the car has to be translated 2.5 meters per frame. This can be done using a program such as:

```
create CAR(...);
for FRAME := 1 to 120 do
    draw CAR;
    TRANSLATION (CAR, ⟨⟨2.5, 0, 0⟩⟩, CAR);
    record CAR;
    erase CAR;
```

The car motion given above is very easy to produce with a user-oriented system. However, when a car moves its wheels also have to rotate at a given angular speed. This can easily be programmed. In the above program, for example, we would add wheel rotation in the loop statement. However, the most appropriate concept for animating an object like a car with rotating wheels is that of "actor." An actor possesses its own animation. This concept was first introduced in ASAS [Reynold 1982] and then generalized by the definition of **actor types** in the CINEMIRA language [Magnenat-Thalmann and Thalmann 1984a]. For example, a CAR type can be defined as:

```
type CARTYPE = actor (SPEED: VECTOR; T1, T2: REAL);
            time T1 .. T2;
            type TPOS = animated VECTOR;
                ...
            TANGLE = animated REAL;
                ...
            var  POS: TPOS;
                ALPHA: TANGLE;
                I: INTEGER;
            begin
                init POS, ALPHA;
                create CAR(...);
                for I := to 4 do create WHEEL[I] (...);
                TRANSLATION (CAR, POS, CAR);
                include CAR;
                for I := 1 to 4 do
                    begin
                        TRANSLATION (WHEEL [I], POS, WHEEL[I]);
```

```
              ROTATION (WHEEL[I], CENTER, WHEEL[I]),
              ALPHA, WHEEL[I]);
              include WHEEL[I]
          end
      end;
```

In this excerpt, we see that the position POS of the CAR and the angle ALPHA of rotation of the wheels are defined as **animated** types. This means that POS and ALPHA are values that vary with time. Of course, the laws of variation governing the two are not independent. When an actor type is defined, variables of this type can be initialized by an **init** statement. For example:

var CAR1, CAR2: CARTYPE;
$\vdots$

init CAR1 ($\langle\!\langle\!\langle 0, 30, 0 \rangle\!\rangle\!\rangle$, 3, 5);
init CAR2 ($\langle\!\langle\!\langle 10, 40, 0 \rangle\!\rangle\!\rangle$, 4, 6);
shoot until 6;

This means that two cars have been initialized with different speeds and different time limits. The statement **shoot** performs the shooting phase, whereupon actors are automatically placed. In this example, the upper time limit of the scene is 6 seconds, while the lower time limit is the upper limit of the previous scene.

These concepts will be further discussed in Chap. 11.

8. Hidden Surfaces, Reflectance, and Shading

8.1 Hidden Surfaces

A three-dimensional line drawing is generally rather unrealistic, except in a few cases (see the Eiffel Tower in Fig. 8.1). To achieve realism in a computer-generated image, lines which could not really be seen by an observer first must be removed. This process has been a common research theme since the first three-dimensional systems; numerous algorithms have been proposed to solve the problem [Sutherland et al. 1974]. They can be classified into three major categories:

1. **Object space**
   Such algorithms are based on calculations and comparisons between the geometric elements as defined by the user in the three-dimensional space or object space. Although very accurate, their cost grows very fast with the complexity of

Fig. 8.1. The Eiffel tower (from *Dream Flight*. Directors: P. Bergeron, N. Magnenat-Thalmann, D. Thalmann)

scene. Although several of these algorithms are well-known [Appel 1967; Ga-limberti and Montanari 1969], they are not yet well used. The Appel algorithm, however, is conceptually interesting because it has applications in shadow generation (see Sect. 9.8) and is also considered to be the first to perform "ray tracing" (see Sect. 9.1). The Appel algorithm is based on the concept of quantitative invisibility, i.e., a count of the number of surfaces hiding a vertex of the polygonal objects represented. A line segment is visible only if all points on it have a quantitative invisibility of zero. This technique detects changes in quantitative invisibility along a segment and draws the visible portions.

2. **Image space**

These algorithms make extensive use of hardware. They are based on the principle that objects are composed of polygonal faces and one must decide which face is visible at each pixel of the screen. Much more efficient than the previous algorithms, they are also limited in cost because the number of pixels remains constant and does not depend on the complexity of the scene. Moreover, these algorithms tie in well with raster technology, which is the most popular. The most well-known image space algorithms are the work of Watkins [1970] and Warnock [1969].

3. **List priority**

These algorithms represent a compromise between object space and image space algorithms. They involve two steps:
- In object space, processing mainly consists of building a priority list between objects according to their depths.
- In image space, processing mainly consists of determining object visibility.

The most well-known list-priority algorithms have been developed concurrently by Schumacker et al. [1969] and Encarnacao [1970].

We briefly summarize some major algorithms that are currently used in computer animation:

- Z-buffer
- Scan-line
- Warnock subdivision

Z-buffer Algorithm

Developed by Catmull [1975], this algorithm is the simplest method for hidden-surface removal. However, it requires a *depth buffer* (or **z-buffer**) that consists of an array containing the depth value for each pixel of the image to be displayed. The depth (or z value) of a new pixel to be written to the frame buffer is compared with the depth stored in the z-buffer. If the new pixel is in front of the pixel stored in the frame buffer, the new pixel is written to the frame buffer and the z-buffer is updated. Otherwise there is no action.

Z-buffer algorithms are generally implemented on graphics terminals which offer the corresponding technology. Several terminals have this kind of hardware, allowing pixels to be written conditionally to the z-value. This means that the frame-buffer and the z-buffer are parts of the terminal; which means, for example, 40 bits/pixel of graphic memory (24 bits for color and 16 bits for depth).

Scan-line Z-buffer Algorithm

Scan-line hidden-surface algorithms are based on the same principle as the color-filling algorithm used to fill a single 2D polygon (see Sect. 5.8). The main difference between the scan-line color-filling algorithm and the scan-line hidden-surface algorithms is that several polygons are processed instead of a single polygon. This means that polygon identifiers must be added in the TE in order to recognize to which polygon an edge belongs. A **table of active polygons** (TAP) is also updated from the TAE.

Each polygon of the TAP is sequentially processed in order to determine the color of each pixel of the scan-line according to the active polygons. As several polygons may overlap, the color of the pixel is given by the polygon which is the nearest to the observer; this corresponds to the minimum z-coordinate. This means that the value of the z-coordinate also has to be stored each time it is less than the currently stored z-coordinate for this pixel. To obtain the z-coordinate of a polygon for each point of the scan-line, we use a process which is analogous to the calculation of the x-coordinate of the intersection point with the scan-line in the color-filling algorithm; this means that we store for each edge in the TE the initial z-coordinate and its variation relative to a variation of 1 along the x-axis.

The z-buffer scan-line algorithm is the simplest scan-line algorithm. It is a special case of the z-buffer algorithm. To store the information concerning a scan-line, we use an array called the **scan buffer**, with the color and the depth for each pixel of the scan-line. The color is the value computed by the shading algorithm (see Sect. 8.3) and the depth is the z-coordinate. When a scan-line has been completely processed, each pixel of the line is colored using the value in the scan buffer. At the beginning of each scan, the scan buffer is initialized with the background color and a very large depth for each pixel.

Several authors [Romney 1970; Bouknight 1970; Watkins 1970] have proposed important improvements on the basic scan-line algorithm. They have introduced the concept of **spans**, which are segments of a scan-line along which the same polygon is visible.

Warnock Algorithm

In this algorithm, the screen is divided into windows; three cases are considered for each:

1. There is nothing to be seen in the window—there is no problem.
2. What is visible in the window is easy to draw—there is no problem.
3. What is visible is too difficult to draw—the window must be subdivided into several smaller windows.

The algorithm is typically recursive, ending under one of three conditions:

1. There is nothing to see—the window is colored with the background color.
2. The window is reduced to a pixel—since no further subdivision is possible, it must be colored with the appropriate color. The pixel-sized window is examined to see if it is surrounded by any of the polygons in the scene. Two cases are possible:

   i) There are surrounding polygons: these are tested (at the pixel center) to see which one is closer to the eyepoint at this pixel location. The pixel is displayed with the color of the closest polygon.

   ii) There is no surrounding polygon: the pixel is displayed with the background color.

3. The window is easy to color; this is possible when:

   i) A single polygon surrounds the window and there are no other polygons in the window. In this case, the window is colored with the appropriate color.

   ii) Only one polygon intersects the window. In this case, the window is first colored with the background color and then the portion of the intersecting polygon is colored with the appropriate color.

   iii) The polygon closest to the eye surrounds the window. In this case, the window is colored with the color appropriate for the surrounding polygon.

8.2 Light Reflection Models

If we eliminate the hidden faces of a sphere approximated by polygons, and color all the visible polygons with the same red color, we will obtain ... a red circle! This is because our perception of the third dimension is greatly improved by the reflection of light. In the case of the sphere, the different points on its surface do not reflect light in the same way if there are point sources of light. This means that the sphere must not be colored with a uniform color.

Theoretically, there are two extremes of surface types:

– Ideal specular reflectors that are like perfect mirrors
– Ideal diffuse reflectors that correspond to dual matte surfaces

In fact, most real surfaces are neither ideal specular reflectors nor ideal diffuse reflectors. For this reason, reflectance models have been developed. These models break reflection into three components: ambient, diffuse, and specular. The ambient component corresponds to light that is uniformly incident and that is reflected equally in all directions by the surface. The diffuse component consists of light that emanates from a point light source, but is scattered equally in all directions. The specular component represents the highlight, i.e., light concentrated around the impact point of the incident ray. The highlight has the color of the source light.

The first light model that took into account these components was devised by Bui-Tuong Phong [1975]. Intensity in this model is given by:

$$I = I_a + I_d + I_s \tag{8.1}$$

where I is reflected intensity, I_a is reflection due to the ambient light, I_d is diffuse reflection, and I_s is specular reflection. Diffuse reflection is defined as:

$$I_d = K_d \sum_1^{ls} \vec{N} \cdot \vec{L}_j \tag{8.2}$$

where

   K_d is the diffuse reflection coefficient
   $\vec{N}$ is the unit surface normal

$\vec{L}_j$ is the vector in the direction of the jth light source
ls is the number of light sources

Specular reflection is defined as:

$$I_s = K_s \sum_1^{ls} (\vec{N} \cdot \vec{L}'_j)^n \qquad (8.3)$$

where

K_s is the specular reflection coefficient
$\vec{L}'_j$ is the vector in the direction halfway between the viewer and jth light source
n is an exponent that depends on the surface (typically n varies from 1 to 200 and would be infinite for a perfect reflector)

Note that the empirically-derived term for I_s contains a dot product to the nth power which in fact reduces to $\cos^n \alpha$ where α is the angle between the direction of reflection and the viewpoint. This means that the highlight is only important where α is near zero and n is small.

There are two dot products in Eq. 8.1 and Phong [1975] has developed an efficient method for their incremental evaluation along a scan line.

Although the Phong model is realistic, the specular reflection component is not exact and this has a noticeable effect for nonmetallic and edge-lit objects. This is due to the fact that the intensity of the highlight does not change with the direction of the light source. According to Blinn [1977], this fault is especially apparent in computer animation.

Blinn has shown that the theoretical model designed by Torrance and Sparrow [1967] is more realistic. In this model, the surface to be drawn is assumed to be a collection of small mirrors, like facets, that are randomly placed all over the surface. The specular component is considered as reflections coming from all facets oriented in direction of $\vec{L}_j$. The amount of specular reflection K_s is calculated as:

$$K_s = \frac{DGF}{\vec{N} \cdot \vec{E}} \qquad (8.4)$$

where $\vec{N}$ is the unit surface normal, $\vec{E}$ the eye direction, D the distribution function of the directions of the facets on the surface, G the amount by which the facets shadow and mask each other, and F the Fresnel factor. Blinn [1977] discusses these factors in detail.

Whitted [1980] has proposed a simpler model based on global illumination information. The new model takes into account the transmission of light through transparent objects. The model is defined by:

$$I = I_a + I_d + I_s + I_t \qquad (8.5)$$

where I_t is the transmitted intensity.

The diffuse term I_d is calculated like Phong by Eq. 8.2. The specular term is defined as:

$$I_s = K_s S \qquad (8.6)$$

where K_s is the specular reflection coefficient and S the intensity of light incident from the specular direction. The transmitted intensity will be further discussed in Sect. 9.2.

Fig. 8.2. A copper vase by Rob Cook, Cornell University

Whitted has applied this model of light in a technique called "ray tracing," which is presented in Sect. 9.1.

Hall and Greenberg [1983] have improved the Whitted model, as will be shown in Sect. 9.2.

Cook and Torrance [1982] have proposed a reflectance model that describes the behavior of light in terms of energy equilibrium and electronic wave theory. In this model, the brightness of an object is related to the intensity and size of each light source that illuminates it. The intensity of reflected light is given by:

$$I = I_a + \sum_j I_{ij}(\vec{N} \cdot \vec{L}_j)dw_{ij}(K_sR_s + K_dR_d) \tag{8.7}$$

where I_a, $\vec{N}$, $\vec{L}_j$, K_s and K_d have the same meaning as in the other models and dw_{ij} represents the solid angle of a beam of incident light coming from the jth source. R_s is the specular bidirectional reflectance and R_d is the diffuse bidirectional reflectance. A bidirectional reflectance is defined as the ratio of the reflected intensity in a given direction to the incident energy from another direction. Cook and Torrance have also introduced an ambient reflectance, R_a, that is a linear combination of R_s and R_d. R_a, R_s and R_d all depend on the wavelength, and as there exist numerous measures of reflectance spectra, a procedure for calculating RGB values from spectral energy distributions has been developed by Cook and Torrance. Figure 8.2 shows an example.

8.3 Surface Shading

We have already shown that there are three kinds of descriptions for surface models (Sect. 6.2):

- A set of polygons
- The equation of an algebraic surface
- Patches

For each of those descriptions, shading can be calculated using the reflection models presented in the previous section. However, reflection models do not directly provide ways of calculating the surface shading of an object, but only the intensity of light at specific points. The shading techniques used depend on the type of object.

For polygon meshes, three basic ways of shading objects have been developed: constant shading, Gouraud shading, and Phong shading.

Constant Shading

This model involves calculating a single intensity for each polygon. It implies the following assumptions:

1. The light source is at infinity.
2. The observer is at infinity.
3. The polygon is not an approximation of a curved surface.

The two first assumptions are required so that the dot products $\vec{N} \cdot \vec{L}_j$ and $\vec{N} \cdot \vec{L}_j'$ are constant in calculation of intensity. The third assumption is made because each polygonal facet of an object will have a slightly different intensity from its neighbors. This produces good results for a cube, but very poor ones for a sphere. Moreover, constant shading produces the Mach band effect, described by E. Mach in 1865 as follows:

> "Wherever the light-intensity curve of an illuminated surface (the light intensity of which varies in only one direction) has a concave or convex flection with respect to the axis of the abscissa, that particular place appears brighter or darker, respectively, than its surroundings."

Figure 8.3 shows an example of constant shading.

Gouraud Shading

Gouraud [1971] introduced an intensity interpolation shading method that eliminates the discontinuities of constant shading. However, the Mach band effect is still visible where the slope of the shading function changes. The principle of Gouraud shading is as follows:

1. For each vertex common to several polygons, the normal to each polygon is computed as a vector perpendicular to the plane of that polygon.
2. For each vertex, a unique normal is calculated by averaging the surface normals obtained previously (see Fig. 8.4).
3. Vertex intensities are calculated by using the vertex normals and one of the light models presented in Sect. 8.2.
4. As each polygon has different shading at each vertex, the shading at any point inside the polygon is found by linear interpolation of vertex intensities along each edge and then between edges along each scan-line (Gouraud shading is based on scan-line algorithm like Watkins' algorithm). Figure 8.5 shows an example of interpolation calculation.

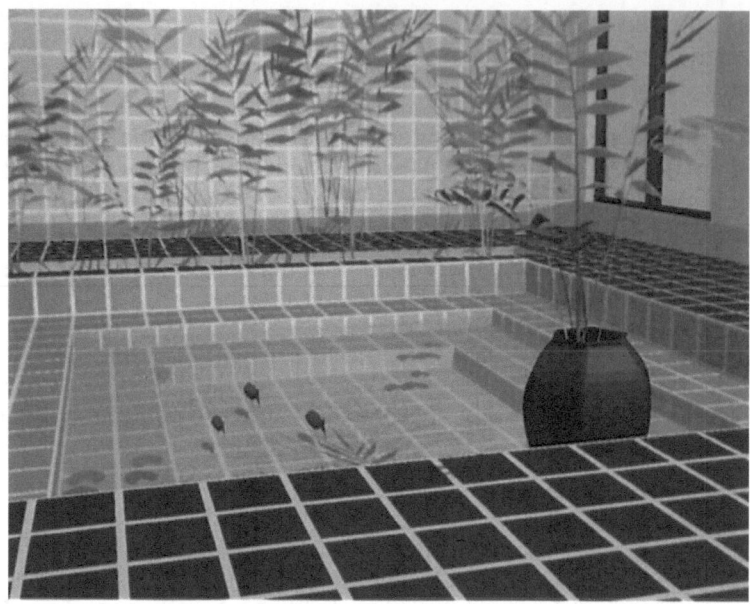

Fig. 8.3. Pool (constant shading) (designer: Marie Andrée Allaire; © Nadia Magnenat-Thalmann and Daniel Thalmann 1987)

Phong Shading

Bui-Tuong Phong [1975] has proposed a normal-vector interpolation shading method. This means that instead of interpolating intensities like Gouraud, Phong interpolates the surface normal vector (as shown in Fig. 8.6). With this approach, the shading of a point is computed from the orientation of the approximated normal. With Phong shading, a better approximation of the curvature of the surface is obtained and highlights due to the simulation of specular reflection are much better rendered. However, the method requires more computation. For this reason, the animator may prefer to choose a different type of shading, according to the kind of object used. The next section will show how it is possible to make this choice in a structured way.

Apart from computation time, there is another great problem in the computer animation of shaded objects with the Gouraud and Phong algorithms. If an object and its light source are rotated together in the image plane, the shading of the object can change contrary to expectations. This is due to the fact that the interpolation of intensities (or normals) is carried out using values on a scan-line, and when objects and lights are rotated, the scan-lines do not cut the edges at the same points. Duff [1979] has proposed to alleviate this problem by interpolating intensities (or normals) in a rotation-independent manner; this would mean avoiding the use of values on a scan-line and adopting an appropriate interpolator depending only on the vertices of the polygon.

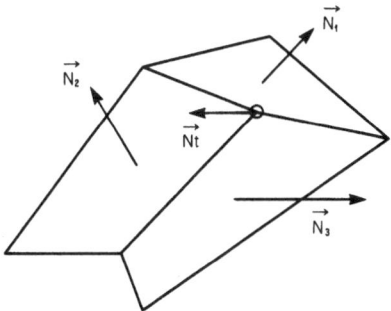

Fig. 8.4. Calculation of the vertex normal $\vec{N_t} = (\vec{N1} + \vec{N2} + \vec{N3})/3$

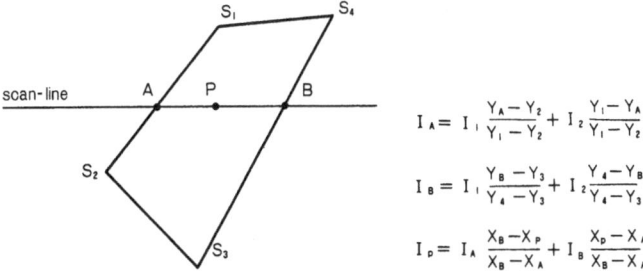

Fig. 8.5. Intensity interpolation (Gouraud shading)

$$I_A = I_1 \frac{Y_A - Y_2}{Y_1 - Y_2} + I_2 \frac{Y_1 - Y_A}{Y_1 - Y_2}$$

$$I_B = I_1 \frac{Y_B - Y_3}{Y_4 - Y_3} + I_2 \frac{Y_4 - Y_B}{Y_4 - Y_3}$$

$$I_P = I_A \frac{X_B - X_P}{X_B - X_A} + I_B \frac{X_P - X_A}{X_B - X_A}$$

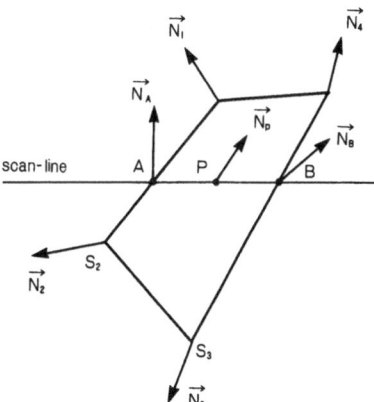

Fig. 8.6. Normal interpolation (Phong shading). $\vec{N_P}$ is calculated by linear interpolation between $\vec{N_A}$ and $\vec{N_B}$; $\vec{N_A}$ is calculated by linear interpolation between $\vec{N_1}$ and $\vec{N_2}$ and $\vec{N_B}$ is calculated by linear interpolation between $\vec{N_3}$ and $\vec{N_4}$

8.4 Rendering of Parametric and Patch Surfaces

Curved surface segments (also called patches) can be used instead of polygons to model free-form curved surfaces. Catmull [1975] has proposed a method for producing computer-shaded pictures of such curved surfaces. This method involves three steps:

1. Establishing a correspondence between points on the surface and the pixels
2. Removing hidden parts of patches
3. Calculating light intensities

The hidden-surface algorithm used was Catmull's Z-buffer algorithm. Calculation of light intensity can be performed with the Phong method by using an intensity function or by mapping intensities from a picture or a photograph. The first step is solved by a recursive subdivision algorithm similar to the Warnock algorithm discussed in Sect. 8.1. According to Catmull [1975], the algorithm can be described as follows:

> "If the patch (or subpatch) is small enough so that its projection covers only one sample point, then compute the intensity of the patch and write it into the corresponding element of the frame-buffer; otherwise, subdivide the patch into smaller subpatches and repeat the process for each subpatch."

This method is time-consuming; in practice, it can be used only with bicubic patches. However, it is of interest because it produces images of superior quality. Carlson [1982] has proposed a modified recursive subdivision to find the space curve which is the intersection of two bicubic patches.

More general algorithms for producing shaded images of parametric surfaces are based on scan-line methods. Three different algorithms have been proposed and compared [Lane et al. 1980]: the Blinn, the Whitted, and the Lane-Carpenter algorithms. In each, patches are surfaces defined by three bivariate functions:

$$X = X(u, v)$$
$$Y = Y(u, v)$$
$$Z = Z(u, v)$$

Patches are then transformed to a display space with X going to the right, Y going up, and Z going into the screen. Silhouette edges are defined as curves in the surface for which the Z-component of the normal is zero.

Blinn Algorithm

This is an algebraic approach that generalizes the concept of scanning a polygon to scanning a patch. In a first phase, boundary curve and silhouette edge intersections with the current scan-line are determined. All intersection calculations are performed using bivariate Newton-Raphson solutions of the equations. The process results in a list of boundaries for the current scan-line. In a second phase, the boundaries are sorted in order of x value on the scan-line. For each picture element, the Z information for the surface is generated and the required shading can be represented. This algorithm tends to be generally robust and relevant, except when the Newton iteration fails.

Whitted Algorithm

In this algorithm, bicubic surface patches are defined in terms of "edges" that are cubic curves. Patches have four cubic edge curves. Extremely curved patches may also have additional interior curved edges which subdivide the patch into sub-patches. The silhouette curve is approximated by a cubic hermite interpolation function. After the silhouettes have been determined, intersections of the edges with the scan-line are calculated using Newton's method. Depth and surface normals are then linearly interpolated between the endpoint values of scan-line segments. Visibility is calculated for each segment by comparing the average depth of segment endpoints to establish the priority of segments. Shading is computed using the Phong model. The major disadvantage of the Whitted algorithm is that it fails if it tries to find silhouettes that do not intersect the boundary of the patch.

Schweizer and Cobb [1982] have proposed an algorithm that is partially based on the Whitted algorithm. Their approach consists of essentially two parts:

1. Preprocessing steps for converting bivariate cubic surface descriptions into a standard internal form and deriving curved-edge polygons; a general surface intersection method is used to detect silhouette edges.
2. Rendering of the curved-edge polygons by calculating a cubic approximation to the normal surface and performing an interpolation of the bounding edge normals across the scan-line.

Lane-Carpenter Algorithm

In this algorithm, a polygonal approximation to the smooth surface is derived and the polygons are rendered. A subdivision technique similar to the Catmull algorithm, combined with a polygon scan-line algorithm, this method can be summarized as follows:

1. Patches are sorted by maximum possible y values.
2. As each scan-line is processed, patches with this maximum possible y value are subdivided until:
   i) Any one piece no longer overlaps the scan line and therefore is placed in the inactive patch list; or
   ii) The patch is within a set of tolerances of being a four-sided planar polygon, at which time it may be processed with a polygon scan-line algorithm.

A variant of the Lane-Carpenter algorithm has been described by Riesenfeld et al. [1981].

The algorithms described above deal with bivariate parametric surfaces generated by three functions of two variables. Another class of surfaces includes shapes like spheres, cones, or hyperboloids of revolution. These fall into the class of quadric surfaces that is a subset of implicit surface solutions to some equation:

$$F(X, Y, Z) = 0$$

Blinn [1982] has proposed a general solution to the imaging problem for such surfaces. The implicit form is ideally suited to raster conversion algorithms. The pixel coordinates are substituted for X and Y and the equation is solved for Z. Blinn has also shown how to solve the problem for the summation of several Gaussian density distributions.

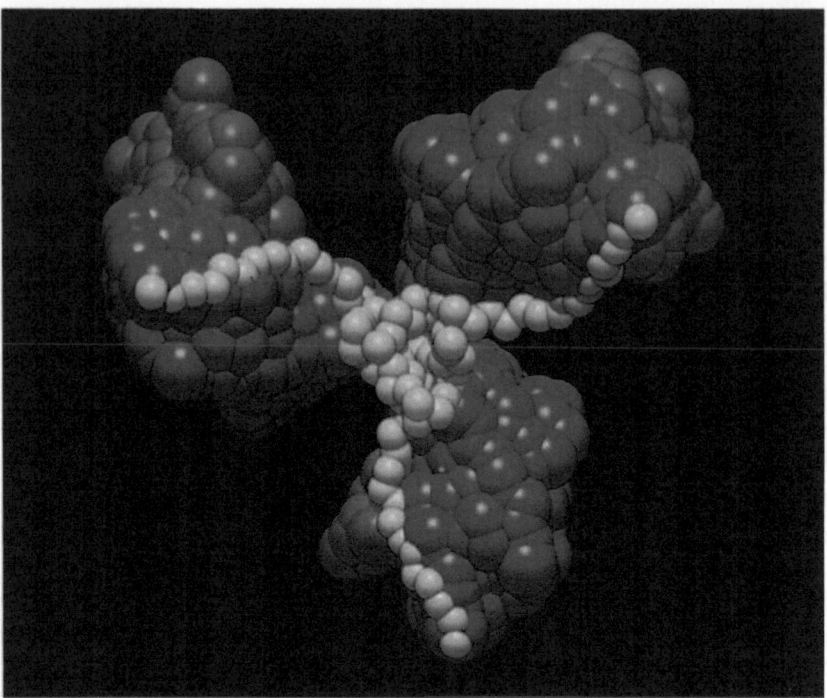

Fig. 8.7. Molecule by Nelson Max. Lawrence Livermore National Laboratory and Department of Energy

The method has been applied to the representation of electron density maps of molecular structures. The results more closely resemble what a real electron density cloud might look like for a covalent bond than do classical molecular models based on intersections of spheres and cylinders [Knowlton and Cherry 1977; Porter 1978; Max 1979]. Although classical models are suitable for animation, as shown by the films produced with Atom LLL [Max 1979], bond-stretching and breaking is more easily controlled with the density distribution approach. Figure 8.7 shows a beautiful picture produced by N. Max.

8.5 Complex Light Sources

As discussed by Verbeck and Greenberg [1984], a complete intensity calculation must incorporate light-source properties and environmental shadowing effects. An accurate description of physical characteristics of light sources should include three attributes to be modeled:

1. Light-source geometry
2. Emitted spectral distribution
3. Luminous intensity distribution

Most published light-reflection models (described in the previous sections) assume point light sources and do not include the effect of light-source geometries.

Warn Spotlights and Floodlights

Warn [1983] introduces a model with new lighting controls based on observations of the lights used in a studio of a professional photographer. The two basic lighting controls are **direction** and **concentration**. The main idea behind the model is as follows: for real lights, direction and concentration are produced by reflectors, lenses, and housings; it would be very expensive in CPU time to model these components; a good approach would be to model their overall effect, rather than the individual causes. Warn's directed lights are modeled as the light emitted by a single point specular reflecting surface illuminated by a hypothetical point source of light.

Radiosity Method for Diffuse Surfaces

To model the interaction of light between diffusely reflecting surfaces, a new procedure has been introduced at Cornell University [Goral et al. 1984; Cohen and Greenberg 1985; Cohen et al. 1986]. This procedure, called **the radiosity method**, describes an equilibrium energy balance within an enclosure. It determines surface intensities for diffuse environments independent of observer position. The main assumption in this method is that all emission and reflection processes are ideal diffuse (Lambertian) reflectors. This means that after reflection from a surface the direction of a ray is lost.

The radiosity B_i is the total rate of energy loss from a surface; it is the sum of emitted energy E_i and reflected energy R_i:

$$B_i = E_i + R_i \tag{8.8}$$

The reflected energy may be expressed as:

$$R_i = \rho_i \int_{env} B_j F_{ij} \tag{8.9}$$

where ρ_i is the reflectivity, which is the fraction of incident light that is reflected back into the environment. F_{ij} is the **form factor**, which is defined as the fraction of the energy leaving one surface which lands on another surface. B_j is the radiosity of the other surface. Equation 8.8 shows the relationship between the two surfaces. The radiosity of the first surface is obtained by the sum of two terms—the self-emitted light and the reflected light. This last term is equal to the radiosity of the other surface multiplied by the fraction of that light which reaches the surface and the reflectivity of the receiving surface.

In this approach, the environment is divided into discrete patches for which a constant radiosity is assumed. This allows the integral (in Eq. 8.9) to be approximated by a summation over the patches.

9. Transparency, Texture, Shadows, and Anti-aliasing

9.1 Ray-tracing Algorithms

Ray tracing is an old technique, based on the numerical simulation of geometric optics. Intuitively, it can be seen that light rays could be traced from a light source along their paths until they reach the observer. However, this is a wasteful approach, because only a few rays coming from a given source actually arrive at the observer. This is why algorithms involving ray tracing carried out the process in the opposite direction. Rays are traced from the observer to the objects in the scene, as shown in Fig. 9.1. The first practical use of the ray-tracing technique in computer animation was the MAGI system [Goldstein and Nagel 1971], which used the algorithm developed by Appel [1968].

A ray-tracing algorithm consists of shooting pixel rays, computing the intersections of these rays with the objects in the scene, and obtaining the photometric information required to color the current pixel.

At each surface struck by a ray, a reflected and/or refracted ray may be generated. For each of these new rays, the process must be recursively applied to determine which other surfaces they intersect. For each pixel, an intersection tree must be

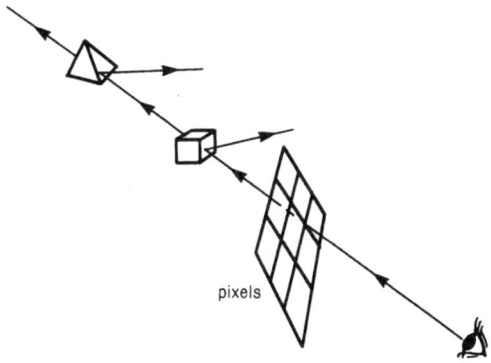

pixels

Fig. 9.1. Principle of ray tracing

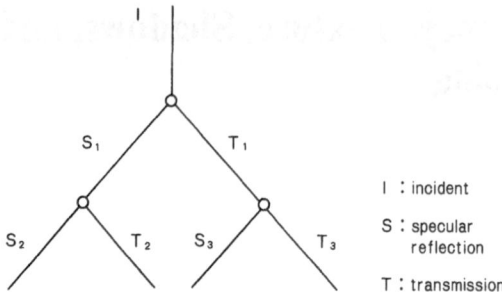

Fig. 9.2. Intersection tree

constructed (see Fig. 9.2). When the tree has been created, it is traversed, applying an equation at each node to calculate intensity. With the recursive process, the intensity for the current node is obtained when all its subnodes have been evaluated.

The equation applied at each node to calculate intensity is one of those already presented in Sect. 8.2: Phong [1975], Whitted [1980] or Hall and Greenberg [1983].

But the heart of a ray-tracing algorithm lies in its intersection algorithms. Whitted [1980] stated that up to 95% of CPU time in computing a ray-traced image is spent on the intersection calculations. Kajiya [1982, 1983] has described methods for calculating the intersection of different objects with rays.

Sphere

Because of the sphere's symmetry, it is a fairly simple process to compute its intersections with a ray. An intersection may be tested by finding the minimal distance between the ray and the center of the sphere. If this distance is less than the radius, there is an intersection. As such calculations only require a few floating operations, the sphere is often used as a primitive to model more complex objects like ellipsoids.

Polygonal Surfaces

For this type of surface, the intersecting point between the ray and the plane of each polygon is first calculated. Then, the algorithm checks if the point is in the interior of the polygon.

Algebraic Surfaces

An algebraic surface is a surface defined by the equation:

$$P(X, Y, Z) = \sum_{ijk} a_{ijk} X^i Y^j Z^k = 0 \qquad (9.1)$$

If we substitute the ray equation $R(t) = R_0 + V \cdot t$ where R_0 is the origin and V a unit vector pointing in the direction of the ray, we obtain a polynomial equation in t which can be solved by various methods of numerical analysis. Pat Hanrahan

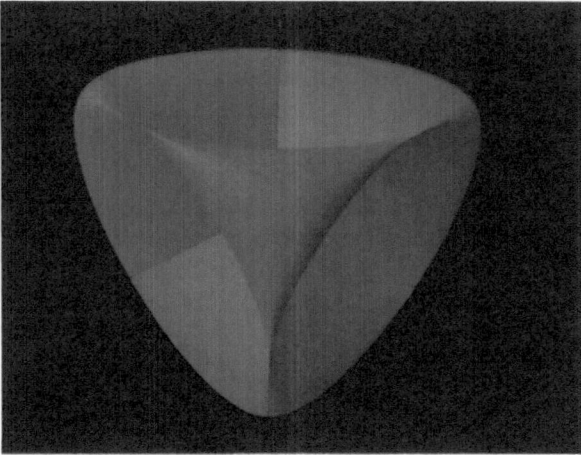

Fig. 9.3. The Steiner surface: an algebraic surface ray traced by programs developed by Pat Hanrahan

[1983] has developed a method to automatically derive the equation of intersection between the ray and the surface. Figure 9.3 shows an example.

Parametric Patches

There are two main methods for calculating the intersection between parametric patches and rays:

1. The recursive method of Whitted [1980] generates bounding spheres for each patch. If the bounding sphere is pierced by a ray, then the patch is subdivided into subpatches and bounding spheres are produced for each subpatch. The process continues until the intersected bounding sphere is smaller than a pre-defined minimum or no more bounding spheres are intersected. This algorithm is similar to Catmull's [1974].
2. The algebraic method of Kajiya [1982] transforms the problem of computing a ray-patch intersection into the problem of intersecting two sixth-degree algebraic curves. The solution of this problem is given by Bezout's theorem [Walker 1950].

Surfaces of Revolution and Cylinders

For this kind of object, the problem can be reduced to two dimensions. For surfaces of revolution, a cut plane is defined as passing through the ray and parallel to the axis of revolution. Intersections between the ray and the curves formed by intersecting the cut plane with the surfaces are then computed. For cylinders, the ray is projected onto the base plane. Then, intersections between the projected ray and the boundary curve of the base are calculated. In both types of objects, the solution of the two-dimensional ray-tracing problem is obtained using strip trees [Ballard 1981], a hierarchical structure which represents the curve at varying resolutions.

9.2 Ray-tracing Problems

Ray-tracing is a very popular technique, because of the super-realistic images that can be produced. However, it also has disadvantages. The major disadvantage is the time needed to generate an image. Another problem is that there is not enough information associated with a ray to perform good anti-aliasing.

One important part of the ray-tracing algorithm is the communication of reflected and transmitted illumination information between the elements of the ray tree. Generally, this is implemented using a pushdown ray stack. Following Kajiya [1983], a skeleton ray-tracing algorithm using a stack can be written as follows:

```
for each pixel
    emit a ray
    push it onto the stack
    while ray stack is not empty do
        for each object
            if no intersection then
                color with background
                exit
            else
                color pixel with the current ray
                pop ray
                generate and push reflection, refraction, and illumination ray
    write the pixel
```

We see that the heart of a ray-tracing algorithm lies in its intersection algorithm. Various approaches have been attempted to speed up ray-tracing. They may be classified into two categories:

1. Speed up the intersection process itself
2. Reduce the number of ray-object intersection calculations

Ray-tracing CSG Models

The MAGI original ray-tracing algorithm [Goldstein and Nagel 1971] was based on objects defined by CSG trees. The CSG model is internally represented as a binary tree. Each leaf node is a primitive object; each intermediate node is the composite formed by applying the operator (intersection, union, difference) at the node to the subobjects defined by the left and right branches of the node; the root node corresponds to the complete object.

The basic CSG ray-tracing algorithm, as described by Roth [1982], works as follows:

"Given a ray and a binary tree representing a scene, the ray is classified with respect to the solid. The classification is the information describing the ray-solid intersection. It designates which parts of the ray are inside rather than outside the solid. The process starts at the root of the CSG tree, recursively descends to the bottom, classifies the ray with respect to the primitive solids, and then returns up the tree combining the classifications of the left and right subtrees."

Fig. 9.4. Ray-traced images of CSG objects (designer: Benoit Lafleur; © Nadia Magnenat-Thalmann and Daniel Thalmann 1989)

For convex primitives, such as cylinders, cones, boxes, and spheres, there are four possible ray-solid intersection cases:

1. The ray misses the primitive.
2. The ray touches the primitive.
3. The ray enters and exits the primitive at two different points.
4. The ray lies on a face of the primitive.

Figure 9.4 shows an example of ray-traced image using CSG models.

9.3 Optimization Techniques for Ray-tracing

Hardware Solutions

Nishimura et al. [1983] have developed LINKS-1, a parallel pipelined multi-microcomputer system for ray-tracing. With this machine, an image to be generated is divided into several subimages and each of the computers generates one or more subimages independently. LINKS-1 has been used for computer-generated films by the Japanese commercial production house TOYO-LINKS.

Plunkett and Bailey [1985] propose the vectorization of a ray-tracing algorithm. This is possible because the intersection calculations belonging to the different pixels and the intensities of the different pixels are calculated independently.

Cleary et al. [1986] have analyzed the performance of a multiprocessor algorithm for ray-tracing. They use a cubic and a square array of processors with only local communication between near neighbors.

Software Solutions

Bounding Volumes and Clusters

Determining the intersections of a ray with a particular object may be computationally very expensive. One simple way of eliminating the unnecessary intersections is to perform a preliminary intersection test of the ray with a **bounding volume** (also called an **extent**) of the object. If there is no intersection between the ray and the bounding volume, it is certain that the ray does not intersect the object. Otherwise, an expensive test is required. This technique works well only if the intersection test with the bounding volume is much more efficient than the test with the object. This implies that the bounding volume must be very simple, for example, a sphere, rectangular parallelepipeds, or ellipsoids.

The technique of bounding volumes was suggested by Clark [1976] and implemented by Whitted [1980].

Space Division for Ray-tracing

Clark [1976] uses hierarchical geometric representations to speed both clipping and visibility calculations. Each level of the hierarchy consists of bounding volumes which enclose the lower levels. Terminal nodes represent primitive object elements such as polygons. Rubin and Whitted [1980] propose using a similar strategy to reduce the number of intersection tests. They describe a scene using a hierarchical tree of bounding boxes. Since the bounding volumes of the children lie entirely within the bounding volumes of the parent, the child volumes need only be searched if the ray intersects the parent volume.

An alternative approach is to decompose space into a set of disjoint volumes containing a list of those surfaces contained within each volume. The total number of objects in each volume has to be a small number, which implies a fine subdivision. The search for an object intersection proceeds along the path of the ray through the subdivision. Four techniques have been proposed:

- Techniques based on a space decomposition with an octree
- Techniques based on a binary space partitioning tree (BSP tree)
- Techniques based on digital differential analyzers (DDA)
- Techniques based on CSG models

9.4 Transparency

A surface may allow some light to be transmitted through it from behind. Depending on the type of material used, the transmittance can be specular (transparent material) or diffuse (translucent material). Little work has been done with diffuse transmission.

Specular transmission methods have been developed. However, they often do not take the whole phenomenon into account.

Physically, the three Descartes laws fix the rules concerning reflection and refraction of light. According to Fig. 9.5:

1. The reflected and refracted rays are in the plane passing through the normal and the incident ray.
2. The incident angle i_1 is equal to the reflected angle r.
3. For monochromatic light, Snell's law is applied:

$$n_1 \sin i_1 = n_2 \sin i_2 \qquad (9.2)$$

where n_1 and n_2 are refraction indices.

The simplest transparency algorithms have two major drawbacks:

1. The intensity of light transmitted through the object does not take into account the depth of the object.
2. Refraction is ignored; this means that, in Fig. 9.6, ray R_2 (which is incorrect) would be used rather than ray R_1.

These simple algorithms simulate transparency by modifying a background image. The color C of the modified pixels is calculated [Newell et al. 1972] by the following expression:

$$C = tC_1 + (1 - t)C_2 \qquad (9.3)$$

where C_1 is the color of the pixel on the background image, C_2 is the color that would be applied to the transparent object if it was opaque and t is the transparency of the object (0 for completely opaque, 1 for completely transparent).

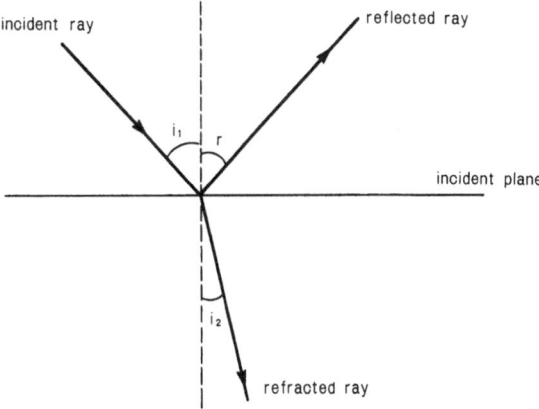

Fig. 9.5. Reflection and refraction of light

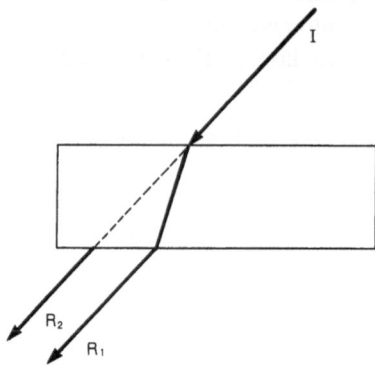

Fig. 9.6. Refraction through an object with depth

This technique can be easily applied in shading algorithms like Gouraud and Phong. For example, during the operation of a scan-line algorithm, when a given polygon in the foreground is transparent, the nearest of the other polygons behind it is visible. The intensity I is calculated as a weighted sum of the individual intensities I_1 and I_2 calculated for the two polygons:

$$I = tI_1 + (1 - t)I_2 \qquad (9.4)$$

If the transparent object is curved, this algorithm is very inaccurate. One way to improve realism is to decrease the transparency near the edges, using a function like:

$$t = (t\max - t\min)(1 - (1 - n_z)^p) + t\min \qquad (9.5)$$

where $t\max$ and $t\min$ are extreme values of the transparency t for the object, n_z is the z component of the unit normal vector to the surface and p is the cosine power factor.

Kay and Greenberg [1979] have proposed an algorithm, based on ray tracing, which takes refraction into account. This means that each ray is modified whenever it strikes a new transparent surface. In a slight modification of the simple algorithm seen in Eq. 9.3, the value C_2 is not necessarily at the same X, Y location as the new value C and the transparency t is a function of the thickness of the material through which the light ray must travel.

To trace the path of a ray through thick material, Kay and Greenberg use the following process:

1. Find a unit vector $\vec{U}$ that defines the direction of the refracted ray by using an approximation of Snell's law (Eq. 8.2).
2. Find the distance D that the ray must travel within the transparent material.
3. Multiply $\vec{U}$ by D to obtain the ΔX and ΔY shift values.
4. Add ΔX and ΔY to the X, Y location. This gives the location of the sight ray as it emerges from the transparent meterial.

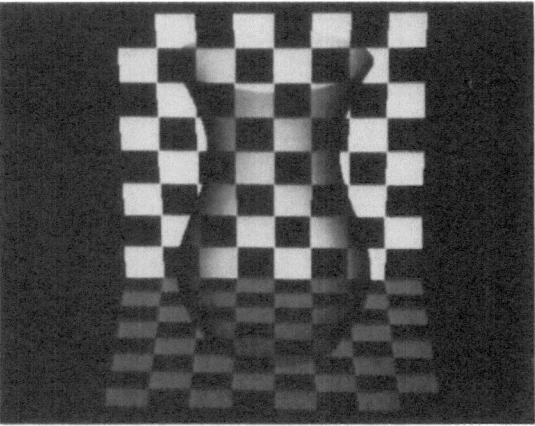

Fig. 9.7. Simulated transparent vase by D.S. Kay and D. Greenberg, Cornell University

The following equation calculates the intensity of a transmitted ray:

$$t = T^d \tag{9.6}$$

where t is the transparency for path of the current ray. T is the transparency for one unit distance, and d is the number of distance units making up the path through the transparent material.

This refraction solution was implemented with a Z-buffer algorithm. However, several iterations were required, because the surfaces must be processed in inverse order. Figure 9.7 shows an image created by Kay and Greenberg.

As already indicated in Sect. 8.7, Whitted [1980] also used ray tracing to determine the global illumination in an image plane. In Eq. 8.5 there is a transparency term I_t, which is calculated as:

$$I_t = K_t T \tag{9.7}$$

where K_t is the transmission coefficient and T is the intensity of the transmitted ray. The direction of this ray is calculated using Snell's law.

Hall and Greenberg [1983] have further improved the model by including Fresnel's relationships for wavelength and angle-of-incidence as suggested by Cook and Torrance [1982], as well as the scattering of transmitted light from sources and the attenuation of previous nodes. The model is as follows:

$$K = K_d \underbrace{\sum_j (\vec{N} \cdot \vec{L}) R_d I_j}_{\substack{\text{diffuse from} \\ \text{light sources}}} + K_s \underbrace{\sum_j (\vec{N} \cdot \vec{H})^n R_f I_j}_{\substack{\text{specular from} \\ \text{light sources}}}$$

$$+ K_s \underbrace{\sum (\vec{N} \cdot \vec{H}')^n T_f I_j}_{\substack{\text{transmitted from} \\ \text{light sources}}} + \underbrace{AR_d}_{\substack{\text{global} \\ \text{diffuse}}} + \underbrace{K_s R_f RF_r d_r}_{\substack{\text{global} \\ \text{specular}}} + \underbrace{K_s T_f TF_t d_t}_{\substack{\text{global} \\ \text{transmitted}}} \tag{9.8}$$

Fig. 9.8. Images of gallery with mirrored walls and local light sources by R. Hall and D. Greenberg, Cornell University

$\vec{H}$ is the unit mirror-direction vector based on the reflected ray and $\vec{H}'$ is the unit mirror-direction vector based on the transmitted ray; R_f is the Fresnel reflectance, T_f the Fresnel transmissivity, A the intensity of global ambient illumination, R the intensity of the reflected ray, T the intensity of the transmitted ray. F_r the transmittance per unit length of material of the reflected ray, F_t the transmittance per unit length of material of the transmitted ray, d_r the distance travelled by the reflected ray, and d_t the distance travelled by the transmitted ray. All other terms are defined as in Sect. 8.2. Figure 9.8 shows an example.

9.5 Texture

Computer-generated images can achieve a high degree of realism with hidden surface removal and shading. However, in many cases they tend to look artificial because surfaces appear very smooth. Images of metallic or plastic cups, for example, look very realistic, but images of oranges or human skin do not. Almost all physical surfaces, in fact, have a microstructure visible to the human eye. This microstructure, called **texture**, provides a great deal of information about the nature of the surface.

Catmull [1975] has shown with his algorithm (see Sect. 8.4) that photographs, drawings, or any picture can be mapped onto bivariate patches. However, this approach fails when the number of points to be displayed on a patch is less than the number of elements in the picture to be mapped. Catmull suggests alleviating this problem by mapping areas onto areas rather than points onto points, subdividing the patch and the picture at the same time.

Blinn and Newell [1976] have extended the Catmull technique by introducing a more sophisticated filtering method; in effect, applying a controlled blur to the pattern to be mapped. This is implemented by computing a weighted average of regions in the pattern definition function. The shape of this weighting function is determined using digital signal processing theory. The quadrilateral formed in texture definition space by the (U, V) corners of the pixel forms the base of a square pyramid which is used to weight the texture values. This function was originally used by Crow [1977] to solve the aliasing problem in computer-synthesized shaded images (see Sect. 9.9).

For a sample object, Blinn and Newell use a plain teapot constructed of 26 bicubic patches. They discuss different techniques for creating and mapping texture patterns such as (U, V) functions, hand drawings, and scanned photographs. Techniques for simulating texture and reflection are combined to produce images of objects having patterned shiny surfaces. The amount of light coming from a given direction is modeled to the texture mapping and then added to the intensity obtained from the texture mapping.

Schweizer [1983] also describes a texturing technique that approximates the changes caused by distance and orientation without attempting to exactly render a realistic surface texture. Since it does not reproduce the actual texture pattern, it is called an **artificial texture**. It is an inexpensive aid for visualizing the shape of a shaded surface.

These approaches are quite interesting but they do not simulate rough surfaces. One application of textured-surface representation is in the area of flight simulators [Schachter 1981]. Schachter distinguishes two basic categories of textures: natural and man-made. For the first category, he proposes [Schachter 1980a] Gaussian random patterns to model natural phenomena. For man-made textures which are more regular, Schachter [1980b] uses patterns modeled with an equation involving a priority function.

Blinn [1978] has developed a method which uses a texturing function to slightly alter the direction of the surface normal before using it in the intensity calculations. This technique was previously used by Batson et al. [1975] to generate shaded relief images. Blinn uses a function $F(u, v)$ that measures the displacement of the irregular surface from an ideal smooth one. A new point $\mathbf{Q}$ on the wrinkled surface is given by the following equation:

$$\mathbf{Q} = \mathbf{P} + F\mathbf{n} \qquad (9.9)$$

where $\mathbf{P}$ is the original point and $\mathbf{n}$ the unitary normal vector. Figure 9.9 shows a cross section of a smooth surface (v is constant), and the function $F(u)$ and the corresponding cross section of the wrinkled surface.

The new normal $\mathbf{M}$ may be calculated as:

$$\mathbf{M} = \mathbf{N} + \mathbf{D} \qquad (9.10)$$

with $\mathbf{N}$ the original normal and $\mathbf{D}$ obtained by:

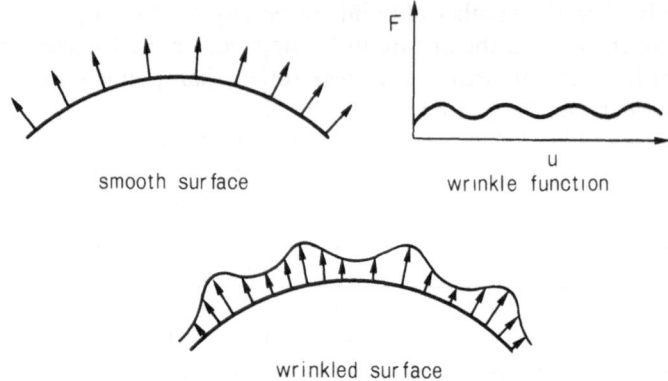

smooth surface   wrinkle function

wrinkled surface

Fig. 9.9. Cross section of a smooth surface

$$\mathbf{D} = F'_u(\mathbf{n} \times \mathbf{P}'_v) - F'_v(\mathbf{n} \times \mathbf{P}'_u) \qquad (9.11)$$

The choice of the function F is very important. Blinn has proposed different techniques:

- F is defined analytically as a bivariate polynomial or bivariate Fourier series; this is generally an expensive approach because of the large number of coefficients required.
- F is defined by a lookup table using a doubly indexed array of values between 0 and 1; the results are not very smooth unless an enormous array is used.
- F is defined by a lookup table as in the previous case and an interpolation is performed for values between table entries; B-splines can be used, but Blinn has shown that a cheaper, continuous interpolation scheme for derivatives consists of taking the difference of the interpolated function along the parametric directions.

Table entries can be generated algorithmically. However, when irregular textures are required, the best approach is to construct a table manually. This can be achieved with a video frame buffer and a painting program that utilizes a digitizing tablet to control the alteration of the table values. The user "paints" in the function values; black areas correspond to small values of the table and white areas to large ones.

Another important way of producing texture is based on fractal surfaces, to be discussed in Sect. 9.6.

Solid Texturing

We saw that existing techniques which apply a texture to an object are restricted to parametrically defined surfaces. Several authors [Peachey 1985; Perlin 1985;

Brossard et al. 1985] propose texture algorithms that can be applied to any 3D surface. This approach is commonly called **solid texturing**.

A **solid texture function**, as defined by Peachey [1985], for a shading parameter ρ is simply a texture function defined at the points on a surface in terms of their 3D coordinates rather than their surface coordinates u and v:

$$\rho = \rho(x, y, z) \tag{9.12}$$

Such a solid texture function is generally defined throughout a given volume of space and is often made periodic so that it is defined at all points in the space. The 3D scene coordinates of the point being rendered may be used as an argument of the texture function; however, it is often more convenient to use a local coordinates system.

As indicated by Perlin [1985], the solid texture approach has several advantages over texture mapping:

1. Shape and texture become independent.
2. The database is extremely small.

Choice of Solid Texture Functions

In 2D, digitized texture plays an important role, but in 3D synthetic textures are more flexible than digitized textures. For this reason, it is essential to find adequate functions to define these textures. In this section, we present a number of popular functions introduced by Peachey and Perlin.

1. **Bombing** is a stochastic texture model which consists of randomly dropping bombs of various shapes, sizes, and orientations onto the texture space. A 3D extension may be easily implemented by using spherical bubbles as bombs.
2. **Fourier synthesis functions** may be used to simulate marble. The solid texture function consists of a sum of sinusoidal functions of $\langle x, y, z \rangle$.
3. **Projection functions** are a class of solid texture functions based on 2D textures projected through 3D space.
4. **Combination functions** are functions which produce a solid texture function from several simpler solid texture functions.
5. **Noise functions** are scalar-valued functions which take a 3D vector argument and have the following properties: statistical invariance under rotation, a narrow bandpass limit in frequency, and statistical invariance under translation. For example, a simple random surface texture may be created by using:

    color = white * noise(point)

    The instantaneous rate of change of noise( ) along the x, y, and z directions provides a simple way of specifying a normal perturbation. Perlin uses this function to create waves.
6. A **turbulence function** provides a realistic representation of turbulent flow and may be used to simulate the appearance of marble, fire, clouds, or bubbles. The turbulence function may be created using a noise function.

9.6 Fractals

Modeling techniques generally assume that an object is a collection of lines or polygons, or that it can be described by high-order polynomials like Bézier, Coons, or B-spline patches. While these techniques efficiently model solid objects like cars, roads, and houses, they are not well-adapted to the representation of natural features like terrain, snow, sand, or smoke. The representation of snow by a collection of polygons is not only too expensive but also too regular to be realistic. Based on the theoretical work of Mandelbrot [1975, 1977, 1982], Fournier et al. [1982] have modeled both primitives and their motion as a combination of deterministic and stochastic elements. With this approach, the surface of an object can be a polynomial function or a stochastic function of predetermined location. Motion can also be a smooth function or it may vary irregularly.

A stochastic model of an object represents that object by a sample path of some stochastic process of one of more variables. Stochastic objects can be constructed from several stochastic modeling primitives. In summary, stochastic modeling requires:

− An object or a phenomenon to be modeled
− A stochastic process
− An algorithm to compute the sample paths of this process.

A very common natural entity to be represented is terrain, which is characterized by randomly distributed features. To model it, a stochastic process is required. Mandelbrot has introduced a fractal model of terrain as an application in computer graphics of a family of one-dimensional Gaussian stochastic processes called a **fractional Brownian motion**. A family of random functions $B_H(u, w)$, forming what Mandelbrot and Van Ness [1968] call reduced fractional Brownian motion, have been introduced. In these functions, u is a real parameter, w the set of all values of a random function taken from a sample space W, and H is a real parameter where $0 < H < 1$. When $H = 0.5$, ordinary Brownian motion is obtained.

Fractional Brownian motion can be chosen for modeling terrain, but an algorithm for computing sample paths must be found. This algorithm must be efficient, because up to 10^6 sample points frequently have to be generated. Mandelbrot has proposed several methods for calculating discrete approximations to Fractional Brownian motion. These methods are based on three approaches: a fractional Poisson field, a modified Markov Process and an inverse Fourier transformation.

Because all these methods are very costly in terms of computation, Fournier et al. have proposed a recursive subdivision algorithm to generate approximations to the sample paths of one-dimensional fractional Brownian motion.

One-dimensional Fractals

The algorithm corresponds to the construction of a "fractal polyline" primitive from an initial deterministic line segment. It recursively subdivides the interval, as shown in Fig. 9.10, and generates a scalar value at the midpoint. This value is taken as a displacement of the midpoint at each step in the recursion and is used as an offset from that midpoint along a vector normal to the original line segment. This offset d is calculated by the following equation:

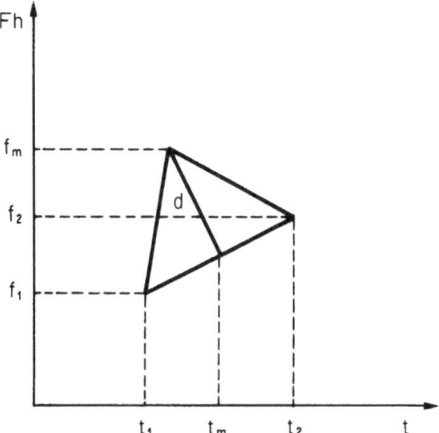

Fig. 9.10. One-dimensional fractal

$$d = s \cdot \text{gauss}(sd, tm) \qquad (9.12)$$

where s is the current standard deviation, gauss is a function that returns a Gaussian random variable with zero mean and unit variance, sd is the seed and tm is the middle of the interval ((t1 + t2)/2).

One-dimensional fractal primitives can be combined in arbitrary ways to represent natural phenomena like rivers or coastlines. By choosing an appropriate value for H, it is possible to generate realistic shapes.

Two-dimensional Fractals

Fractal polygons can be created similarly to fractal polylines. For example, surfaces consisting of triangles can be easily used to represent stochastic surfaces. Each triangle is subdivided into four by connecting the midpoints of the sides, as shown in Fig. 9.11. The positions of the midpoints are obtained by the same process as for polylines. A similar method can be used to subdivide quadrilaterals, and the process can be generalized to a mesh of triangles or quadrilaterals.

Fournier et al. also show how to generate stochastic parametric surfaces by defining a surface description which is stochastic in nature rather than deterministic. Figure 9.12 shows an example.

Three-dimensional Fractals

Norton [1982] has described a system for generating and displaying geometric fractals in three dimensions. The algorithm used to generate the surfaces, well adapted for an array processor, requires space and time. As three-dimensional surfaces are assumed to have an interior and an exterior, the technique is based on "point determinations;" this means that calculations determine whether a point is inside or outside a specified invariant set. The technique involves iterating a function

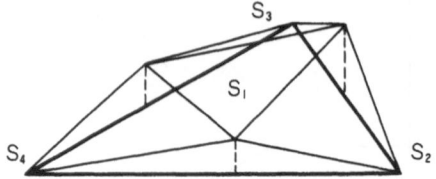

Fig. 9.11. 2D fractal subdivision. The midpoint of each edge of the triangle is displaced in x by a random variable

Fig. 9.12. Planets produced using a stochastic model by Alain Fournier, University of Toronto

repeatedly and keeping track of the points which satisfy certain criteria. A three-dimensional grid is used; the output of the algorithm consists of a list of boundary points on the grid. The surface is displayed using a two-stage method:

1. Assign illumination intensities to each vertex by imagining a light source.
2. Produce an image depending on viewer direction.

The display process is based on Z-buffers. Figures 9.13 and 9.14 show examples of three-dimensional fractals.

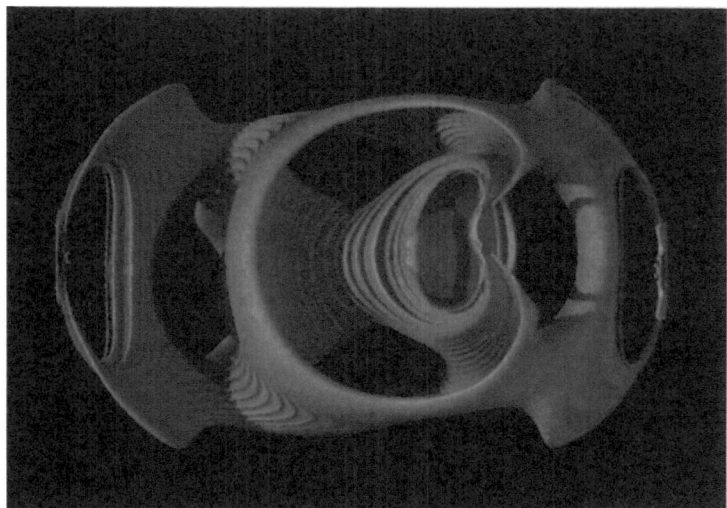

9.13

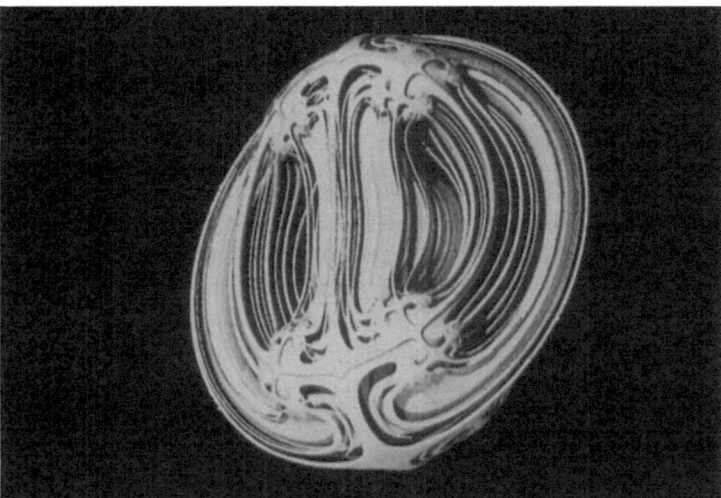

9.14

Figs. 9.13–14. By Alan Norton, IBM Research. These mathematical shapes result from the dynamics of simple formulas in 3-dimensional space. Repeatedly applying such a formula is like a process of erosion: we see here what remains after the process is repeated many times. The resulting object is a fractal [Mandelbrot 1982], possessing roughness and fragmentation at all scales of magnification. The generation technique, described in [Norton 1982], effectively simulates the erosion process inside the memory of a computer, then displays the resulting shape by simulating the reflections of light from such a surface. Calculations were performed on an IBM 3033 computer using an FPS 190L array processor. Pictures were displayed at resolution 1024 × 1280 on a RAMTEK 9400 system

Fig. 9.15. Synthetic fractal mountain. © Loren Carpenter 1980

Four-dimensional Fractals

The introduction of fractals to model motion can be very effective in handling complex irregular moving objects, such as a leaf in the wind. Used by Loren Carpenter in the film *Vol Libre* (see Appendix) to model the path of a lightning bolt, the sequence of positions was created by extending fractional Brownian motion from one dimension into three and by changing the random numbers generated. The complete path was obtained by interpolation as in keyframe systems. Figure 9.15 shows an image created by Loren Carpenter.

Fractal Surfaces with Ray Tracing

Kajiya [1982] has introduced a method of intersecting rays with fractal surfaces. The algorithm, which involves calculating all the intersections between rays and polygons, is of course impractical, because a typical scene requires the tracing of a million rays on a surface of a million polygons. To cut dramatically the number of intersections to be computed, Kajiya proposed generating the fractal surface and tracing it at the same time, thereby discarding very early the parts of the surface which do not contribute to the current pixel.

The Kajiya rendering algorithm maintains a list of active nodes which are to be traced by the current ray. A facet is a polygon representing the surface at this level of recursion, and the extent encloses the surface given by the subtree at N. A node is active if its extent intersects the ray and no primitive polygonal facet shadows it. Assume that the fractal surface can be represented as a tree of branching ratio four, with a facet and an extent associated with each node.

The algorithm works as follows:

> Remove the closest node N from the active node list. For each of the four extents E_i, if there is an intersection with the ray, add the corresponding nodes N_i to the active node list. If the new nodes contain primitive facets that intersect the ray, then remove all nodes shadowed by the closest facet from the active node list.

9.7 Fuzzy Objects Modeling and Particle Systems

Fuzzy objects, as defined by Reeves [1983], are objects that do not have smooth, well-defined and shiny surfaces. Their shapes are irregular and ill-defined and may change with time. In computer animation these objects, most importantly clouds, smoke, fire, and water, are frequently required but difficult to represent. Fuzzy objects can of course be represented by geometric primitives. For example, Schachter [1983] describes the simulation of cumulus cloud layers by a concatenation of cloud groups, each consisting of about 75 sunshaded ellipsoids confined to a circular envelope. Schachter also shows how smoke trails can be simulated by strings of long, thin, translucent ellipsoids. The results, however, are quite unrealistic, although they are useful especially in the case of flight simulators.

Csuri et al. [1979] have proposed a model for representing a cloud of smoke. The cloud is first generated by a three-dimensional mathematical approximation. Then a two-dimensional array of the intensities is created by ray tracing. A procedure model has been well described by Marshall et al. [1980] and is one of the first attempts to model objects as collections of particles. Blinn [1982b] has produced images of the rings of Saturn using light reflection functions for simulating clouds and dusty surfaces. The technique consists of simulating light passing through and being reflected by layers of particles.

A systematic method for modeling fuzzy objects has been developed by Reeves [1983], called the **particle systems** method. A particle system is a collection of particles that together represent a fuzzy object. Over a period of time, particles in the system are born, move, change, and die. Reeves describes how to compute each frame in a motion sequence with the following steps:

1. Generate new particles and assign them individual attributes.
2. Extinguish particles whose lifetime is over.
3. Move and transform the remaining particles according to their dynamic attributes.
4. Render the image of the living particles in a frame buffer.

Particles are generated by means of controlled stochastic processes. The number of particles generated at a given frame can be determined by an equation involving either the mean number generated at a frame and its variance, or the mean number generated per unit of screen area and its variance. For each new particle generated, values are determined for the following attributes: initial position, velocity, size, color, transparency, shape, and lifetime. Global dynamic attributes like "rates of change" are also defined in the particle system to control motion and transformations. A particle is killed when its lifetime reaches zero, accomplished by decrementing the current lifetime at each frame.

Particle rendering can be complex because particles can hide each other and transparency and shadows are also often required. However, for explosions and fires, Reeves describes a very simple algorithm based on the assumption that each particle is displayed as a point light source.

A pixel gains light when it is covered by a particle; the amount depends on attributes like the particle's transparency and color. A particle's size and shape determine the covered pixels. A hierarchy of particle systems can also be defined to control complicated fuzzy objects.

Particle systems were used to produce the Genesis Demo sequence (see Appendix) from the Lucasfilm Ltd. movie, *Star Trek II: The Wrath of Khan*. Fireworks have also been modeled using particle systems.

In Reeves' work, particle systems do not intersect with other surface-based modeling primitives. Objects modeled using other techniques are combined together with particle system objects in a postrendering composition stage. This composition stage is performed by splitting the image of the particle system into subimages based on clipping planes defined in the model coordinate space. An experiment for combining particles and polygons is described by Wyvill et al. [1985], but they consider particles as single pixels or spheres, which may be very expensive in terms of CPU time. An algorithm which integrates particle and polygon rendering has been developed by Magnenat-Thalmann et al. [1986] based on an A-buffer algorithm.

Other extensions to Reeves' work have been proposed. In particular, Wyvill et al. [1985] introduce particles as fuzzy balls with a radius of influence. At the rendering stage, a particle is treated as a sphere of radius r, with varying translucency. The edge of the sphere is almost perfectly translucent, contributing almost nothing to the image, while at the center the full color intensity of the particle is added to the pixel value.

Yaeger et al. [1986] describe a specific application of special particle systems for modeling the planet Jupiter. Particles are moved using a real physical model based on fluid mechanics. The particle renderer produces 2D output, which serves as a texture map in a polygonal rendering system.

9.8 Shadows

As noted by Crow [1978], algorithms for shadows require considerable computation time and are rarely used in computer-animated films.

However, unless the light source is located at an eyepoint, or illumination is very diffuse, as with an overcast sky, an image is not complete without shadows.

Before studying several algorithms for implementing shadows, we must define the term "shadow." This is the darkness cast by an object that intercepts light. This shadow falls from the side opposite the source of light and, as already mentioned, it is only visible when the eyepoint moves away from the light source.

The first algorithm for generating shadows was suggested by Appel [1968] as an extension of his hidden-line algorithm [1967]. The segment parts that lie in shadow are determined by computing for all vertices the quantitative invisibility with respect to the light source.

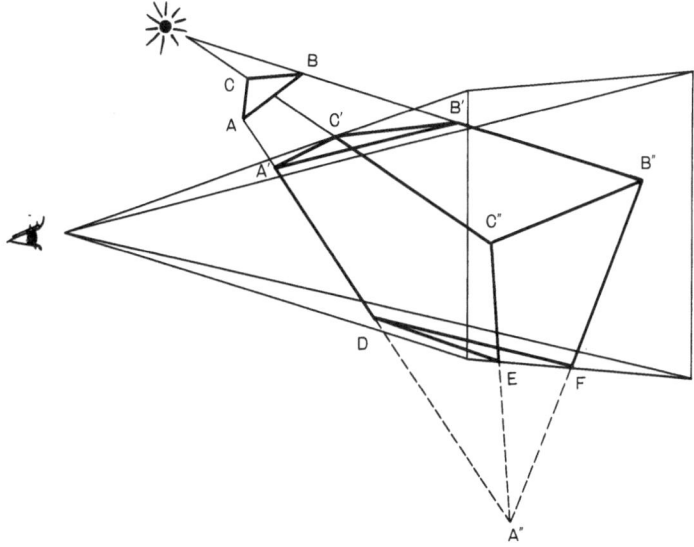

Fig. 9.16. Shadow volume

Bouknight and Kelley [1970] have designed a method that scans an object row by row to determine visibility. When a polygon boundary is crossed, the polygonal surface nearest the observer is found by a depth sort. A secondary scan is used to detect shadow boundaries calculated by projecting edges upon the surfaces being scanned.

Another way of generating shadows is to use a hidden-surface algorithm to detect which surfaces are hidden from the light source. As this information (on shadow boundaries) must be used in a second pass to generate an image, an object-space hidden-surface algorithm such as that described by Sutherland et al. [1974] must be used. Calculations can be optimized by using hierarchical data description as proposed by Clark [1976], because the shadow algorithm may be driven by the hierarchical organization of the data. A priority order is used to treat groups of objects.

Nishita and Nakamae [1974] have proposed a method for generating shadows by using a convex polyhedron-clipping algorithm in a first step, and then a method similar to that used by Bouknight and Kelley to remove hidden surfaces.

An algorithm based on a "shadow volume" approach was designed by Crow [1977b]. The shadow volume is the space region within which an object "intercepts" light. The boundary surface of the shadow volume is obtained, as shown in Fig. 9.16, by all planes defined by the light source and the contour edges of the original object. This volume is theoretically unlimited; however, it is normally restricted to the view volume. Polygons which bound the shadow volume are added to the list of polygons for display processing, just like the polygons of objects. During display processing, shadow polygons are considered invisible, and when they are crossed over, a transition inside or outside the object shadow is produced. This means that shadow polygons are included in the z-sort of a scan-line hidden-surface algorithm and the parity of the shadow polygons in front of a visible surface is counted to determine whether it is in shadow.

Two kinds of shadow polygons have to be considered—**front-facing polygons** and **back-facing polygons**. Any point in front of a back-facing polygon and behind a front-facing polygon is in the shadow. Consider now a line from the camera eye to a polygon. This polygon is front-facing if the shadow volume is entered, but back-facing if it is left. A number $+1$ is given to front-facing polygons, and a number -1 to back-facing polygons. The general idea of the algorithm is to consider a line from the eye to the graphic object and to examine the shadow polygons that are crossed by the line. If the sum of their associated numbers is greater than zero, the pixel is in shadow because more front-facing than back-facing polygons have been entered.

One way of accelerating the algorithm and saving memory is to consider the silhouette of the object as viewed from the light source. This silhouette is obtained by considering the edges of the object. There are two kinds of edges:

1. Edges in the boundary of the object (category 1)
2. Edges shared by two polygons with only one lighted (category 2)

Problems may occur, where there are edges of both categories in the same object. One way of solving this problem is to associate a value of 1 to category 1 edges and a value of 2 to category 2 edges. The method is satisfactory except with translucent objects.

The best approach is probably the polygon shadow generation algorithm proposed by Atherton et al. [1978]. The method is based on an object space polygon-clipping algorithm designed by Weiler and Atherton [1977] for hidden surface removal. This algorithm removes all surfaces that lie behind each unique polygonal area and within its borders. Shadows are created in three steps:

1. Shadow descriptions are found by viewing the environment from the light source.
2. By using the hidden-surface removal algorithm, illuminated polygons are detected. These polygons are those that are not in shadow and they are determined by considering hidden surfaces removed when viewed from the light source.
3. Illuminated polygons are added to the original polygons.

The transformations are performed using view and shadow matrices. The first shadow matrix transforms the polygonal data environment to the environment from a viewpoint at the light source position. Illuminated surfaces are then obtained by using hidden-surface removal. The second shadow matrix is used to obtain illuminated surfaces and a copy of the environment at any orientation. This results in a complete shadowed data file. By applying view matrices and the hidden-surface removal algorithm, hidden-line removed vector displays or hidden-surface removed halftone displays can be obtained.

By using the hidden-surface removal algorithm for each light source, shadowed images with several light sources can be produced, as shown in Fig. 9.17.

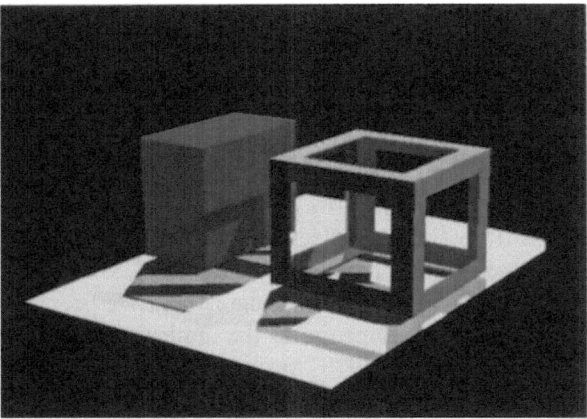

Fig. 9.17. Shadowed image display with two light sources at different locations by P. Atherton, K. Weiler, and D. Greenberg, Cornell University

9.9 Spatial Anti-aliasing

A phenomenon called **aliasing** is a major enemy of the computer animator. The term refers to the fact that this phenomenon occurs when a low-frequency signal appears as an "alias" of a high-frequency signal after sampling. Practically, this means that resolution in the object space is infinite when compared with resolution in the display space.

Typically, the effects of the aliasing problem are as follows:

1. A **stairstepping** effect exists along the edges of a line drawing or border of two contrasting surfaces.
2. Small objects can disappear between the dots because it is possible that no part of them will coincide with a sample point.
3. There is a line breakup effect, wherein the width of a stripe is on the order of a pixel and misses the center of this pixel.

These problems become very obvious in computer animation, where the main anomalies are:

– Objects appearing and disappearing
– Shapes of objects changing
– A scintillation effect

Aliasing effects were mentioned early on by Shoup [1973] and Catmull [1974]. However, the problem was first systematically studied by Crow [1977], who proposed three general classes of anti-aliasing algorithms:

1. As the aliasing problem is due to low resolution, one possibility is to increase that resolution, causing sample points to occur more frequently. However, this approach has severe limits, because it also increases the cost of image production.

2. The image may be generated at high resolution, and then digitally filtered. This method, called **supersampling**, eliminates the high frequencies that are the source of aliases. The technique has been used with excellent results [Crow 1981]. However, it requires a high-resolution copy of the image.

3. The image can be calculated by integrating intensities over neighborhoods to yield pixel values. This kind of algorithm is called a **prefiltering algorithm**. It has been successfully employed by Crow [1977] and Catmull [1978]. In both approaches, the reduction of aliasing effects is obtained by using a display algorithm with a filtering process in the rendering algorithm. Crow [1977] discusses the application of filtering to hidden-surface algorithms. He properly computes the intensity at a sample point. He proposes the implementation of a filtering tiler for convex polygons. Catmull [1978] has proposed a hidden-surface algorithm at the pixel level. The area of a pixel is viewed as a window, against which all nearby polygons are clipped. This determines the area of the pixel covered by each polygon.

The elimination of all aliasing is theoretically possible by limiting the frequency of the input image in the spatial domain to one-half of the sampling frequency [Oppenheim and Shafer 1975]. However, this requires convolving the image with $\sin(x)/x$ functions, which is not feasible with traditional hardware. The function $\sin(x)/x$ must be approximated; the least costly method involves intensity-averaging by area. The intensity of the pixel is computed as a weighted average of the intensities of each region that covers the pixel, as shown in Fig. 9.18.

Such a technique is also applicable to line drawings where each pixel overlapped by the line must have an intensity proportional to the area of the pixel covered by the line. To compute the fraction of each pixel overlapped by the line, algorithms have been proposed by Crow [1978] and Fuchs and Barros [1979].

Research in anti-aliasing methods is still making progress and different directions are being explored. Piller [1980] and Gupta and Sproull [1981] have proposed parallel processing approaches using special hardware. Fiume et al. [1982] have proposed a parallel scan conversion algorithm for a general-purpose "ultracompu-

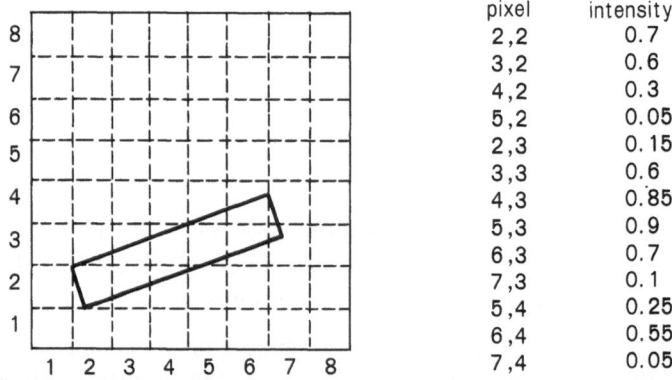

pixel	intensity
2,2	0.7
3,2	0.6
4,2	0.3
5,2	0.05
2,3	0.15
3,3	0.6
4,3	0.85
5,3	0.9
6,3	0.7
7,3	0.1
5,4	0.25
6,4	0.55
7,4	0.05

Fig. 9.18. Spatial antialiasing

ter." In this approach, a parallel anti-aliasing algorithm approximates the subpixel coverage by edges using a look-up table. Turkowski [1982] has introduced a method of calculating anti-aliasing through the use of coordinate transformations. He has studied the use of the perpendicular point-line distance in evaluating the two-dimensional anti-aliasing convolution. This means that the anti-aliasing filter kernel is approximated by a one-dimensional function of the perpendicular distance from a pixel to a line. Extension to polygon rendering has also been described.

Bloomenthal [1983] has presented algorithms for the detection and smoothing of edges and the filtering of an image in accordance with the inferred edges, obtained from the set of vertical and horizontal segments which form the staircase of the aliased line.

Other interesting anti-aliasing techniques have been applied to texture by Blinn and Newell [1976], Dungan et al. [1978] and Feibush et al. [1980]. Whitted [1980] and Roth [1982] have also studied the problem of aliasing in highlighting and Whitted [1983] has described a method of displaying anti-aliased lines by painting with an anti-aliased brush.

The anti-aliasing techniques discussed in this section are spatial in nature. They help to reduce the problem of creating images by sampling processes in the space domain. However, we have not discussed the problem vis à vis time.

9.10 Motion Blur and Temporal Anti-aliasing

As we have seen, spatial aliasing is an effect of spatial undersampling. Temporal undersampling can also be disturbing. Szabo [1978] distinguishes three different temporal effects: the interlace effect, the frame rate update effect, and the stroboscopic effect.

The **interlace effect** is present in all interlaced television. When an object moves up or down the screen of a CRT, it appears to break up into a series of parallel bands. In particular, if the object travels at a rate of one scan-line per field time, only half the number of scan-lines appear. The interlace effect can be overcome by using a wide spatial filter which scans two pixels and two scan lines; of course, this reduces the resolution. The effect can also be reduced by sampling at the frame rate instead of the field rate. However, this introduces another effect, the **frame rate update effect**: when an object (for example, a vertical stripe) moves horizontally to the right, it will appear twice on the eye retina if the position of the stripe is calculated at the frame rate. The **stroboscopic effect** occurs when an object which is supposed to spin so rapidly that it appears as a blur to the eye, seems to be stationary when generated on a display.

Lipscomb [1981] has studied temporal aliasing problems in real-time refresh vector systems. In particular, with many refreshes per update, motion can appear reversed, jerky, or erratic.

More recently, the problem of temporal anti-aliasing in computer animation, also called motion blur, has been investigated by several authors.

Potmesil and Chakravarty [1983] attempt to model motion blur, which they define as "an effect caused by the movement of objects during the exposure time of the camera, and often used to give the viewer the illusion of the motion of objects."

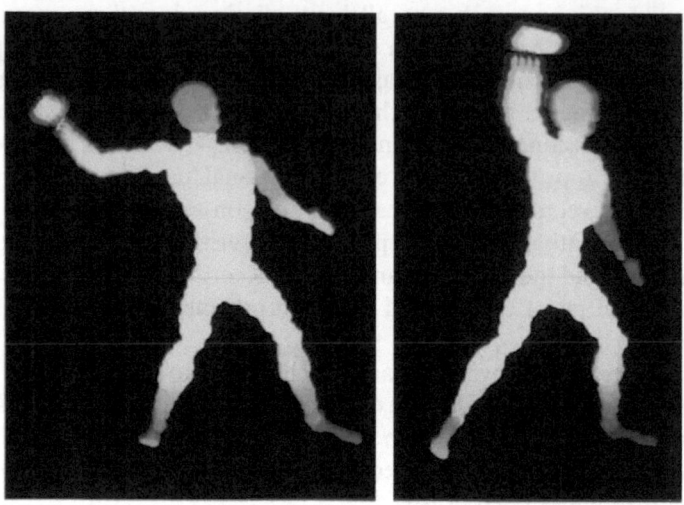

Fig. 9.19. Temporal anti-aliasing by Jan Korein and Norman I. Badler. University of Pennsylvania

In fact, the principle is simple: a movie camera opens its shutter for a short interval of time and motion is represented as a slight blur of the image of the moving object. In computer-animated films, this motion blur is required if the object moves rapidly. This is also the case when the virtual camera moves rapidly.

Potmesil and Chakravarty [1982] have earlier described a technique for modeling the effects of a lens and aperture in a virtual camera. Their model allows the generation of synthetic images which have a depth of field and can be focused on an arbitrary plane. Also, optical characteristics of a lens can be incorporated. This approach is quite interesting in computer animation, because it allows selective highlighting through focusing or other optical effects and permits special techniques like fade-in, fade-out, lens distortions, and filtering (see Sect. 2.4) to be simulated. Image generation consists of two stages:

1. Generation of point samples of intensity in the image using a geometric pin-hole camera; points are generated by the ray-tracing hidden-surface algorithm [Whitted 1980] discussed in Sect. 9.1.
2. Conversion into a raster image by a focus processor.

Image (de)focusing is obtained by introducing a circle of confusion as a projection of a point onto the image plane. Diffraction effects are studied by determining the light intensity distribution within the circle of confusion for defocused points.

The raster image is generated using the point samples, the geometric camera model, and the lens and aperture parameters. Potmesil and Chakravarty have extended their model to motion blur by redefining the two stages of image generation of computer animation as:

9.19

1. The ray-tracing hidden-surface program generates intensity sample points of an instantaneous image, identifying points which are in motion and giving the image path of the projected motion.
2. A processor generates motion blur by convolving moving points with optical system-transfer functions; these functions are derived from the path and the velocity of the objects and the exposure time of the virtual camera.

Korein and Badler [1983] have incorporated motion blur into computer-animated sequences by using two forms of algorithms. The first approach is based on intervals during which each object covers each pixel. For each pixel, objects that cover it during the filtered interval are determined. Subintervals, during which each of these objects projects onto that pixel, are also determined and subintervals associated with occluded intervals are removed. The pixel intensity function is obtained using the remaining subintervals and corresponding object attribute functions. The implementation of the algorithm has been limited to objects composed of spheres like Bubbleman [Badler et al. 1979], which will be further discussed in Sect. 10.3.

The second approach is based on surpersampling. The technique is similar to the corresponding spatial anti-aliasing technique, but multiple intensity buffers for a single frame are generated, each one corresponding to a different point in time. The intensities of each pixel in the different buffers form a function that can be digitized at a greater resolution than the output frame rate. It may then be filtered to obtain the final image. Although Korein and Badler note a few undesirable effects, the technique is simple to implement and can be used with different methods of image rendering. Figure 9.19 shows the effect of temporal anti-aliasing.

The particles in the particle systems introduced by Reeves [1983] and presented in Sect. 9.7 are motion-blurred. Particle positions are calculated at the beginning and about halfway through the frame, and an anti-aliased straight line is drawn between the corresponding screen coordinate positions in the frame buffer.

Motion blur and depth of field blurring are also possible using the visible surface algorithm for independent pixel processing developed by Catmull [1984]. Motion blur is accomplished by shrinking the polygons in the direction of the blur. The transformation is relative to the center of the pixel.

Max and Lerner [1985] propose a $2\frac{1}{2}$ D approach based on sorting the objects in depth and then combining these images into a single picture, starting from the rear. Layers L_i are characterized by an opacity mask value OP_i and a color value C_i and they are built up from back to front. Each L_i is added to an opaque background of color B to obtain an opaque composite. The process is separated into two steps:

1. Applying the mask to provide an intermediate I
2. Adding L_i to I

Motion blur is included by applying a blur process to both the image and its opacity mask, before doing the composition. The motion blur routine is restricted to translations, implying that each layer has a unique blur direction. The algorithm blurs a raster image, called by Max and Lerner the instantaneous raster in the direction of the blur vector $\langle BX, BY \rangle$. It works as follows:

1. Skew the instantaneous raster into a skewed raster S.
2. Blur the skewed image S into a blurred raster B.
3. Unskew the blurred raster B and combine it with the current composite picture.

The skewed raster is blurred by a number of pixels corresponding to the magnitude of the largest blur vector component and written into the blurred raster.

Max [1989] also describes a 3-pass raster motion blur algorithm in the context of texture-mapped polygons, and its applications to blurring objects and surfaces made up of multiple polygons which may move in different directions.

10. Human Modeling and Animation

10.1 Stick, Surface, and Volume Models

As stated by Norman Badler [1982], one of the best-known specialists in this area, modeling realistic human forms remains one of the most difficult and challenging problems.

There are two reasons for this:

1. Geometric and mathematical models used in computer graphics are not very suitable for the shape of the human body.
2. The movement of joints is difficult to model, in particular because of the role of muscle action.

One way of representing realistic human motions is the method of rotoscopy, sometimes called brute force method. It consists of recording the exact motion based on real persons. A typical example is the commercial *Brilliance* produced by Robert Abel and Associates.

To obtain realistic three-dimensional movements, three-dimensional models must be used. There are three general methods for modeling the human body in three dimensions [Badler and Smoliar 1979; Tost and Pueyo 1988]:

- Stick figures
- Surface models
- Volume models

Stick Figures

A stick figure like a skeleton is made up of a collection of body segments and joints. Realism suffers because depths are difficult to evaluate. Several movements are impossible to represent, like twists and contacts. The most well-known stick model was designed by Withrow [1970]. The hero of the film *Dream Flight* [Thalmann et al. 1982], Hipi, is also a stick model. This is further described in Sect. 13.1. Figure 10.1 shows Hipi flying.

Fig. 10.1. Hipi flying (from *Dream Flight*)

Surface Figures

Skeletons can be surrounded by surfaces that are composed of planar or curved patches. Movements that modify these surfaces are now visible and hidden lines can be removed.

Various models have been designed for surface figures. In 1968, Fetter [1982] introduced his first man model with seven segments (parts) for studying the Boeing 747 Instrument panel. A second, more fully articulated, man was introduced in 1969. Then, the third man and woman were designed by Fetter as a hierarchy of figures whose complexity depends on the application and the point of view. The fourth man (Fig. 10.2) and woman (Fig. 10.3) are based on the most recent work of Fetter on the visual effects of hemispheric projections [1981]. These models can be shaded with Phong's algorithm.

Other models are based on data obtained by anthropometrists [Dooley 1982].

Boeman (Boeing Corporation) is based on a 50th-percentile three-dimensional human model. He can reach for objects like baskets but a mathematical description of the object and the tasks is assumed. Collisions are detected during Boeman's tasks and visual interferences are identified. Boeman is built as a 23-joint figure with variable link lengths.

Buford (Rockwell International) is based on the 50th-percentile three-dimensional model of Dreyfus. He has difficulty moving and has no vision system. Buford is composed of 15 independent links that must be redefined at each modification.

Cyberman (Chrysler Corporation) was designed for the automobile industry. Although he was created to study the position and motion of car drivers, there is no check to determine whether his motions are realistic. It is based on 15 joints; the position of the observer is predefined.

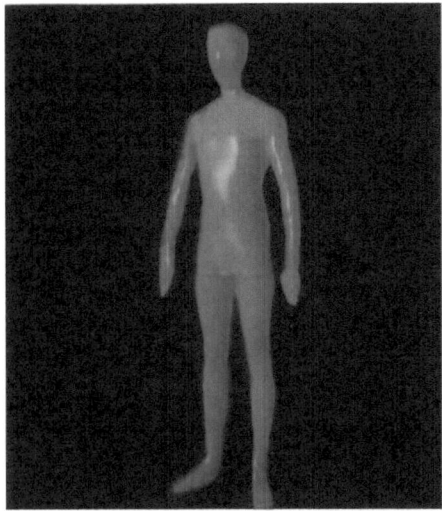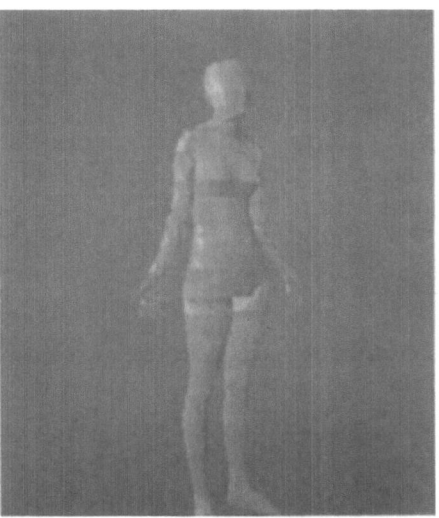

Fig. 10.2. *"Fourth Man"* by William Fetter. Steven Williams, Craig Wittenberg, James Wallace. SIROCO, Bellevue, Washington, USA

Fig. 10.3. *"Fourth Woman"* by William Fetter, Steven Williams, Craig Wittenberg, James Wallace. SIROCO, Bellevue, Washington, USA

Combiman (Aerospace Medical Research Center) was specifically designed to test how easily a human can reach objects in a cockpit. Motions have to be realistic and the human can be chosen at any percentile from among three-dimensional human models. The vision system is very limited. Combiman is defined using a 35 internal-link skeletal system.

Sammie was designed in 1980 at the University of Nottingham. This is, so far, the best parameterized human model and it presents a choice of physical types: slim, fat, muscled, etc. The vision system is very developed and complex objects can be manipulated by Sammie, based on 21 rigid links with 17 joints.

Volume Figures

In this approach, the body is decomposed into several primitive volumes. Three kinds of elementary volumes have been used to create such models:

– Cylinders by Evans [1976] and Poter and Willmert [1975]
– Ellipsoids by Herbison-Evans (see Sect. 10.2)
– Spheres by Badler (see Sect. 10.3)

The use of cylinders is very difficult because of the joints, and hidden-surface removal is very time-consuming. For these reasons, we examine only the two other models in the next two sections.

10.2 The NUDES System

The NUDES system (Numerical Utility Displaying Ellipsoid Solids), designed by
Don Herbison-Evans [1978, 1980, 1982], provides real-time animation of human
figure drawings with hidden lines omitted. The human figures are stick figures
fleshed out by ellipsoids. Figures 10.4 and 10.5 show examples of such human
figures.

The principle behind the use of ellipsoids is very simple. Assume we have two
ellipsoids, A and B, where B hides part of A (Fig. 10.6a). The points where the
elliptical outlines disappear and reappear must be of one of the following types:

1. **Obscuration points**—these are intersection points between the elliptical outlines
   (Fig. 10.6b)

Fig. 10.4. "*Rina*" by Don Herbison-Evans. Figure from the "Computers and Dance" program at the University of Sydney

Fig. 10.5. "*Horse and Jockey*" by Don Herbison-Evans, University of Sydney

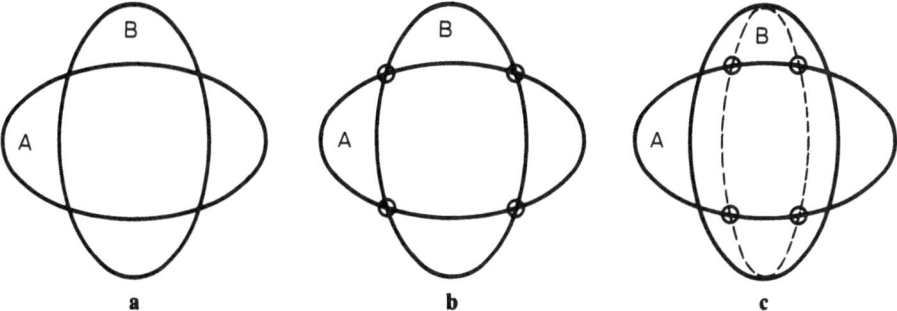

Fig. 10.6a–c. Two intersecting ellipsoids. **a** two ellipsoids. **b** obscuration points. **c** interpenetration points

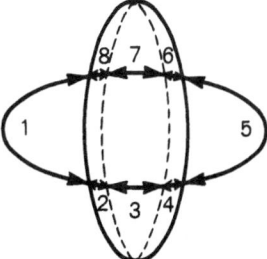

Fig. 10.7. 8 possible arcs

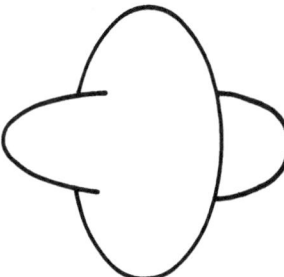

Fig. 10.8. Visibility of intersecting ellipsoids

2. **Interpenetration points**—these are the intersections between the outline of ellipsoid A and the section of ellipsoid B which is cut by the plane of the outline of ellipsoid A (Fig. 10.6c)

These points can generate eight possible arcs (Fig. 10.7). We now have to decide which ones should be visible. A very simple algorithm involves testing to see whether the center of the arc should be visible; if so, the arc must be visible. For example, in Fig. 10.8, arcs 1, 2, 5 and 8 are visible.

10.3 The Badler Bubbleman

Designed by N. Badler et al. of the University of Pennsylvania [1979, 1980], Bubbleman is a three-dimensional human figure consisting of a number of spheres or **bubbles**. The model is based on overlap of spheres, and the appearance (intensity and size) of the spheres varies depending on the distance from the observer. The spheres correspond to a second level in a hierarchy; the first level is the skeleton.

Skeleton

The Bubbleman skeleton is a set of joints and segments organized in a tree structure. The nodes are the segments and the edges are the joints. One segment is defined as the reference segment.

To simplify processing, the logical window concept was introduced. The segments taken into account in the computation of motion are only those which fall within the logical window, or those along a path from the reference segment to some segment within the logical window. For example, if we assume that the logical window includes only the left elbow, then the head segments, right arm and legs will not be involved in motion processing. The shape and size of each segment is described independently, and each has its own local coordinate system. The origin of the coordinate system is the center of gravity of the segment. The notation used follows the conventions of Labanotation, discussed in Sect. 10.4.

Spheres

It would be possible to draw the human figure by representing each segment by a line linking joints. However, this is quite unrealistic. A simple but advantageous way of improving the figure is to use overlapping spheres. Spheres are useful for three reasons:

1. Sphere projections always produce circles on vector displays and can be represented by shaded discs on raster displays.
2. Hidden-face removal can be implemented with a z-buffer method.
3. Unlike cylinders or ellipsoids, spheres have no privileged direction.

Spheres are used to create a kind of skin for each segment. In the Badler model, 310 spheres are used. They are produced with a decomposition algorithm [O'Rourke and Badler 1979], and then the choice is interactively improved. Spheres that belong to a segment are linked to it. Positioning the segment positions all the spheres. Any transformation on the segment is applied to the center of the sphere. The radius remains unchanged. Spheres of adjacent segments may overlap.

One important property of spheres is that they have the same shape from any point of view. Their projection is always a circle or a disc; the radius does not change for an orthographic projection nor decrease in perspective when the observer is far away.

Hidden surfaces and shading can be economically processed using a depth buffer algorithm as described in Sect. 8.1, but adapted to the topology of the sphere. The screen is considered as an array of pairs of values: depth and intensity. At the beginning, the array is initialized with a maximum depth and 0 intensity (black) at each point.

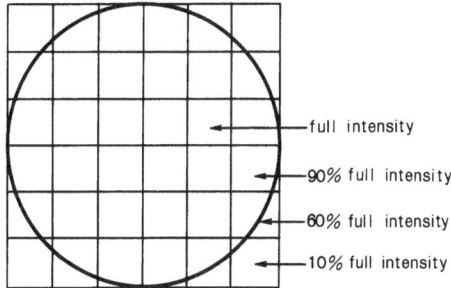

Fig. 10.9. Anti-aliasing in a spherical representation

Each sphere is processed as a solid disk, using the value of the nearest point to the observer as the depth value. For each processed sphere, values in the depth buffer are only modified if the depth of this sphere is less than the current value. With this approach, hidden parts are erased in the depth buffer by overlapping parts. Overlapping spheres have of course similar depth and thus similar intensities; the result is a smoothly shaded picture.

Aliasing problems are solved using a technique similar to that presented in Sect. 9.9. Figure 10.9 indicates the main principles of the method. The screen is considered to be an array of cells; a cell which is completely covered by a disc receives the full intensity; a cell that is partly covered has an intensity in proportion to the area of the cell covered.

Problems with the model and methods for dealing with the intersection of spheres associated with different segments are described in Badler et al. [1979].

10.4 Labanotation

Computer-modelled human motion can only be improved by studying real human movement. Two forms of notation for recording human movement have been established and may form the basis for computer-represented human movement. These are Labanotation or Kinetography Laban [1966] and Eshkol-Wachmann notation [1958]. In Labanotation, the body is viewed as a set of joints connected by limbs. In Eshkol-Wachmann notation, limbs are connected at joints. Only Labanotation, which provides an abstraction of the human body as shown in Fig. 10.10., will be discussed in this text.

For each joint, a position is specified with respect to a set of axes that can be oriented in many ways. Two specific joints have a role: the **distal joint** is the active joint and the **proximal joint** is the one from which movement is carried out. Movement of the distal joint is expressed through operations that are classified into five categories:

1. **Direction signs** that describe the translation of joints
2. **Revolution signs** that describe the rotations of joints

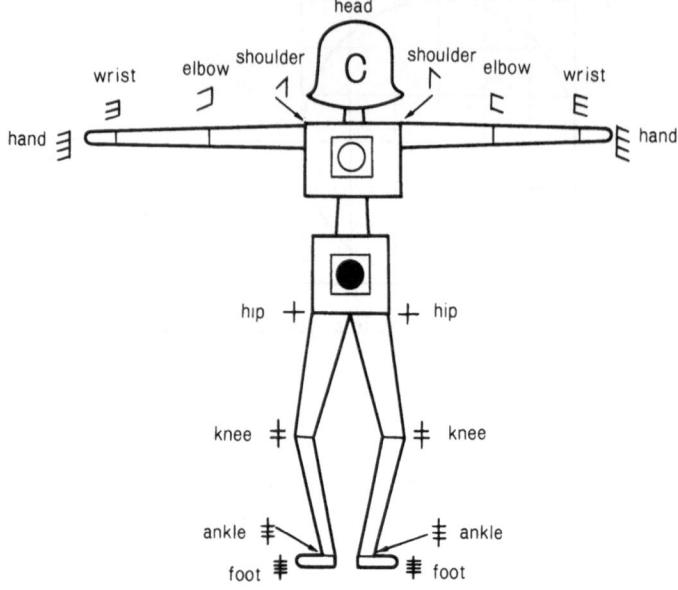

Fig. 10.10. Labanotation

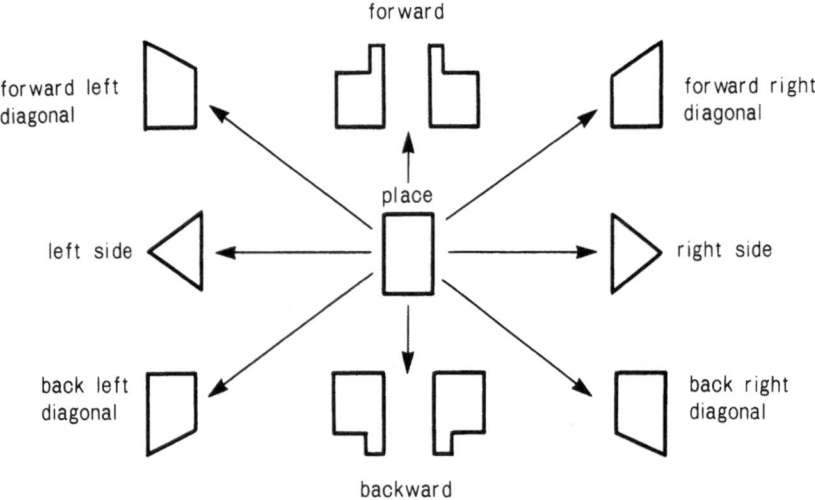

Fig. 10.11. The direction symbols

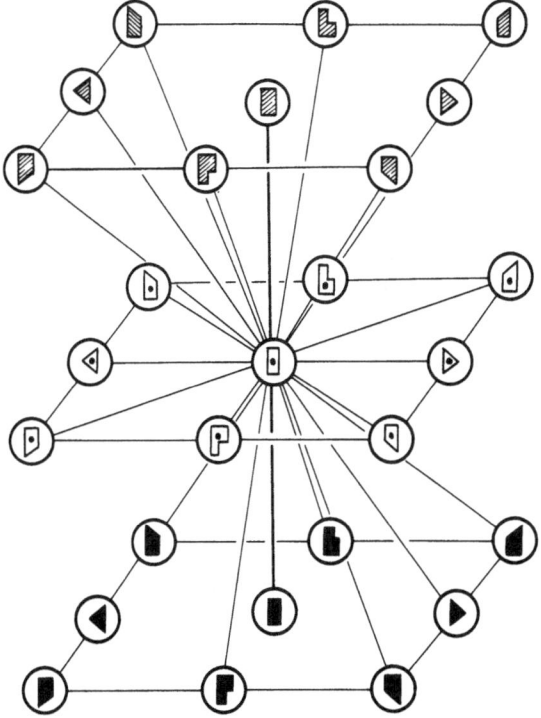

Fig. 10.12. 3D space directions

3. **Facing signs** that describe the orientation of points on surfaces (e.g., the orientation of a palm)
4. **Contact signs** that describe the contact of two body parts or the contact of a body part with an object
5. **Shape signs** that describe the tracing of a path or formation of a shape by some body part

In Labanotation, symbols have been introduced to describe the operations of these five classes. Each symbol has a shape to describe the movement, an intensity to express its level, and a size to define the duration of the motion. For example, Fig. 10.11 shows the shape of the nine direction symbols in a plane.

To describe the 27 three-dimensional space directions, shading is used, as shown in Fig. 10.12.

The description of the movement of a human body is noted in columns. One column represents one body part, as shown in Fig. 10.13.

Figure 10.14 shows an example of a walking cycle. Interactive editors and programming languages based on Labanotation have been developed [Weber et al. 1978; Smoliar and Tracton 1978; Smoliar and Weber 1977; Calvert and Chapman 1978; Calvert et al. 1980, 1982, 1982b].

arm
body
leg gesture
left support
right support
leg gesture
body
arm
head

Fig. 10.13. Simplified description of the movement of a human body

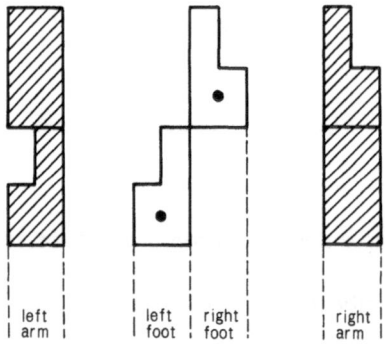

Fig. 10.14. A walking cycle

10.5 Parametric Keyframe Animation of Articulated Bodies

The animation described in this section is based on parametric keyframe animation. As already discussed in Sect. 7.6, the animator creates keyframes by specifying the appropriate set of parameter values; parameters are interpolated and images are finally individually constructed from the interpolated parameters. For each parameter, interpolation has to be computed using a good method. To animate (to move) a human body, it is necessary to use specific software for human motion. This software runs using a certain number of values of angles (key values) provided by the user. These angles are angles between the various body parts at certain times.

Name	Number	Angles
VERTEBRA 1	2	FTP
VERTEBRA 2	3	FTP
VERTEBRA 3	4	FTP
VERTEBRA 4	5	FTP
VERTEBRA 5	6	FTP
LEFT CLAVICLE	7	FP
RIGHT CLAVICLE	11	FP
LEFT SHOULDER	8	FTP
RIGHT SHOULDER	12	FTP
LEFT ELBOW	9	FT
RIGHT ELBOW	13	FT
LEFT WRIST	10	FP
RIGHT WRIST	14	FP
LEFT HIP	15	F
RIGHT HIP	20	F
LEFT THIGH	16	FTP
RIGHT THIGH	21	FTP
LEFT KNEE	17	F
RIGHT KNEE	22	F
LEFT ANKLE	18	F
RIGHT ANKLE	23	F
LEFT TOE	19	F
RIGHT TOE	24	F

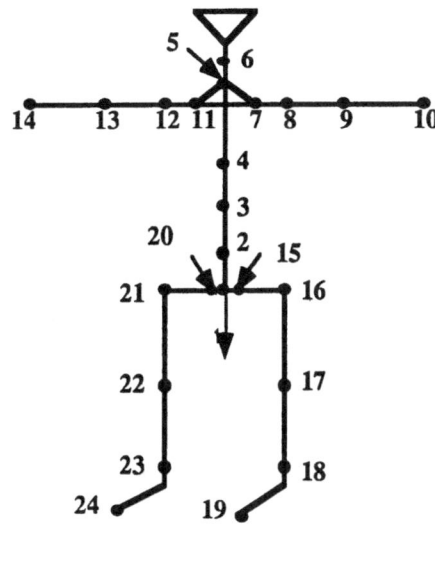

Fig. 10.15. A basic skeleton

For example, to bend an arm, it is necessary to enter into the computer the elbow angle at different selected times. Then the software is able to find any angle at any time.

Consider a skeleton as a connected set of segments, corresponding to limbs, and joints, as shown in Fig.10.15. A joint is the intersection of two segments, which means it is a skeleton point where the limb which is linked to the point may move. The angle between the two segments is called the joint angle. A joint may have at most three kinds of position angles: flexion, pivot, and twisting. The **flexion** is a rotation of the limb which is influenced by the joint and causes the motion of all limbs linked to this joint. This flexion is carried out relative to the joint point and a flexion axis has to be defined. The **pivot** makes the flexion axis rotate around the limb which is influenced by the joint. **Twisting** causes a torsion of the limb which is influenced by the joint. The direction of the twisting axis is found similarly to the direction of the pivot.

Motion is specified by giving key values for each joint angle. In-between values may be calculated using cubic splines [Kochanek and Bartels 1984].

10.6 Body Deformations and JLD Operators

Body Mapping

Once the motion of the 3D character is designed, the character needs to be covered with surfaces. Ideally, the topology of the surfaces should be completely separated from the skeleton. The animation system should transform the surfaces according to the wire-frame model ensuring an automatic continuity between the different surfaces. This correspondence is based on a changing of reference systems independent of the segment length. This means that for the same set of surfaces, several bodies of different sizes may be obtained according to the segment length in the wire-frame models.

When the animator specifies the animation sequence, he/she defines the motion using a skeleton, as shown in Sect. 10.4. In order to animate full 3D characters, the animator also has to position this skeleton according to the body of the character to be animated. This operation must be very accurate and is generally long. However, it is necessary, because the animation is completely computed from the skeleton. When the skeleton has been correctly positioned, the software will transform the character according to the angles required by the animation without any animator intervention.

One technique, introduced by Magnenat-Thalmann and Thalmann [1987c, 1989b] is based on specific local deformation operators depending on the joint nature; they are called **Joint-dependent Local Deformation (JLD)** operators. These JLD operators control the evolution of surfaces and may be considered as operators on these surfaces. Each JLD operator will be applicable to some uniquely defined part of the surface which may be called the domain of the operator. The value of the operator itself will be determined as a function of the angular values of the specific set of joints defining the operator.

This means that a body shape state is a frame-dependent state defined from three kinds of data:

- The set of angles for this frame obtained by interpolation or evaluation of some law
- The neutral synthetic actor body (surface)
- The JLD operators (knee, shoulder, elbow, finger)

The general algorithm for covering a body may be summarized as follows:
for each segment of the skeleton
    for each point P of the original synthetic actor body corresponding to the segment do
        associate P to the nearest bound of the segment
        select the JLD operator based on the type of joint

Surfaces covering most of the joints may be considered as flexible pipes; in this case, standard JLD operators may be applied on these surfaces. A flexing is applied on the bound of the segment corresponding to the joint. New coordinates of the points of the body surface are calculated by a changing of reference system. However, for a large flexing angle, the body surface around the segment is made thinner along the direction of the normal towards the segment, which is unnatural of course; these problems have been described earlier by Badler and Smoliar [1979]. To overcome this problem, a correction is applied to the points of the surface. The correction is obtained by adding to each point P_i' of the corresponding body surface, a term $(D_i - D_i')$ DIR where D_i is the distance between the point P_i of the surface in the neutral synthetic actor body and the segment in the neutral position, D_i' is the distance between P_i' and its projection K_i' onto the segment after flexing, and

Fig. 10.16. The synthetic actress Marilyn (from the film *Rendez-vous à Montréal*, © Nadia Magnenat-Thalmann and Daniel Thalmann)

DIR is the direction of the correction $P'_i - K'_i$. Note that this approach is also compatible with torsions; for example, the normal at the center of the segment is rotated by an angle which is half the angle of torsion.

For the neck vertebrae or the shoulder, JLD operators must be different from the previous ones. In case of a flexing on the first neck vertebra, the previous technique will cause points at the neck base to go inside the body volume for a positive angle and outside the body volume for a negative angle. One trivial solution to this problem is to calculate the new reference axes perpendicular to the segment before the flexing instead of after the flexing. It has a drawback: the correction to avoid a thinness effect cannot work anymore; however the correction is not necessary, because the flexing angles at the neck base are limited to 40°.

The shoulder is the most complex joint and it is generally poorly processed in computer-animated films. The problem is mainly due to the approximation of the skeleton by a set of straight line segments; this is an acceptable simplification for most joints but may cause problems for the more complex ones. This means that the location of the joint cannot be the same for any value of the flexing angle. When the joint is far enough from the body surface, the results are good for a large angle; but for small angles, the shoulder looks like a flexible pipe. With a joint near the body surface, the results are good for small angles; but we can observe that vertices tend to go inside the body for large angles. Thus, we have to use a moving joint. In fact, two choices are possible: move the joint by shortening the arm length or lengthening the clavicle. The second solution is more natural and provides better results. Figure 10.16 shows the mapped surface for the neck vertebrae and the shoulders.

Chadwick et al. [1988, 1989] propose another approach which combines recent research advances in robotics, physically-based modeling, and geometric modeling. The control points of geometric modeling deformations are constrained by an underlying articulated robotics skeleton. These deformations are tailored by the animator and act as a muscle layer to provide automatic squash and stretch behavior of the surface geometry. Komatsu [1988] describes the synthesis and the transformation of a new human skin model using the Bézier surfaces.

10.7 Hand Animation

As the hand is the most useful tool for the human being, it is not surprising that computer scientists have been interested in its modeling and animation. Two specific attempts are the Catmull and the Badler models. In the MOP system designed by Catmull [1972], hands are decomposed into polygons. Then, the Watkins algorithm is applied to remove hidden surfaces. Gouraud shading allows the designer to achieve realism (Fig. 10.17 shows examples).

The Badler model [Badler and Morris 1982] is based on the same principle. However, a B-spline surface is computed, based on the skeleton of the hand, to improve the simulation of palm movements. Spheres are linked to the B-spline surface, which does not itself appear on the image. It is only used for the placement of the spheres.

Two problems are important in hand animation: skeleton motion and surface deformation. Moreover, a connected problem is the problem of grasping an object, that is discussed in Sect. 12.5. The hand skeleton is also defined as a connected set of segments and joints. Figure 10.18 shows the joint angles for the left hand.

The mapping of surfaces onto the hand skeleton [Magnenat-Thalmann et al. 1988a] may be based on the concept of Joint-dependent Local Deformation (JLD) operators (see Sect. 10.6). The case of the hand is especially complex, as deformations are very important when the fingers are bent, and the shape of the palm is very flexible. Links of fingers are independent and the JLD operators are calculated using a unique link-dependent reference system. For the palm, JLD operators use reference systems of several links to calculate surface mapping. In order to make fingers realistic, two effects are simulated: rounding calculation at the joints, and muscle inflation. For the rounding, it is necessary to determine if the vertices involved are outside of the flexion, and if they are located in some area at a certain distance from the joint to be rounded. If this is the case, the y-coordinates of the vertices have to be modified according to their location on the segment relatively to the joint, and also according to inflation parameters defined by the user. An exponent function is also used to simulate the surface shape. For the inflations, two exponent functions are used; they are joined in a point, which may be modified by the user. The user may also define parameters of inflation to change the exponent functions.

The hand mapping calculations are based on normals to each proximal joint. Several parameters are used in these mapping calculations and they may be modified by the animator in order to improve the realism of muscles and joints. These parameters include:

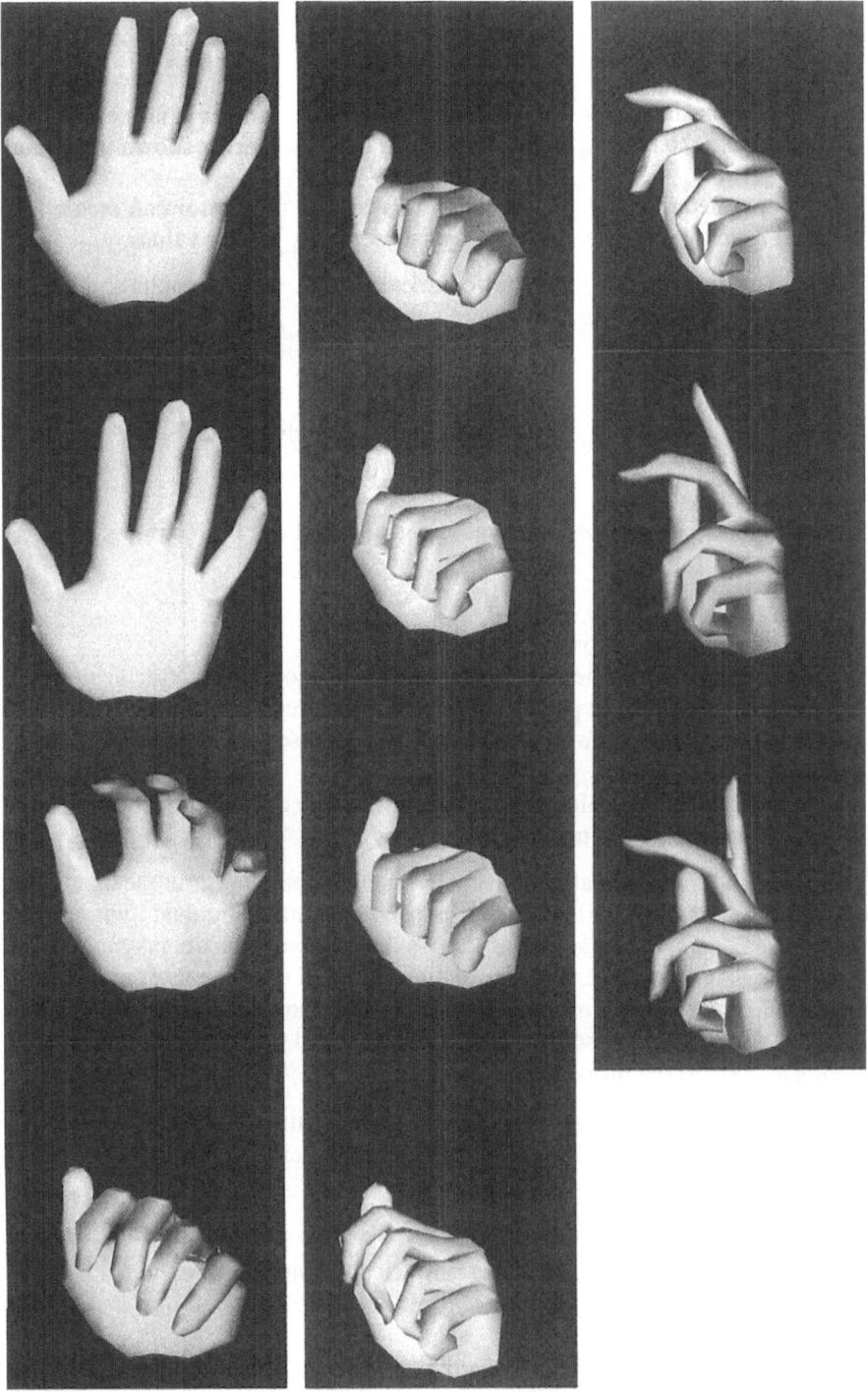

Fig. 10.17. A sequence of 11 frames showing the hand close and open by E. Catmull, University of Utah. Notice the rate of change is not constant

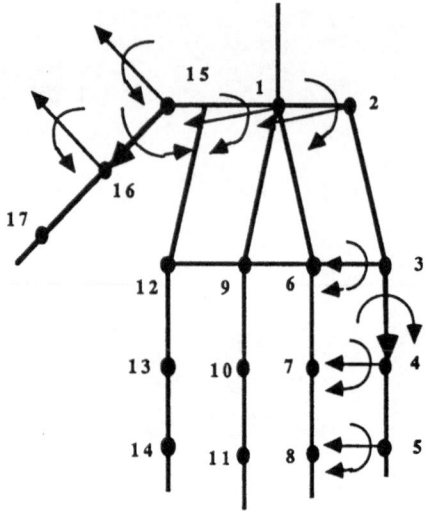

Fig. 10.18. Joint angles for the left hand; rotations 3–4 and 15–16 are pivoting

- The flexion axis at each joint
- A parameter to control the inflation amplitude of a joint during the flexion
- A parameter to define the portion of link to round during a joint flexion
- A parameter to control the inflation amplitude of muscles inside the hand during a flexion
- A parameter to define the location of the point where the inflation of the internal muscles is maximum during a flexion

The initial and final normals are first determined for both joints of the link. Then, a modified normal is calculated as the average of the initial and final joint normal. This modified normal is then used as the y-axis of the coordinate basis and it will allow the simulation of the external rounding of a joint during a flexion. For palm links, normal and modified normal calculations are also required for the neighbor links. Then, a loop is performed on all vertices associated with the link to be covered, and for each vertex, the process is:

Look for the 3D coordinates of the vertex in the digitized character.
Calculate the following information to localize the vertex relative to the link:
Determine a projection of the vertex on the link

$$\text{Calculate the ratio R} = \frac{\text{distance between the projection and the proximal joint}}{\text{distance between the projection and the distal joint}}$$

{The proximal joint is the nearest joint to the wrist, the distal joint is the other joint}.
Calculate the "vertex thickness", which is the distance between the vertex and its projection on the link.

A projection is also determined on the link in its final position. If the link to be covered is a link of the palm, the same projection calculations are performed, but

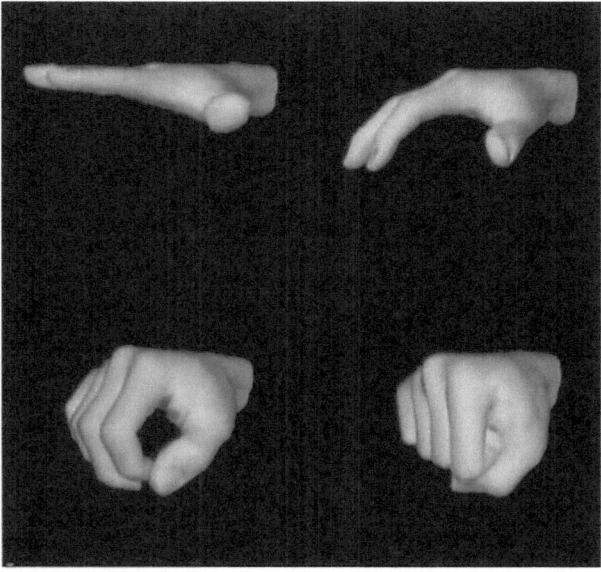

Fig. 10.19. Hand animation (designer: Richard Laperrière, © Nadia Magnenat-Thalmann and Daniel Thalmann 1988)

relatively to the neighbor link, in order to obtain an initial projection and a final projection on this link. These projections are used to simulate a virtual link linking the vertex projection on the link to be covered to the vertex projection on the neighbor link. The projection of the final position is also used as reference point or position relative to the link, in order to allow the transformation from the initial position to the final position. This virtual link allows the calculation of a scale factor:

$$F = \frac{\text{length of the virtual link at the initial position}}{\text{length of the virtual link at the final position}}$$

If the neighbor link in the final position is further from the link to be covered than in the initial position, the scale factor F will be greater than 1, otherwise it is in the range $[0, 1]$. In this latter case, the distance between both links has decreased relatively to the initial position and an inflation should be generated.

Figure 10.19 shows how surface is mapped on the fingers.

Gourret et al. [1989] propose a finite element method to model the deformations of human flesh due to flexion of members and/or contact with objects. The method is further described in Sect. 12.4.

10.8 Facial Animation

Realistic animation of a human face [Magnenat-Thalmann 1989] is extremely difficult to render by a computer. There are two problems:

1. The representation of the face itself. It is difficult to make a realistic image with natural-looking skin. Yau and Duffy [1988] and Nahas et al. [1990] propose a method combining 3D computer graphics with a texture mapping technique to synthesize and animate facial images.
2. The modeling of motion. This is very complex, because there are numerous specific muscles and important interactions between the muscles and the bone structure. This complexity leads to what are commonly called facial expressions. The properties of these facial expressions have been studied for 25 years by psychologist Ekman, who proposed a parameterization of muscles with their relationships to emotions: the FACS system [Ekman and Friesen 1978].

Only the second problem will be addressed in this section.

The Parke Model

The most well-known specialist in facial animation is Frederic I. Parke of the New York Institute of Technology. For him there are two main approaches to applying computer graphics techniques to facial animation [1982]:

1. Using a keyframe system: this means that a certain number of face images are specified and the in-betweens are calculated by computer, as shown in Sect. 5.3.
2. Using parameterized facial models: in this case the animator can create any facial image by specifying the appropriate set of parameter values.

The use of keyframe systems in two dimensions gives good results and is used in cartoons [Stern 1979; Reeves 1981]. Parke used this technique in three dimensions [1972], but it was not very efficient, as too many keyframes were required.

Parameterized models, as introduced by Parke [1975, 1982], are based on the concept of basic parameterization and a model of image synthesis. Basic parameterization consists of choosing the appropriate set of facial parameters. These can be based on observation or on the underlying structures that cause facial expression. The Parke model is based on both types. Parameters are classified into two classes: expression and conformation. The most important expression parameters are related to the eyes (pupil dilation, eyelid opening, direction of vision, etc.) and the mouth (jaw rotation, width of the mouth, smiling, etc.). Conformation parameters include the color of the skin, the color of the eyes, the neck dimensions, nose characteristics, and so on.

Image generation in the Parke model is based on three polygonal surfaces: one for the face and two for the eyes. As shown in Fig. 10.20, the polygons do not all have the same size and shape. According to Parke, the topology provided is the result of trial-and-error. Five types of operations determine vertex positions from the parameter values:

1. Eyes are modeled by **procedural animation**.
2. The forehead, the cheek bone region, the neck, and the mouth are calculated by **interpolation**.
3. The mouth is opened by **rotation**.
4. **Scaling** is used to control the relative size of facial features.
5. For controlling the corners of the mouth or the raising of the upper lip, **position offsets** are used.

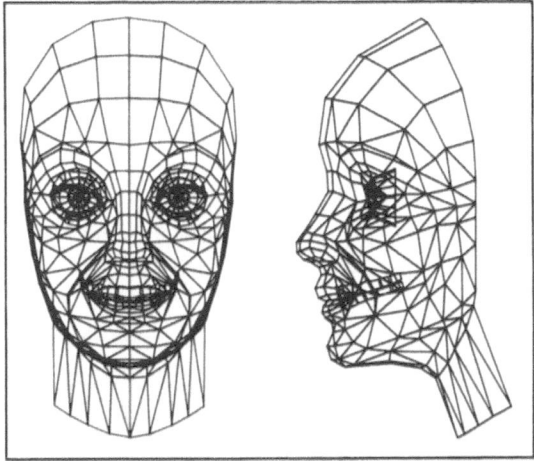

Fig. 10.20. Front and side views of the polygonal network, or topology, used to generate the image shown in Fig. 10.21

Fig. 10.21. Image of facial animation (Phong shading) by Frederic I. Parke, New York Institute of Technology

Phong shading was chosen for image rendering (Fig. 10.21).

Pearce et al. [1986] introduced a small set of keywords to extend the Parke model.

Other Approaches

Platt and Badler [1981] have designed a model that is based on underlying facial structure. Points are simulated in the skin, the muscles, and the bones by a set of three-dimensional networks. The skin is the outside level, represented by a set of

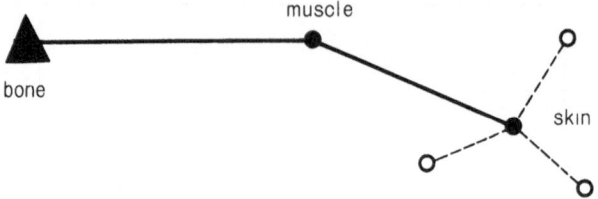

Fig. 10.22. Underlying facial structure

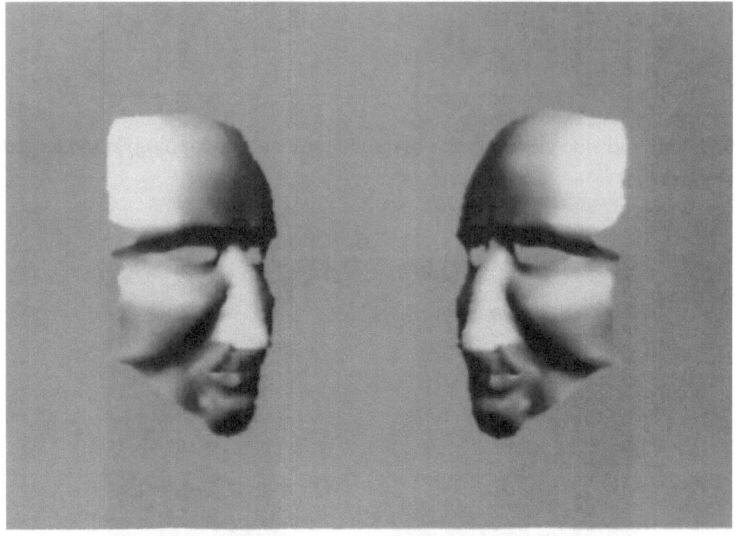

Fig. 10.23. *"Two Faces"* by Stephen M. Platt and Norman I. Badler, University of Pennsylvania

3D points that define a surface which can be modified. The bones represent an internal level that cannot be moved. Between both levels, muscles are groups of points with "elastic" arcs. In Fig. 10.22, when a force is applied to the point M, point B is immovable. Figure 10.23 shows an example.

Nahas et al. [1987] propose a method based on the B-spline. They use a digitizing system to obtain data on the face. Then they extract a certain number of points, and organize them in a matrix. This matrix is used as a set of control points for a 5-dimensional bicubic B-spline surface.

Two recent papers report studies of problems in computer-animated speech: Hill et al. [1987] introduce an automatic approach to animating speech using speech synthesized by rules; Lewis and Parke [1987] automate the lip synchronization between computer-generated imagery and real speech recorded from a real actor.

Waters [1987a, b] represents the action of muscles using primary motivators on a nonspecific deformable topology of the face. Two types of muscles were created: linear/parallel muscles that pull and sphincter muscles that squeeze. The zone of influence depends upon the degree of contraction, and uses FACS as basis.

Guenter [1989] proposes an interactive system for attaching muscles and wrinkle lines to arbitrary rectangular face meshes and then for simulating the contractions of those muscles. A new skin model is described which simulates the extended effects of large facial muscles. Structural analysis techniques are used to solve the resulting elasticity equations efficiently.

10.9 A Three-level Approach Based on Abstract Muscles

How to Animate the Face of a Synthetic Actor?

When you want to animate the face of a synthetic actor, there are two things that have to be considered. First, the muscular structure of the face which causes facial expressions has to be understood and simulated on the computer. But also, at a higher level, there are the expressions themselves, which must represent speech and emotions. The animator must first build a certain number of facial expressions specific to her/his character. The expressions are built by specifying face deformations as they are really caused by muscles: jag opening, eye opening, face folds, etc. These facial deformations are generally different from one person to another person. Let us consider a simple example. We may ask each person to open their mouth as wide as possible; the maximum aperture attained is not the same for everybody.

Once the animator has built the expressions, he/she animates the face by indicating to the computer some of these expressions at certain selected times. For example, "KID" will be pronounced by a character, indicating that the phoneme "K" is used at a given time, the phoneme "I" a short time later, then the phoneme "D". Then the software will progressively transform the facial expression corresponding to the phoneme "K" in order to obtain the facial expression corresponding to the phoneme "I", then to the phoneme "D".

Parameter, Expression, and Script Levels

From the considerations above, we may distinguish three levels of interaction for the animator. The first and the lowest level is the level of control of facial parameters; the animator may decide how a basic deformation acts on a specific synthetic actor. At the second level, the animator creates specific expressions based on the facial parameters. For example, he/she may create phonemes, a smile, or a loving look. At the third level, the animator decides the timing of the animation by fixing some expressions at various times.

Let us consider an example to understand the three levels. At the first level, the animator may decide how the synthetic actress Marilyn may open her mouth; this means setting the maximum horizontal and vertical openings, which are facial parameters. At the second level, the animator may decide the contribution of these facial parameters to an expression like a smile. At the third level, the animator makes Marilyn smile at a certain time.

In other cases, an animator may only work at the script level; however, in this case, he/she may only control the timing and the duration of expressions, or combine expressions. He/she cannot create completely new expressions, except when they are combinations of existing expressions.

The parameter level is not necessary when basic facial parameters for a synthetic actor already exist, as, for example, in the case of Marilyn and Humphrey, created for the film *Rendez-vous à Montréal* (see Sect. 13.2). In this situation, the animator may create any new scene involving the same actors. With the expression level, new expressions may be created using the facial parameters.

Only for a new synthetic actor is the parameter level absolutely necessary, because all facial parameters must be defined for the actor. They are equivalent to the basic physical characteristics of the muscles and the bony structure of the actor's face.

Facial Parameters and AMA procedures

As a muscle is only apparent by the effects of its action, it is not necessary for the animator to know how it works. However, actions are very specific to the various muscles and give the illusion of the presence of a bony structure.

More generally, basic facial animation is based on independent facial parameters simulated by procedures. These procedures, which may be considered as an abstraction of the muscles' actions, are called **Abstract Muscles Action procedures** (AMA procedures) [Magnenat-Thalmann et al. 1988c]. They are more complex than the single parameter approach or a general muscle approach, because they are very specialized; however, a better control of the results may be obtained. AMA procedures work on specific regions of the human face, which need only be defined when the face is constructed. In fact, each AMA procedure is responsible for a facial parameter: e.g., vertical jaw, close upper lip, close lower lip, lip raiser... Facial parameters are not only muscles, as shown in Table 10.1, which presents the main AMA procedures.

Each AMA procedure may have up to 24 parameters. For example, consider the LIP_RAISER procedure which controls how the upper lip may be raised by the action of a particular muscle, the lip raiser on the side of the nose. This is the muscle which shows the teeth when we are smiling or pronouncing the letter "f". The upper lip appears to undergo a kind of a wave, being raised to a maximum point, then lowered. Parameters for this specialized procedure are:

- The highest vertex
- Both commissures
- The maximum percentage of the wave (0 = left commissure, 1 = right commissure)
- The maximum translation at the maximum of the wave
- Parameters affecting the shape of the wave on each side of the maximum
- Parameters affecting the shape according to the distance along the vertical axis

In most AMA procedures, there are some parameters which control the dependancy $f(d)$ on a distance d; these parameters are integer values VAL such that $f(d) = k \cdot d^{VAL}$.

Table 10.1. Most important facial parameters

VERTICAL_JAW	MOVE_RIGHT_EYE_HORIZONTAL
CLOSE_UPPER_LIP	MOVE_RIGHT_EYE_VERTICAL
CLOSE_LOWER_LIP	MOVE_LEFT_EYE_HORIZONTAL
COMPRESSED_LIP	MOVE_LEFT_EYE_VERTICAL
RIGHT_EYELID	RIGHT_RISORIUS
LEFT_EYELID	LEFT_RISORIUS
LEFT_LIP_RAISER	MOVE_RIGHT_EYEBROW
RIGHT_LIP_RAISER	MOVE_LEFT_EYEBROW
LEFT_ZYGOMATIC	MOUTH_BEAK
RIGHT_ZYGOMATIC	

In the case of zygomatic and risorius muscles, the AMA procedures are based on the principle of a traction on the face surface according to an action volume (generally a box). An initial vertex in the action volume is translated by some vector DISP and all other vertices in the volume are translated by a fraction of DISP depending on the location in the volume.

The Expression Level: Phonemes and Emotions

It is possible to animate a human face by manipulating the facial parameters using AMA procedures. However, these procedures have to be considered as a low-level access to the human face. By combining the facial parameters obtained by the AMA procedures in different ways, we can construct more complex entities corresponding to the well-known concept of facial expression. A facial expression is a group of facial parameter values which together transform the neutral face into an expressive face. For the neutral expression, facial parameters have an initial predefined value, let us say 0%. An active facial parameter is assumed to have a maximum value of 100%.

A facial expression for a synthetic actor is a percentage of actions for each active facial parameter. For example, a smile is a combination of 30% of the parameter A, 50% of the parameter G and 0% of all other parameters.

We may also say that an expression of a synthetic actor is defined as a state characterized by a unique face for the actor, a set of regions, and a set of parameter values. An actor personality is defined as the set of expressions for the actor. Even for the same set of parameters, expressions may be different, because of a different basic face and/or different regions.

Two types of facial expressions are possible: phonemes and emotions. A phoneme is a facial expression which only uses mouth motion and directly contributes to speech. It is a combination of several mouth motions corresponding to specific sounds useful for speaking. For example, for the phoneme "I", the teeth are slightly open and the commissures are horizontally pulled towards the outside (risorius muscle). To produce the sound "I", we select 10% of the AMA procedure VERTI-CAL_JAW, 50% of the AMA procedure LEFT_RISORIUS, and 50% of the AMA procedure RIGHT_RISORIUS. An emotion is a facial expression which may act

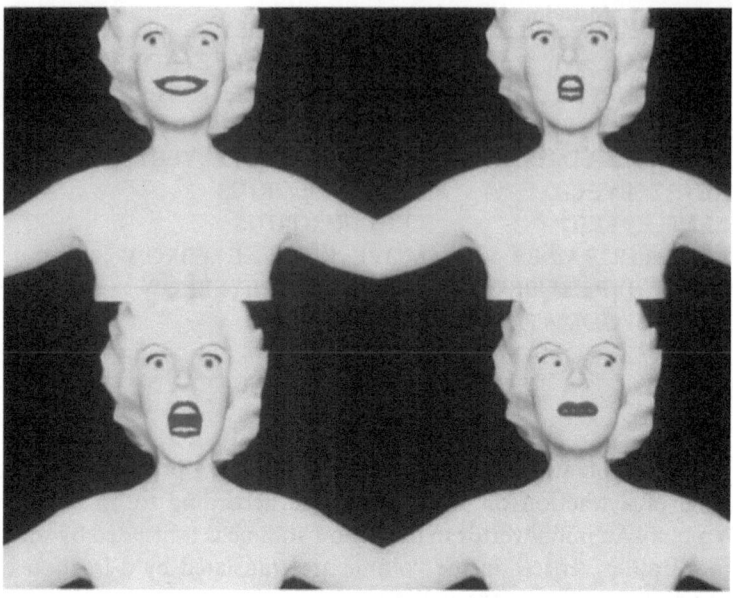

Fig. 10.24. Facial expressions (© Nadia Magnenat-Thalmann and Daniel Thalmann 1989)

on any part of the face: it may correspond to a cry, a smile, a laugh, a kiss, or an expression of love.

Figure 10.24 shows various facial expressions.

Multiple Tracks and Script Level

A script in facial animation is a collection of multiple tracks as described in Sect. 7.5. A track is a chronological sequence of keyframes. There is one track per facial parameter (or AMA procedure). A track for a specific facial parameter or muscle allows the animation of this parameter or muscle independently of all other parameters or muscles. A script may then be considered as multiple parallel parameter animations of the various facial parameters. On each track, a percentage of the facial parameter or the facial expression may be fixed for a given time. Tracks are independent, but they may be mixed exactly in the same way as sound is mixed in a sound studio.

At any time, a track for a facial parameter may be modified, and then mixed with the facial expression. With such an approach, it is easy to modify, for example, an eye in an expression corresponding to a phoneme.

The animation itself is performed by a spline interpolation; this interpolation is assumed to be applied to the mixed track. This means that the animator does not work directly with parametric interpolation but with expression interpolation. This is very important, because it provides the user an access to a higher facial animation level.

11. Object-oriented and Actor Languages and Systems

11.1 Classes, Modules, and Processes

As indicated in Chap. 6, modeled computer animation involves three main activities:

- Object modeling
- Motion specification and synchronization
- Image rendering

In this chapter, we study the impact of new programming languages on object modeling and motion specification and synchronization. Research in image rendering is oriented more towards algorithm development than towards programming languages. Object modeling and motion specification and synchronization can generally be considered simultaneously, as a moving object is by definition an object that is modified during time by motion or some other transformations. As a complex scene involves several moving objects, parallelism is also important. This means that language features of interest for computer animation would include:

- Tools that permit the structured definition of objects with associated operations on them
- Tools that permit the definition of parallelism and quasi-parallelism
- Tools that permit communication between objects

These tools and concepts have been progressively introduced over the years. The first high-level concept for defining a complex object with its own transformations is the class concept in SIMULA-67 [Dahl and Nygaard 1968]. SIMULA, a development of ALGOL, was initially developed for simulation. A class is composed of declarations (variables, procedures, and even classes) and statements. This concept was expanded in the object-oriented languages like SMALLTALK, which will be discussed in next section. The class concept was also introduced in programming languages like Concurrent Pascal [Brinch Hansen 1975] and it is also the basis for the modules defined in the language MODULA-2 [Wirth 1983].

More formally, work on data abstraction [Liskov and Zilles 1974; Guttag 1977] has led to the concept of the abstract data type. This has had important implications for computer graphics, as already shown by Thalmann and Magnenat-Thalmann [1979] and Mallgren [1982].

As mentioned, objects generally move concurrently. This would suggest that the development of concepts and notations for concurrent programming, like those described by Andrews and Schneider [1983], could be important for computer animation. However, this is generally not the case, because these concepts have been designed mainly for applications in system programming, real-time programming or simulation. Frame-by-frame animation requires the presence of all actors, cameras, and decor at each frame, and the synchronization mechanisms provided by process-oriented languages like SIMULA, CONCURRENT PASCAL, or ADA are too complex for animation. However, these concepts can be very useful for real-time animation, as demonstrated by the GALATEA system [Futrelle 1974].

Although the conventional concurrent programming approach has not had a great impact on computer animation, the object-oriented concepts introduced by Kay [1969] and Hewitt's actor theory [1971] have been very influential.

11.2 Kay's Work and SMALLTALK

The first well-known graphics system was SKETCHPAD [Sutherland 1963]. This interactive system allowed the creation of "instances" of a basic shape, and "constraints" upon it. Based upon SKETCHPAD and SIMULA, Kay [1969] suggested that a programming system could be based on objects that send messages to each other. This idea met with great interest and two major results developed from it:

1. Kay went to Xerox Palo Alto Research Center and worked with Adele Goldberg to develop the first uniformly object-oriented language: SMALLTALK 72.
2. Projects in artificial intelligence were developed using a similar approach (see Sect. 11.3).

The SMALLTALK language was developed based on Kay's ideas, beginning in 1970 [Goldberg and Kay 1976]. The latest version is SMALLTALK-80 [Goldberg and Robson 1983], its most important concepts being:

1. Every entity is an **object**: numbers, strings, programs, compilers, etc.
2. Each object is an **instance** of a **class**.
3. Objects consist of some private memory and a set of operations.
4. Objects communicate with each other by sending messages.

A graphics system is included in SMALLTALK-80 with capabilities that are very useful for computer animation. It represents images by instances of a class **Form**. A Form has height, width, and a bitmap. Animation can be displayed smoothly by using one Form as the display while the next image to be displayed is prepared in a second Form. As each image is completed, the two Forms exchange roles and the process can start again.

Basic graphical objects are defined as instances of classes Point and Rectangle. There are other display objects besides objects of the class Form. These are all defined in the class DisplayObject that contains three primary subclasses:

- DisplayMedium, which represents images that can be colored and bordered
- DisplayText, which represents textual images

– Path, that corresponds to an ordered collection of points and a Form that can be displayed at each point. The concept is very similar to the P-curves [Baecker 1969] discussed in Sect. 5.6

A conversational extensible system for the animation of shaded images, called SHAZAM, has been implemented in SMALLTALK by Baecker [1976]. More recently, several object-oriented animation systems have been proposed: SOLAR [Chua et al. 1988], CLOCKWORKS [Breen et al. 1987], and FIFTH DIMENSION [Turner et al. 1990].

11.3 Hewitt's Actor Theory

In artificial intelligence laboratories, especially those at Massachusetts Institute of Technology (MIT) and Stanford, numerous systems and languages have been developed around concepts near those of the Smalltalk school. However, research has taken a somewhat different direction, reflecting the artificial intelligence background of the researchers and the influence of LISP.

Based on his PhD thesis, Hewitt [1971] of MIT first introduced the term "actor" [Hewitt et al. 1973] and this has been used in several systems designed by his team: PLANNER-73 [Greif and Hewitt 1975] and PLASMA [Hewitt and Smith 1975].

Hewitt defined an actor as an object than can send or receive messages. All elements of a system are actors and the only activity possible in the system is the transmission of messages between them. Programming consists merely of telling the different classes of actors how to respond to the messages they receive.

There are several advantages in the Hewitt actor approach:

1. Changing a program means simply changing the responses of the actors.
2. Program complexity does not increase as programs grow.
3. It gives a natural representation of the knowledge needed for an application, and intelligence can easily be modeled as an integrated community of rather limited individuals.

Actors are defined by their behaviors. Greif and Hewitt [1975] have given the following definition of a behavior:

"A behavior is a partially ordered set of events which represent transmissions... Behaviors consist of events. An event is a four-tuple, $\langle t\ m\alpha ec \rangle$ where t is the target, m is the transmission, α is the activator, and ec is the event count of the activator α."

This approach implies programs with side-effects, parallelism and synchronization and these concepts have been formally described by Greif and Hewitt [1975] and Hewitt and Atkinson [1977].

11.4 LOGO and the DIRECTOR Actor-based Animation Language

Hewitt's actor is like a person who can receive requesting messages, send messages to other actors, and remember things. It therefore seemed to Kenneth M. Kahn to provide an ideal way of representing dynamic objects in computer animation. Kahn [1976] implemented an animation language called DIRECTOR which is based on actors.

In DIRECTOR, objects and the messages they handle are specified. In particular, an actor can be asked to do all the things that LOGO turtles can do. As the concept of the LOGO turtle is important in DIRECTOR and has also been extended to three-dimensions by Reynolds [1978, 1982] in ASAS, it will be briefly summarized here.

LOGO is a programming language that was developed at M.I.T. primarily for children [Papert 1970]. Its most important concept is the turtle geometry which consists of polar-coordinate graphics. At the beginning of a session, the turtle (a triangle, in fact) is at the center of the screen and is invisible. The turtle appears with the command APPEAR and disappears with the command HIDE. It goes forward with the command FORWARD n and backward with the command BACKWARD n, where n is a number of steps. The commands LEFT α and RIGHT α make the turtle turn left or right and the angle α is always calculated relative to its current orientation. For example, the following sequence of instructions draws a square of vertices $\langle\langle 0, 0\rangle\rangle$, $\langle\langle 20, 0\rangle\rangle$, $\langle\langle 20, 20\rangle\rangle$, $\langle\langle 0, 20\rangle\rangle$, $\langle\langle 0, 0\rangle\rangle$, where $\langle\langle 0, 0\rangle\rangle$ is the center of the screen:

> APPEAR
> REPEAT 4 [FORWARD 20 LEFT 90]

Message passing is the mechanism of communication between two actors in DIRECTOR. The most important and the basic message-passing command is ASK. The syntax is as follows:

> ASK ⟨actor name⟩ (⟨message⟩)

For example, ASK CORVETTE (FORWARD 10), means that a message is sent to the actor CORVETTE, and this actor is asked to go forward 10 units.

Messages begin with a key word corresponding to the action required of the actor. Among the most important key words are:

- The turtle commands: FORWARD, BACK, RIGHT, LEFT, APPEAR, HIDE, SHOW, PENUP, and PENDOWN
- MAKE, that tells the actor to create a new actor and UNMAKE, that tells the actor to destroy another actor
- RECEIVE, that enables the actor to increase the set of messages it can understand
- REMEMBER and FORGET, that tell the actor to remember or forget an item, REPLACE, that tells it to replace a value, and WHAT, that gives it a value.
- PLAN, that tells the actor to schedule things to do at later times

There are also transformation commands like GROW or conditional commands like IF. Moreover, an ASK command can be repeated several times by using REPEAT.

As an example, we present the script of a short movie, designed by Kahn [1976]:

"a garden in which seeds are born, wait, grow into flowers, create new seeds, continue growing, and die."

The DIRECTOR script is shown in Fig. 11.1 with comments.

```
TO DEFINE.FLOWER                        --LOGO command
10 ASK OBJECT(MAKE FLOWER)              --flower creation
20 ASK FLOWER(REMEMBER SIZE 10)         --flower size
30 ASK FLOWER(REMEMBER DRAW             --to draw a flower using
           USING DRAW-FLOWER)             a LOGO procedure
END


TO DEFINE .SEED
10 ASK SOMETHING(MAKE SEED)             --seed creation
20 ASK SEED (IF RECEIVE?SEED(START)     --start message and
           THEN DO.SEED.THING:?SEED)    --appropriate procedure call
END


TO DO.SEED.THING:SEED                   --procedure for handling seeds
10 LOCAL A FLOWER                       --local flower name
20 ASK FLOWER (MAKE A.FLOWER)
30 ASK A.FLOWER (APPEAR RIGHT 90)       --turtle commands
40 ASK A.FLOWER (APPEAR FORWARD
           (*100 (RANDOM)))
50 ASK A.FLOWER (APPEAR LEFT 90)
60 ASK A.FLOWER (PLAN:SHOW IN 10 TICKS)--the message ASK A.FLOWER
                                          (SHOW) will occur after
                                          A.FLOWER has received
                                          10 ticks
70 REPEAT 15 (ASK A.FLOWER             --ASK A.FLOWER (GROW 10)
           (PLAN:GROW 10 AFTER 2         will be called 15 times,
           MORE TICKS))                  2 ticks after the last
80 ASK SEED (PLAN:ASK (SEED (MAKE))    --creation of another seed that
   (START) AT THAT TIME)                 must start at the same time
                                         as the last thing scheduled
90 ASK A.FLOWER (PLAN:HIDE
       AFTER 60 MORE TICKS)
END
```

Fig. 11.1. A DIRECTOR script

SOMETHING and OBJECT are predefined actors which are hierarchically organized. SOMETHING is at the top of the hierarchy and receives all messages that are not understood by the other actors: editing of actors, print out, creation of new actors, etc. OBJECT is an actor directly below SOMETHING and as such, inherits all of its abilities. Moreover, OBJECT can behave like a LOGO turtle. This is why, in the garden example, OBJECT is asked to create FLOWER (which does turtle-like things) and SOMETHING is asked to create SEED (which does not do turtle-like things).

For computer animation, the message-passing and matching involved are much slower than other mechanisms. However, Hewitt's concept of an actor was a significant innovation which has been influential in computer animation systems.

11.5 ASAS: The Actor/Scriptor Animation System

ASAS [Reynolds 1978, 1982] is a procedural programming language for animation and graphics. It was developed at the Architecture Machine Group at MIT by C.W. Reynolds as a thesis project. ASAS was then integrated into the Digital Scene Simulation System of Information International Inc. The latest version, ASAS 3.0, was in fact a preprocessor for three-dimensional software.

ASAS was influenced by Hewitt's work and it is also a LISP-based language, from which it borrows its "parenthesized prefix notation." There are eight types of geometric objects in ASAS:

1. *vector*, i.e., a 3D position
   For example: (*vector* 1 2 3)
2. *color* defined either in the RGB (red, green, blue) system or in the IHS (intensity, hue, saturation) system
   For example: (*rgb* 0.5 0.4 0.3)
                  (*ihs* 0.33 0.5 1)
3. *polygon* defined by its color and a list of vertices
   For example: (*polygon* yellow a b c)
4. *solid* defined by a list of polygons
   For example: for the tetrahedron:
             (*solid* yellow
                     (*vertices*: (a 1 2 3) (b 4 5 6)
                             (c 3 2 0) (d 7 9 1))
                     (*polygon* blue a b c)
                     (*polygon* * a d b)
                     (*polygon* * a c d)
                     (*polygon* * c b d)))
5. *group*, i.e., a concatenation of simpler objects
   For example: (*group* head body)
6. *point of view* (*pov*) representing the relationship between an object's local coordinate system and the external global system. The *pov* object is used to define the point of view of an observer (virtual camera) or of an object. A *pov* object is defined by four vectors: the base position vector and three vectors parallel to the local coordinate axes.
   For example: (*pov*(*vector* a b c) xvec yvec zvec)
7. *subworld*, i.e., an object associated with a *pov*. A complex object can be manipulated by modifying only the *pov*.
   For example: (*subworld*(*pov* vl vx vy vz) corvette)
8. *light* composed of a position vector and a color
   For example: (*light*(*vector* 1 2 3) (*rgb* 0.33 0.5 1))

The geometric operations are implemented as functions which produce a copy of the object on which they are applied. When these functions are used as local operators in a subworld, the effect corresponds to a three-dimensional extension of the "turtle" of the LOGO language shown in Sect. 11.4. Objects will be defined in such a way that their centers will be the origin of the local coordinate space. The major local operators are as follows:

grow	scale up about local center
shrink	scale down about local center
forward a	move distance a along local $+Z$ axis
backward a	move distance a along local $-Z$ axis
left α	rotate to left by angle α about local Y axis
right α	rotate to right by angle α about local Y axis
up α	rotate upward by angle α about local X axis
down α	rotate downward by angle α about local X axis
cw α	rotate clockwise by angle α about local Z axis
ccw α	rotate counter-clockwise by angle α about local Z-axis
zoom-in a	scale up of a along local Z axis
zoom-out a	scale down of a along local Z axis

Figure 11.2 shows the effect of the different operators. All these operators are applied to an object specified as the last parameter or, if this is omitted, to the current object defined by the operator *grasp*. For example:

(*grasp* corvette)
(*forward* 3)
(*left*(quotient pi 4))
(*forward* 2)
(*right*(quotient pi 5))
(*forward* 10)

An ASAS script (main program) generally has "animate blocks" in its main body. These are loops that automatically produce a frame at each loop step. In an animate block, object can be made visible by the operator *see* or actors can be started and stopped at specific times with the operator *cue*.

For example, a script called transportation that starts two actors airplane (at time 10) and ship (at time 20) can be coded as:
(*script* transportation
    (*animate*(*cue* (*at* 10)
              (*start* airplane))
        (*cue*(*at* 20)
            (*start* ship))
        (*cut* 30)))

"*cut* 30" means that the animate block is exited at time 30.

An ASAS actor is, as defined by Reynolds [1982], basically a "chunk" of code that is executed once each frame. It is started by a *start* operator and stopped by a *stop* operator. It can also be displayed by the operator *see*. Figure 11.3 shows an example of an actor which consists of an object that is rotated.

Actors can switch messages that are handled by two operators, *send* and *receive*.

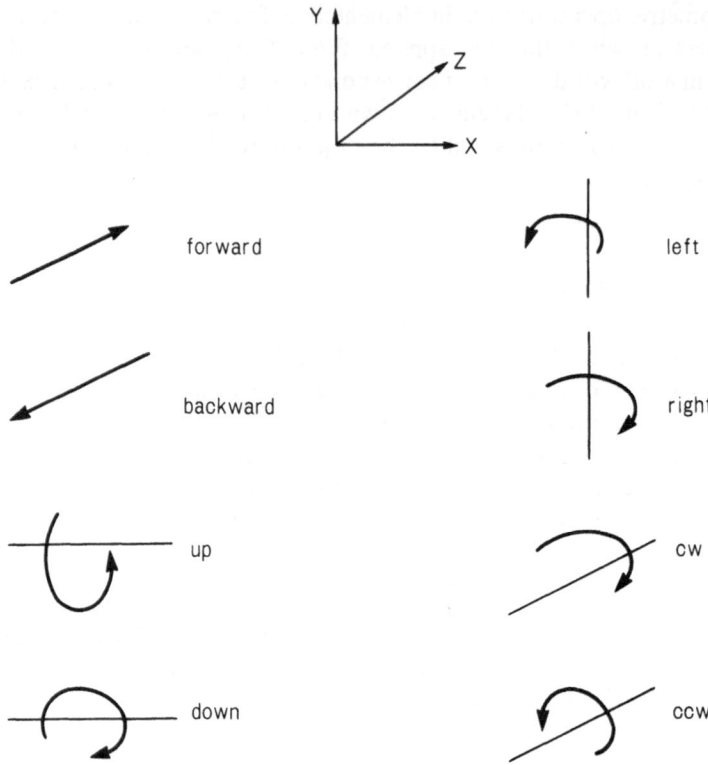

Fig. 11.2. The ASAS operators

```
(actor (local: (angle 0)
               (step (quo 2 runtime))
               (octa octahedron))
       (see (rotate angle y-axis octa)
       (define angle (plus angle step))))
```

Fig. 11.3. An ASAS actor

11.6 CINEMIRA: A Language Based on Actor and Camera Data Types

CINEMIRA [Thalmann and Magnenat-Thalmann 1984] is a high-level three-dimensional computer animation language based on data abstraction. It allows the animator to write structured scripts by defining animated basic types, actor types, and camera types. Static graphical objects are defined as figures and decor. Messages can be switched between actors and cameras. A director, who can also communicate with actors and cameras, assumes scene control.

Animated Basic Types

Image transformations are defined by functions depending on variables of three basic types: INTEGER, REAL, and VECTOR. For example, a translation is defined by a vector translation, and a rotation by a vector (the center) and a real number (the angle). Attributes like color, intensity, or source lights are also defined by parameters of these types. Viewing transformations are also based on these types. For example, a perspective projection is defined by its center, which is a vector. Animation of objects (actors) and cameras can then be based on the animation of basic parameters.

A good way of defining animation of these parameters is to introduce **animated basic types**. This concept is a generalization of the Newton concept defined in ASAS (see Sect. 11.5). Each variable of an animated basic type—INTEGER, REAL, and VECTOR—can itself be animated. An animated type is defined by giving the starting and ending values of the number or the vector, the starting and ending times, and a function or law which describes how the value varies with time. During the specified interval, variables of animated basic types are automatically updated to the next value according to the function. For example, suppose we wish to define a vector that starts at time 10 and moves with a constant speed $\langle\langle 3,0,0\rangle\rangle$ from the point $\langle\langle 0,10,4\rangle\rangle$ and stops at time 13. This is expressed as follows:

type TVEC = *animated* VECTOR;
        val $\langle\langle 0,10,4\rangle\rangle$ .. UNLIMITED;
        time 10 .. 13;
        law $\langle\langle 0,10,4\rangle\rangle + \langle\langle 3,0,0\rangle\rangle * (\text{CLOCK-10})$
        end;
var VEC:TVEC;

As the end position and the ending time are redundant values, they are not both required. It is possible to use UNLIMITED to avoid specifying a value.

Of course, starting and ending values of the number or vector, and starting and ending times have to be defined either by calculation or by direct input. This is why expressions can be defined using both the *val* and *time* specifications. Formal parameters can be defined in an animated basic type. These parameters must be value parameters and they can be used in *val*, *time*, and *law* expressions. For example:

type TVEC = *animated* VECTOR (STARTTIME, ENDTIME:REAL;
                               (STARTVAL, SPEED:VECTOR);
        val STARTVAL .. UNLIMITED;
        time STARTTIME .. ENDTIME;
        law STARTVAL + SPEED * (CLOCK-STARTTIME)
        end;

Expressions in the law can also involve "CLOCK" that is the current time and "CURVAL" that is the current value of the animated basic variable.

type TVEC = *animated* VECTOR (DELTA:VECTOR);
        ⋮
        law CURVAL + DELTA
        end;

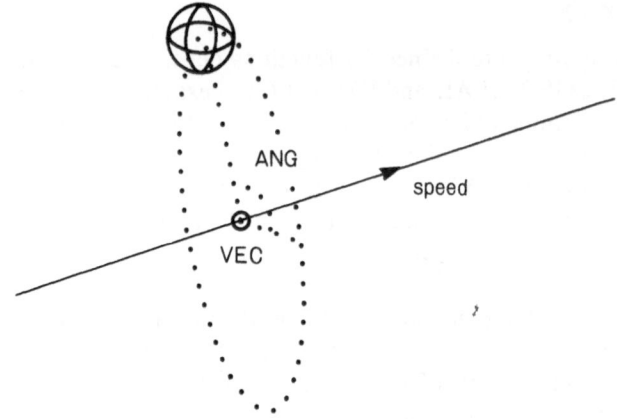

Fig. 11.4. A motion

Initialization of the animated basic variables is performed by the *init* statement. It is at this stage that values of the parameters are given, as shown:

init VEC (10, 13, ⟨⟨0, 10, 4⟩⟩, ⟨⟨3, 0, 0⟩⟩)

Animated basic variables can be used wherever a variable of the same basic type would be used. This feature is very powerful. For example, a point can be moved along a line and a sphere S can be rotated around this point, as shown in Fig. 11.4. This can be described by a single rotation where the center is an animated vector, and the angle an animated real number.

```
type   TVEC = animated VECTOR (...)
                (* as defined previously *)
       TREAL = animated REAL (STARTTIME, ENDTIME: REAL);
                val 0..UNLIMITED;
                time STARTTIME..ENDTIME;
                law CURVAL * 1.2
                end;
       TREAL = animated REAL (STARTTIME, ENDTIME: REAL);
                val 0..UNLIMITED;
                time STARTTIME..ENDTIME;
                law (CURVAL + PI/20) mod (2*PI)
                end;
var VEC: TVEC;
    ANG: TREAL;
    S: SPHERE;
    ⋮
init VEC(10, 13, ⟨⟨0, 10, 4⟩⟩ ⟨⟨3, 0, 0,⟩⟩);
init ANG (10, 13);
    ⋮
ROTATION (S, VEC, ANG, S)
```

Actor Data Types

An *actor* type is an animated abstract graphical data type. Animated basic types and variables can be defined within an *actor* type. *Actor* types can only be defined in a script. The syntax of an actor type is as follows:

⟨actor type⟩:: = *actor* ⟨formal parameter list⟩; ⟨time interval⟩;
⟨actor block⟩

An actor can be constructed using *figures* that can be manipulated. The time interval specifies when the actor exists. If the actor type BALL is defined as:

type BALL = *actor* (TINIT:REAL);
        time TINIT..20;
        ...

actors of BALL type will be on the scene between the time TINIT and 20.

As in the case of animated variables, actor variables are initialized by the *init* statement. For example, two differents variables of BALL type can be initialized:

var BALL1, BALL2:BALL;
        ⋮
init BALL1 (10);
init BALL2 (12);

We now give an example of an actor type: we define an actor that is a stone (of icosahedric shape) that falls from a position P until it arrives at the level 0 (Y = 0); for example, a water surface. The *actor* type stone is defined as follows:

STONE = *actor* (P:VECTOR; TINIT, TSTART:REAL);
        time TINIT..UNLIMITED;
        type TVEC = *animated* VECTOR;
          val P..⟪P.X, 0, P.Z⟫;
          time TSTART..⟪P.X, 0, P.Z⟫;
          law P − 0.5∗9.81∗SQR (CLOCK-TSTART)
          end;
        var VEC:TVEC;
          ICOSA:ICOSAHEDRON;
        begin
          init VEC;
          create ICOSA (VEC, CFA, DIR);
          include ICOSA
        end;

A variable ROCK of STONE type is animated by the following sequence:

init ROCK (⟪10, 8, 20⟫, 10, 12);
        ...

This means that the *actor* ROCK exists from time 10, but starts moving at time 12.

In many cases, it is difficult to decide in advance when an *actor* must start moving. In our example, suppose that the stone has to begin moving when a person (another *actor*) drops it. This can be performed by removing the TSTART parameter in the

STONE *actor* and replacing the lower time limit TSTART in the TVEC type by SIGNAL:

> STONE = *actor* (P: VECTOR; TINIT: REAL);
>   *time* TINIT .. UNLIMITED;
>   *type* TVEC = *animated* VECTOR;
>   *val* P .. ⟪P.X, 0, P.Z⟫;
>   *time* SIGNAL .. UNLIMITED;
>   *law* P − 0.5∗9.81∗SQR (CLOCK-SIGNAL)
>   *end*;
>   *begin*
>   ...
>   *end*;

The animation sequence is as follows:

> *unit* PERSON (...);
> *init* ROCK (⟪10, 8, 20⟫, 10);

PERSON is a variable of *actor* type, which must contain a *start* ROCK statement at the right time.

Similarly, we may start a new actor WAVES, consisting of circular waves that begin as a stone hits the water by rewriting the STONE *actor* type as:

> *begin*
>   *init* VEC;
>   *create* ICOSA (VEC, CFA, DIR);
>   *include* ICOSA;
>   *if* VEC.Y = 0 *then start* WAVES
> *end*;

More generally, a *start* A statement has the immediate effect of replacing all lower SIGNAL time limits of the actor A by the current runtime. It can make the *actor* appear and/or start the motion of animated variables declared within the *actor* type. Similarly, a *stop* B statement has the immediate effect of replacing all higher SIGNAL time limits of the *actor* B by the current time. It can make the *actor* disappear and/or stop the motion of animated variables declared within the *actor* type.

Camera Data Types

A *camera* type is also an animated abstract type. Its syntax is exactly the same as that of an *actor* type, replacing *actor* with *camera* keywords. Time limits have the same meaning as for an *actor*. Animated basic types and variables can be defined within a camera type, but no *actor* or other *camera* types can be used. As expected, *camera* type can only be defined in a *script*. The goal of a *camera* type is to define the values of the visual parameters and how they vary with time. Typically, statements in a *camera* type are viewing procedure calls. Their parameters can, of course, be animated variables, as shown:

```
type TCAM = camera (TINIT, TEND:REAL);
            time TINIT..TEND;
            type TVEC = animated VECTOR (VSTART,
                                         VSTEP:VECTOR);
                val VSTART..UNLIMITED;
                time TINIT..TEND;
                law CURVAL + VSTEP
                end;
            var V1, V2:TVEC;
            begin
                init V1 (《0,0,1》, 《0,0.1,0》);
                init V2 (《20,25, −20》
                        《0,1, −0.5》);
                VIEWPORT (《0,0》, 《1,1》);
                WINDOW (《−20, −5》, 《20,35》);
                PLANENORMAL (V1);
                PERSPECTIV (V2);
            end;
```

Scripts

A CINEMIRA *script* is a subprogram dedicated to computer animation. A program can invoke several scripts, but only one at a time. A script is under the control of a **director** which is normally not apparent, but can communicate with other entities of the system by messages. Actor and cameras can also exchange messages. A script has the following syntax:

⟨script declaration⟩:: = *script* ⟨script identifier⟩
⟨formal parameter list⟩; ⟨script block⟩;

A script has a name that is an identifier and can have parameters like a procedure.
A script block is composed of declarations (constants, types, variables and subprograms), statements, and *scenes*. The syntax of a script block is as follows:

⟨script block⟩:: = ⟨declaration part⟩ *begin* ⟨statement⟩
{;⟨statement⟩}*⟨scene⟩ {;⟨scene⟩}*end;

The declaration part can include animated basic types, *figure* types, *actor* types, *camera* types, and message variables.
A script is a sequence of scenes. The scenes can be preceded by a sequence of statements to initialize objects that are common to several scenes.
Each scene has the following syntax:

⟨scene⟩:: = *scene* ⟨scene identifier⟩; ⟨statement⟩;
{⟨statement⟩;}*⟨shoot statement⟩ *end* ⟨scene identifier⟩

The scene has a name and consists of a sequence of statements that serve mainly to initialize actors, cameras, and decor. The decor is a collection of graphical objects that do not move or change during the entire scene. In CINEMIRA, a decor is defined by the statement *decor* ⟨figure list⟩ where the figure list is an enumeration of figure variables. For example:

create HOUSE (…);
create SKY;
create SUN (…);
decor HOUSE, SKY, SUN;

The *shoot* statement performs the shooting phase, during which decor, actors and cameras are automatically placed. The shoot statement can take a very simple form:

shoot until ⟨expression⟩

where the expression is the upper time limit of the scene in seconds. The lower limit is the upper limit of the previous scene (0 at the beginning).

Each scene can have initializations and must have a *shoot* statement. *Actors, cameras, decor,* and animated basic variables can be activated for several scenes or parts of scenes. In this case, they have to be initialized before the first scene and not within one.

Special effects like fade-in, fade-out, and cross dissolves are only possible by overlapping scenes. This can be done by declaring an overlap of the next scene in the *shoot* statement and by specifying the overlap time, as shown:

scene ONE:
⋮

shoot until 20 *overlap* 3
end ONE;
scene TWO;
⋮

We give an example where scene ONE begins to disappear 2 seconds before the end and scene TWO appears simultaneously. The visual effect is shown in Fig. 11.5. The CINEMIRA code is presented in Fig. 11.6.

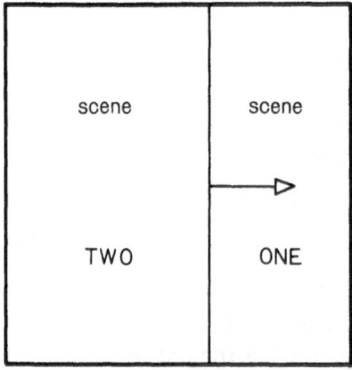

Fig. 11.5. Wipe effect

```
type
   TREAL = animated REAL(R1,R2,TSTART:REAL);
            val R1..R2;
            time TSTART..UNLIMITED;
            law R1+0.01*(CLOCK-TSTART)
         end;

   TCAM1 = camera(EYE,INTEREST:VECTOR; TWIPE:REAL);
         time 0..UNLIMITED;
         var R:TREAL;

         begin
            init R(0,1,TWIPE);
            PERCAMERA(EYE,INTEREST,1);
            CLIPEXT(« R,0 », «1,1 »)
         end;

   TCAM2 = camera(EYE,INTEREST:VECTOR; TWIPE:REAL);
         time 0..UNLIMITED;
         var R:TREAL;
         begin
            init R(0,1,TWIPE);
            PERCAMERA(EYE,INTEREST,1);
            CLIPINT(« R,0 », «1,1 »)
         end;

var
   CAM1:TCAM1;

   CAM2:TCAM2;

   ...
begin
   init CAM1(EYE1,INTEREST1,18);
   init CAM2(EYE2,INTEREST2,18);

   scene ONE;
   ...actor and decor initializations
      shoot until 20 overlap 2
   end ONE;

   scene TWO;
   ...actor and decor initializations
      shoot until 35
   end TWO;
end.
```

Fig. 11.6. CINEMIRA code

11.7 MIRANIM: An Extensible Director-oriented 3D Animation System

Although there are problems in computer-aided animation, various animator-oriented systems have been developed that work. They can be used by non computer-expert artists. In modeled animation, the problem is more complex and always centers around the question: programming language or animator-oriented system? The production of three-dimensional computer-animated films using a graphical programming language is time-consuming.

Moreover, such an approach implies that animators also have to be programmers. User-friendly interactive systems can have the great advantage of being dedicated to artists, but they impose limits on creativity and fail to exploit all the possibilities of a computer. Special effects like the ones shown in Fig. 11.7 are difficult to produce without programming. Apart from three-dimensional key-frame animation systems like BBOP or MUTAN [Fortin et al. 1983], discussed in Sects. 4.8 and 7.5, there are not many examples of artist-oriented 3D systems except ANTTS, presented in Sect. 4.6. Some of the spectacular effects in *TRON*, for instance, were produced by Information International Inc. using ASAS, a typical programming language used for computer animation.

Artists who do not know how to program a computer (they are in the majority) have to use an artist-oriented system. That system must offer the possibility of making most scenes of a computer-animated film. It must provide facilities for controlling main actor motions, virtual cameras, and lighting. In the case of very complex motions, procedural models can be programmed by a programmer, but it is essential that the control of this procedural model be given to the animator in the interactive system. This means that the new motion must be added to the system, which must therefore be extensible. Such a system, called MIRANIM, has been designed and implemented. It is composed of an animator-oriented system and an animation sublanguage called CINEMIRA-2 [Magnenat-Thalmann et al. 1985, Magnenat-Thalmann and Thalmann, 1985c]

The Animator-Oriented System MIRANIM

With the MIRANIM system, the animator can specify a complete script without any programming. He or she can create actors with their motions and transformations as well as virtual cameras with their motions and characteristics. Backgrounds can also be built interactively. Multiple light sources can be defined and moved around at will. Eight modes are defined in the system, each with specific commands.

1. **Motion mode**
   This mode allows the animator to create constants and animated variables. Such variables, which drive the motion of actors, cameras, and lights, are defined by evolution laws describing how their values change over time. Among the available laws are the Catmull laws and the main physical motions. To define a point PT that turns from time 0 to time 10 with a circular motion around an axis passing through the vector $\langle 8, 4, 0 \rangle$ and the plane normal vector $\langle 0, 0, 1 \rangle$, with an angular velocity of 1 rad/s and angular acceleration of 0 rad s^2, we type:

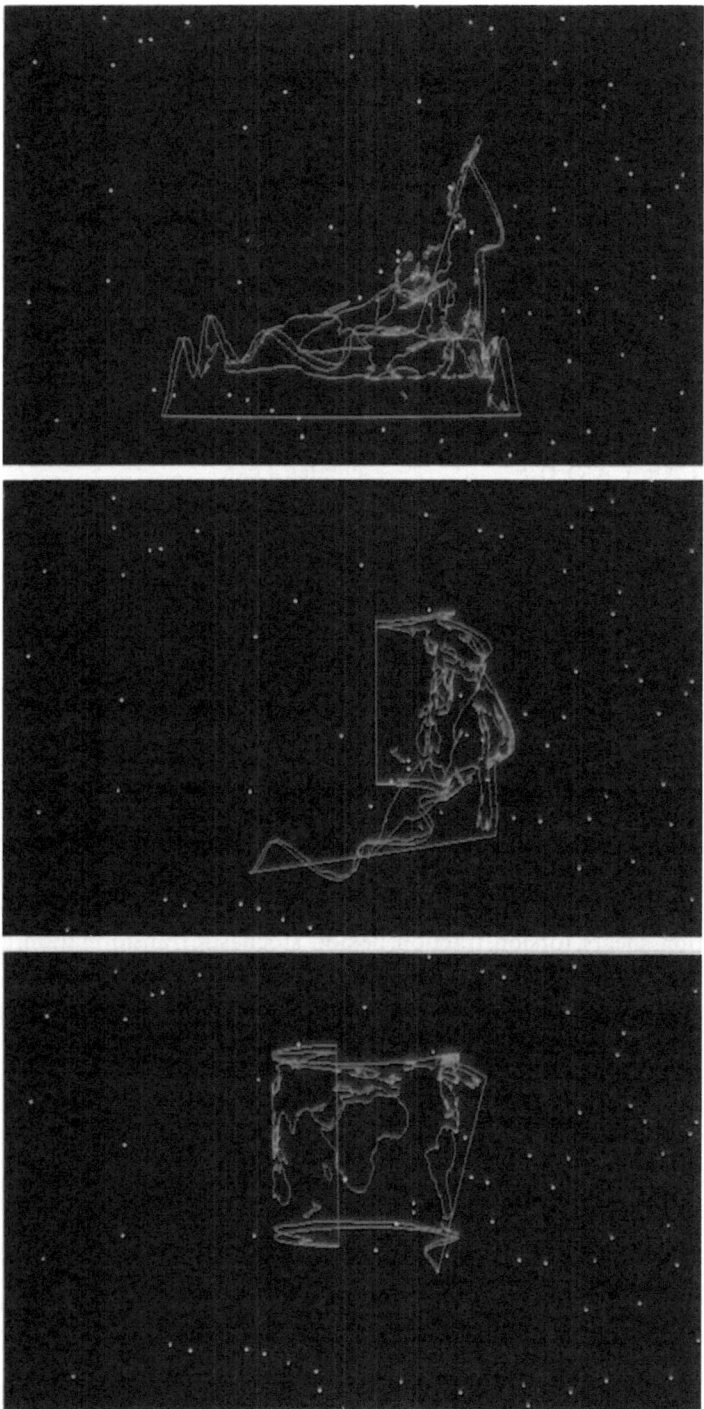

Fig. 11.7. Formation of the earth (from *Dream Flight*)

VVEC, PT $\langle 0,0,0 \rangle$ – defines point PT as a vector with an initial value.

MVTCIRC MYLAW $\langle 8,4,0 \rangle$ $\langle 0,0,1 \rangle$ 1 0 – defines the law MYLAW as a specific circular motion.

EVOLUTION PT, MYLAW, 0, 10   – associates the law with the point from time 0 to time 10.

2. **Object mode**

This mode offers the same possibilities for creating objects as a limited three-dimensional graphics editor. In fact, basic objects must be built outside the animation system. But they can be modified in the object mode by rotations, translations, scaling, and coloring. For example, if we wish to use objects such as a car which is an actor and mountains which form part of the background, or decor, the objects are read from a file and they can be colored or translated.

READ CAR, CARFILE   – creates a car.
READ MOUNT1 MOUNTFILE – creates a mountain.
COPY MOUNT1 MOUNT2   – duplicates the mountain.
MOVE MOUNT2 $\langle 5,15,20 \rangle$ – translates the second mountain.
COLOR CAR 0.33, 0.5, 1   – colors the car red.

3. **Decor mode**

This mode allows the animator to build up a decor with objects and to view it. For example, to build a decor with a house and two mountains:

    DECOR D1, HOUSE, MOUNT1, MOUNT2

4. **Actor mode**

This mode is the most important one. The animator defines actors (animated objects) and then gives a list of transformations which have to be applied to each. At present, 16 kinds of transformations are available, including rotation, sizing, translation, shears, torsion, traction, flexion, stochastic transformation, and color changing. The parameters of a transformation may be animated variables; the latter are also generally used to specify time dependence. For example, in a rotation, the angle can be an animated real number and the direction of the axis can be an animated vector. The number of transformations associated with an actor is not limited and the transformations are driven by the animated variables. For example, suppose the following transformations are to be performed on a tree:

i)   Changing the size
ii) Flexion (or bending)
iii) Changing the color from green to red

This can be performed by the following commands:

ACTOR TREE, TREEOBJ   – defines the actor tree with the object THREEOBJ as basis.

SIZE TREE, V   – V is an animated vector which defines how the size changes.

FLEXION TREE, V1, V2, V3, V4 – V1, V2, V3 and V4 are flexion parameters.

COLOR TREE, VC   – VC is an animated vector which changes from the HLS value of green to the HLS value of red according to a law.

5. **Camera mode**

In this mode, the animator can define one or several virtual cameras. Each camera has an eye point and an interest point, which can be animated vectors. Moreover, clipping, spin, viewpoint, and zoom can be specified for a camera as well as animation. The eye point or the interest point of a camera can also follow the motion of a specific actor. By using several cameras at the same time, special effects like wipes can easily be achieved.

For example, it is possible to use C1 as a constant eye point and to have an animated interest point moving along a circle. We also include the use of a varying zoom. The camera will be defined as:

CAMERA C1, EYE, PT   – PT is the interest point defined previously in the variable mode.

ZOOM C1, VALZOOM   – VALZOOM is an animated real variable.

6. **Light mode**

In this mode, the animator can define one or several light sources and their motion(s). For example, two moving lights can be defined by:

LIGHT S1, POS1
LIGHT S2, POS2 (POS1 and POS2 are two animated vectors)

7. **Director mode**

This mode belongs to the director's mode; starting time and duration of actors, cameras, and decor are decided here. Shooting and playback are also activated in this mode.

ACT CAR, 0, 10, 0   – the car is at the beginning and transformations begin at the same time.

ACT TREE, 0, 100, 5   – the tree is at the beginning but transformations start only at time 5.

DEC D1, 0, 100   – the same decor is used all the time.

CAM C1, 0, 100   – the same camera is used all the time.

LIGHT S1, 0, 100
LIGHT S2, 0, 100   – two light sources are moving all the time.

SPEED 24   – the number of images per second is 24.

SHOOT 0, 100   – the shooting time is from 0 to 100.

8. **Control mode**

This mode allows the animator to enter other modes, to save or retrieve actors, cameras, decors or to obtain a list of the script under the form of an "abstract table" of all variables, laws, actors, transformations, cameras, lights, and so on.

The CINEMIRA-2 Sublanguage

This sublanguage is limited to the programming of entities to be used by MIRANIM. What is innovative about this approach is that an entity programmed in CINE-

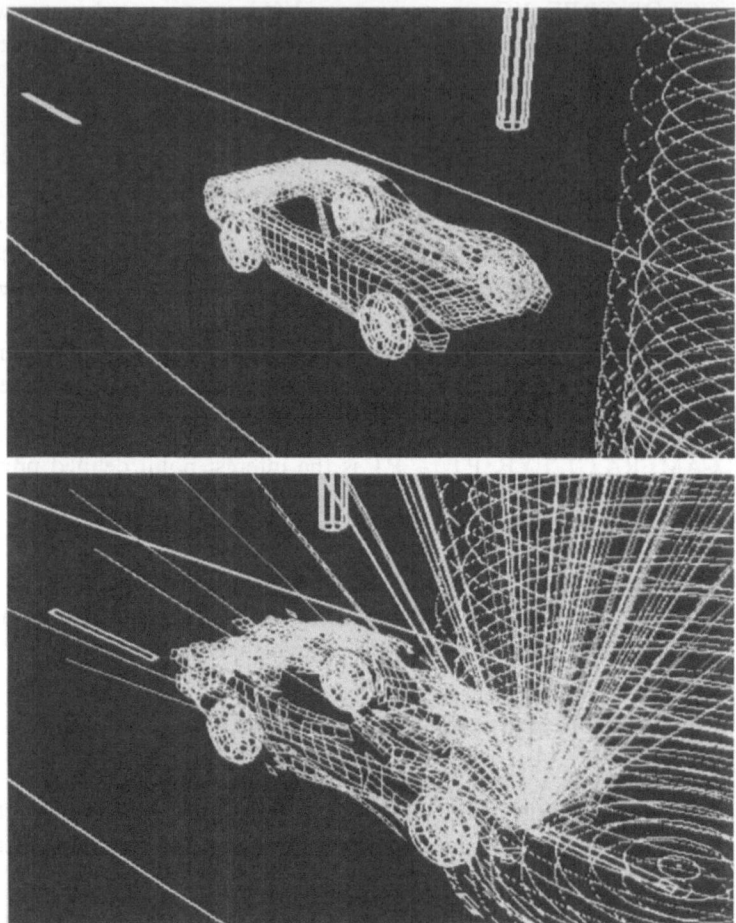

Fig. 11.8. Explosion of a Corvette (four frames from NIRVANA. © N. Magnenat-Thalmann and D. Thalmann 1983)

MIRA-2 is directly accessible to MIRANIM. For example, suppose an animator would like to introduce a transformation EXPLOSION in a scene where an actor CAR is running, crashes, and is destroyed by an explosion. The animator would like to control the EXPLOSION by parameters like the speed of the car V and the distance from an obstacle D. We assume that the animator does not know how to program. He or she asks a programmer to implement a transformation EXPLO-SION (V, D). With this done, the animator can define in the actor mode:

EXPLOSION CAR, V, D

whre V is an animated vector and D an animated real variable. Figure 11.8 shows an explosion.

11.8

Apart from actor transformations, CINEMIRA-2 allows the programming of four kinds of entities:

– Animation blocks
– Laws
– Transformations
– Subactors

Commands in MIRANIM give the animator access to these entities. These commands have parameters corresponding to the parameters of the entities defined in CINEMIRA-2.

An animation block is a subprogram executed at each frame. For instance:

```
block BALL (CENTER:VECTOR);
var SPH:SPHERE;
begin
   create SPH (CENTER, 3); draw SPH
end;
```

The animator can activate a block in the editor by invoking the block name and then choosing the parameters, as shown:

BALL 10, 5, CENTER – where 10 is the activation time, 5 the duration time and CENTER an animated vector.

Laws can be defined in a similar way to functions in PASCAL. However, the function type is necessarily REAL or VECTOR and these laws are functions of time (CLOCK). For example:

law MVTACC (SPDINIT, ACC: VECTOR): VECTOR;
begin
    MVTACC := 0.5*ACC*SQR (CLOCK) + SPDINIT*CLOCK
end

These laws can then be used by the animator with the editor command MVTACC.

Subactors can either be treated as parts of an actor in the editor or as complete actors. Synchronization between actors and subactors is assured by parameters, which can themselves be animated variables. For example, we can define, in the editor, an actor CAR with a velocity V. The car possesses 4 wheels which are subactors. These wheels have a rotation speed depending on the speed of the car. The wheels are implemented in CINEMIRA-2 in the form:

type WHEEL = *subactor* (CENTER, V : VECTOR)
            begin
            :
            end;

In the editor, the CAR with animated wheels is created as:

ACTOR CAR, CARFILE
TRANSLATION CAR, A, POSITION
SUBACTOR WHEEL1, WHEEL, POINT1, SPEED
SUBACTOR WHEEL2, WHEEL, POINT2, SPEED
SUBACTOR WHEEL3, WHEEL, POINT3, SPEED
SUBACTOR WHEEL4, WHEEL, POINT4, SPEED
HIERARCHY CAR, WHEEL1, WHEEL2, WHEEL3, WHEEL4

12. Automatic Motion Control

12.1 Mechanics, Robotics, and A.I. in Computer Animation

In future animation systems, based on synthetic actors, motion control will be automatically performed using artificial intelligence (A.I.) and robotics techniques [Badler 1986, 1989; Boisvert et al. 1989; Calvert 1988; Magnenat-Thalmann and Thalmann 1987a, 1989c–e; Thalmann 1989; Wilhelms 1987a]. In particular, motion will be planned at a task level and computed using physical laws. In the next sections, five steps to automatic motion control are described.

12.2 First Step: Positional Constraints and Inverse Kinematics

Consider the important problem of limb positioning, e.g., what are the angle values for the shoulder, elbow, and wrist if the hand has to reach a certain position and orientation in space? The problem involves the determination of the joint variables given the position and the orientation of the end of the hand with respect to the reference coordinate system. This is a key problem, because the independent variables in a human being are joint variables. This problem is well-known in robotics [Korein 1985; Morasso 1983; Sugimoto and Duffy 1981] and is called **the inverse-kinematics problem** [Featherstone 1983; Hollerbach and Sahar 1983; Low and Dubey 1986]. In a typical animation system based on inverse kinematics, the animator specifies discrete positions and motions for end parts; then the system computes the necessary joint angles and orientations for other parts of the body to put the specified parts in the desired positions and through the desired motions. Such an approach works well for simple linkages. However, the inverse kinematic solutions to a particular position become numerous and complicated when the number of linkages increases. Let us take an example. It is not difficult to determine how much to bend an elbow and a wrist to reach an object with the hand. It is much more difficult if we bring into play the rotation of the shoulder and the flexing of the fingers. The transformation problem from Cartesian coordinates has no closed-form solution in general. However, there are a number of special arrangements of the joint axes for which closed-form solutions have been suggested in the context of animation [Badler et al. 1985; Girard and Maciejewski 1985; Girard 1987; Korein and Badler 1982; Forsey and Wilhelms 1988].

In order to make a synthetic actor sit down on a chair, for example, it is necessary to specify the relevant constraints on the feet, on the pelvis, and on the hands. A system which allows us to specify only one constraint at a time is not a very efficient way to solve this problem. Badler et al. [1986, 1987] have introduced an iterative algorithm for solving multiple constraints using inverse kinematics. In their system, the user has to specify also the precedence of each constraint in case they cannot all be simultaneously satisfied.

A simple algorithm solving the positional constraint problem has been described by Boisvert et al. [1989]. The animator may impose constraints at the hands, the feet, and the pelvis levels. The position and orientation of the hand or the feet may be specified in the local coordinate system attached to the limb (arm or leg), or in the actor system or the world system. A constraint may be a fixed position/orientation or a 6D trajectory. Tools are available for constructing constraints as functions of the actor environment and his envelope (e.g., contact of the foot and the floor). In order to solve the constraints, the system makes use of the position and orientation of the pelvis and the trunk angles (vertebrae and clavicles) for finding the origin of the hips and the shoulders. It then calculates the limb angles required to reach the intended position. In the case where no solution exists, the closest possible position is calculated by projecting the intended position on the volume of possible motion of the arm (leg). The human skeleton has seven degrees of freedom at the arm (leg) level and the constraint has six degrees of freedom (position/orientation). Since the model is redundant from a kinematics point-of-view, this implies the existence of an infinity of solutions to reach the intended position. This is a well-known situation; as an example, when an actor is sitting down with a foot resting on the floor, he may rotate his knee around a hip-ankle axis. The variation of the rotation angle is constrained by the physical limitations of the joints. It may also be pointed out that the comfortable position for the knee (elbow) depends on the orientation of the foot (hand). One solution consists of minimizing the variation of the angle between the leg (arm) and the foot (hand). It is also possible to have the user select the solution by giving an opening parameter. The position/orientation/ opening constraint allows us to select a unique solution from the arm's (or the leg's) seven degrees of freedom. Other criteria, such as the collision of the limb with an object, may play a role in the selection of the solution.

The key framing technique and the positional constraints may be considered as the low-level commands of an animation system. The higher-level commands may produce keyframes and joint constraints. The animator must have access to the various levels of the hierarchy in order to be able to do the fine-tuning of the actor motion.

Figure 12.1 shows an example of the use of positional constraints to define a motion.

12.3 Second Step: Motion Control Using Dynamics

A more complex, but more realistic approach is based on dynamics. The motion of a synthetic actor is governed by forces and torques applied to limbs. Two problems may be considered: the direct-dynamics problem and the inverse-dynamics pro-

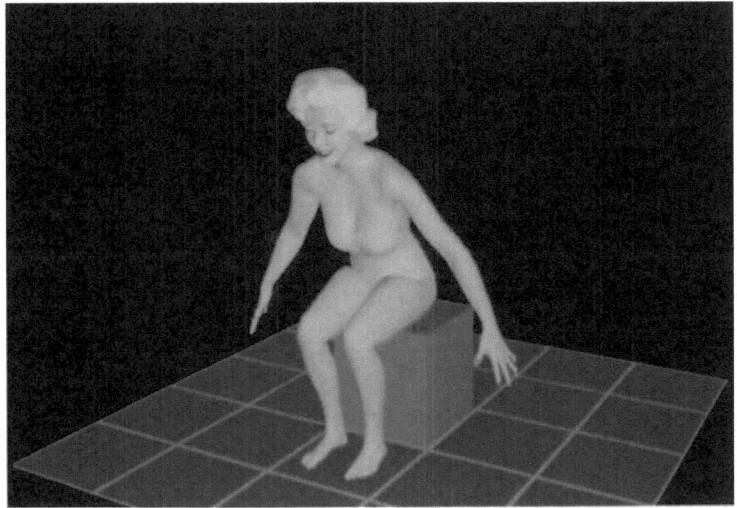

Fig. 12.1. Constraint-based motion (designer: Dominique Boisvert, © Nadia Magnenat-Thalmann and Daniel Thalmann 1989)

blem. The direct-dynamics problem consists of finding the trajectories of some point as the end effector with regard to the forces and torques that cause the motion. The inverse-dynamics problem is much more useful and may be stated as follows: determine the forces and torques required to produce a prescribed motion in a system. For a synthetic actor, it is possible to compute the time sequence of joint torques required to achieve the desired time sequence of positions, velocities, and accelerations using various methods.

The equations of motion for articulated bodies can be derived through the application of the Lagrange's equations of motion for nonconservative systems. The Newton-Euler formulation is based on the laws governing the dynamics of rigid bodies. The procedure in this formulation is first to write the equations which define the angular and linear velocities and accelerations of each link and then write the equations which relate the forces and torques exerted on successive links while under this motion. Armstrong [1979] calculated the angular and linear velocities in link coordinates as well. The Armstrong method is based on the hypothetical existence of a linear recursive relationship between the motion of and forces applied to one link, and the motion of and forces applied to its neighbors. A set of recursion coefficients is defined for each link and the coefficients for one link may be calculated in terms of those of one its neighbors. The accelerations are then derived from the coefficients. The method is only applicable to spherical joints, but its computational complexity is only $O(n)$, where n is the number of links. Based on this theory, Armstrong et al. [1987] designed a near real-time dynamics algorithm and implemented it in a prototype animation system. To reduce the amount of computer time required, Armstrong et al. [1987] make some simplifying assumptions about the structure of the figure and can produce a near real-time dynamics algorithm. They use frames which move with the links and an inertial frame considered fixed and nonrotating. The transformation from one frame to another is done by multiplying a column vector on the left by a 3×3 orthogonal matrix.

Wilhelms [1987b] used the Gibbs-Appel formulation for her animation system Deva, but this formulation does not exploit the recursive nature of the terms, and has a cost of $O(n^4)$. However, it is more general than the Armstrong approach.

As discussed by Arnaldi et al. [1989], three main factors lead to introduce dynamics in animation control:

- Dynamics frees the animator from the description of the motion due to the physical properties of the solid objects.
- Reality of natural phenomena is better rendered.
- Bodies can react automatically to internal and external environmental constraints: fields, collisions, forces, and torques.

Techniques based on dynamics have already been implemented for computer animation [Armstrong and Green 1985a, b; Badler 1986; Wilhelms and Barsky 1985; Wilhelms 1986, 1987b, 1989; Wilhelms et al. 1988 a, b; Isaacs and Cohen 1987; Arnaldi et al. 1989a, b; Hégron et al. 1989], but only for simplified and rigid articulated bodies with few joints, geometrical bodies (cylinders), and without any deformation. The use of dynamics in an animation system of articulated bodies, like the human body, has several important disadvantages.

First, the animator does not think in terms of forces or torques to apply to a limb or the body in order to perform a motion. The design of a specific user interface is essential.

Another problem is the amount of CPU time required to solve the motion equations of a complex articulated body using numerical methods. This considerably reduces the possibility of interaction of the system with the user. Only very short sequences have been produced, because of the lack of complete specification for complex motions and because of the CPU time required for certain methods.

Moreover, although dynamics-based motions are more realistic, they are too regular, because they do not take into account the personality of the characters. It is unrealistic to think that only the physical characteristics of two people carrying out the same actions make these characters different for any observer. The behavior and personality of the human beings are also essential causes of the observable differences. Several ideas for gracefulness and style in motion control are proposed by Cohen [1989].

Bruderlin and Calvert [1989] propose a hybrid approach to human locomotion which combines goal-oriented and dynamic motion control. Knowledge about a locomotion cycle is incorporated into a hierarchical control process. Decomposition of the locomotion determines forces and torques that drive the dynamic model of the legs by numerical approximation techniques. Rather than relying on a general dynamic model, the equations of motion of the legs are tailored to locomotion and analytically constrained to allow for only a specific range of movements. Isaacs and Cohen [1988] discuss mixed methods for complex constraints in dynamic figure animation. They propose an integration of direct and inverse kinematics specifications within a mixed method of forward and inverse dynamics simulation. Lee and Kunii [1989] present a design method for animation systems which includes scene analysis. Analytic forces such as those of gravity, friction, and air resistance are then applied to the objects modeled out of the extracted data. Shapiro-Brotman and Netravali [1988] solve the motion interpolation problems in the context of keyframe animation. They model motion of objects and their environment by differential equations obtained from classical mechanics and use external control to force the motion to satisfy constraints imposed by keyframes.

12.4 Third Step: Impact of the Environment

Adaptive Motion Control

Adaptive motion control of an actor means that the environment has an impact on the actor motion and vice versa. Information about the environment and the actor must be available during the control process. Traditional animation techniques like rotoscopy or key framing cannot be considered as adaptive control techniques, because the animator has to explicitly control by hand the relation between the environment and the actors. The purpose of adaptive control motion is to decrease the amount of information entered into the computer by the animator. This is done by using existing information about the scene and the actor. The system should also have an efficient representation of the geometry of the objects in order to automatically plan tasks as well as prevent collisions.

Girard [1987] gives a good example of this type of control applied to the motion of humans and animals on a flat terrain. At the low level, the animation is performed on a sequence of key positions of the limbs which define angle trajectories (direct kinematics) or Cartesian positions (inverse kinematics). These trajectories are calculated using optimizing criteria with kinematics or dynamics constraints. Actors may walk on flat terrains, on slopes, or even climb stairs without any intervention from the animator [Sims and Zeltzer 1988; Sims 1989].

Trajectory Planning and Obstacle Avoidance

An animation system should determine possible trajectories for the actor based on the environment. This obstacle avoidance may be subdivided into two subproblems:

1. Avoidance of static obstacles (decor) or objects grasped by actors
2. Avoidance of dynamic obstacles

The trajectory planning problem is classical and was extensively studied in artificial intelligence and robotics [Maciejewski and Klein 1985; McGhee and Iswandhi 1979], but also aesthetic criteria are very important in computer animation. For example, given the starting position of a hand and objects on a table, the problem in robotics is to find the trajectory to follow in order to avoid obstacles. For a synthetic actor, the problem is more complex due to the nonrigidity of the actor. For the problem of walking without collision among obstacles, one strategy used is based on the 2D Lozano-Perez algorithm [Lozano-Perez and Wesley 1979]. Obstacles are assumed to be polygonal, while the moving object is convex and its shape is constant. The first step consists of forming a graph. Vertices of this graph are composed of the vertices of the obstacles, the start point S and the goal point

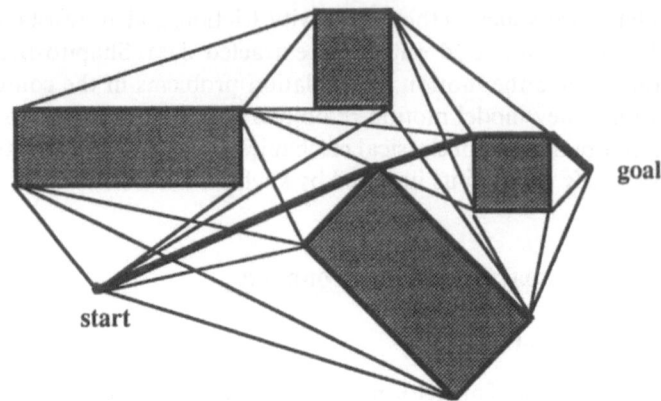

Fig. 12.2. Visibility graph

G. Arcs are defined such that a straight line can be drawn joining the vertices without overlapping any obstacle. This graph is called a visibility graph, since connected vertices can see each other. Figure 12.2 shows an example of a **visibility graph** with obstacles O_i, start point S, and goal point G. The shortest collision-free path from S to G is the shortest path in the graph from S to G. The method may be applied to a 2D motion in computer animation. However, it assumes that the moving object is a point; this restricts the application of the algorithm to camera motions, light motions, or motions of very small objects. Lozano-Perez and Wesley [1979] describe a way of extending the method to moving objects which are not points. In the original method, the obstacles may be considered as forbidden regions for the position of the moving point. If the moving object is not a point, obstacles may be replaced by new obstacles, which are forbidden regions for a reference point on the object. In the case of synthetic actors, the result trajectory is then used as input to a positional constraint solver based on inverse kinematics. Schröder and Zeltzer [1988] introduced the Lozano-Perez algorithm into their interactive animation package BOLIO.

Breen [1989] proposes a technique employing cost functions to avoid obstacles. Cost functions can be used to define goal-oriented motions and actions. A cost function can be defined whose variables are the animated parameters of a scene. The parameters are modified in such a way to minimize the cost function. This cost function technique has been encapsulated in the cost_analysis object of The Clockworks, an object-oriented computer animation system [Breen et al. 1987; Breen and Wozny 1989].

Renault et al. [1990] propose a vision-based approach for avoiding obstacles. The method is further described in Sect. 12.6.

Collisions

Analytical methods for calculating the forces between colliding rigid bodies have been proposed by several authors. Moore and Wilhelms [1988] model simultaneous collisions as a slightly staggered series of single collisions and used non-analytical methods to deal with bodies in resting contact. Hahn [1988] prevented bodies in resting contact from interpenetrating by modeling their contact as a series of frequently occurring collisions. Baraff [1989] proposes an analytical method for finding forces between contacting polyhedral bodies, based on linear programming techniques. The solution algorithm currently used is heuristic and allows holonomic geometric constraints to be maintained.

Finite Elements and Local Deformations

The environment of characters is made up of physical objects, which should act as if they had a mind. They should react to applied forces such as gravity, pressure, and contact. The models recently developed by Terzopoulos et al. [1987] are, for example, implemented using the Finite Difference Method, and collisions between elastic objects are simulated by creating potential energy around each object, i.e., intersections between deformable bodies are avoided by surrounding the object surfaces with a repulsive collision force. Terzopoulos and Fleischer [1988a, b] developed deformable models capable of perfectly elastic and inelastic behavior, viscoelasticity, plasticity, and fracture. Miller [1988, 1989] applied dynamic models to the motion of snakes and worms. Platt and Barr [1988] also use repulsive forces and discuss constraint methods in terms of animator tools for physical model control.

Gourret et al. [1989a, b] propose a finite element method to model the deformations of human flesh due to flexion of members and/or contact with objects (see Fig. 12.3). The method is able to deal with penetrating impacts and true contacts. For this

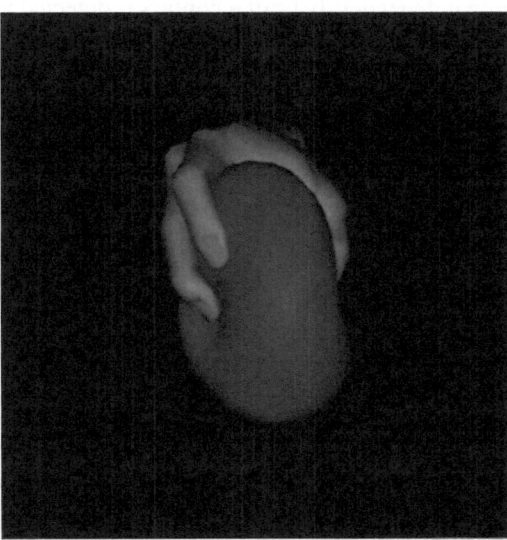

Fig. 12.3. Deformation using finite element theory (© Jean-Paul Gourret, Nadia Magnenat-Thalmann and Daniel Thalmann 1989)

reason, they prefer to consider true contact forces with possibilities of sliding and sticking rather than only repulsive forces. Simulation of impact with penetration can be used to model the grasping of ductile objects, and requires decomposition of objects into small geometrically simple objects. All the advantages of physical modeling of objects can also be transferred to human flesh. For example, the hand grasp of an object is expected to lead to realistic flesh deformation as well as an exchange of information between the object and the hand which will not only be geometrical. This exchange of information using acting and reacting forces is significant for a good and realistic grip and can influence the behavior of the hand and of the arm skeleton. When a deformable object is grasped, the contact forces that act on the fingertips will lead both to deformation of the object and of the fingertips, giving reacting forces which provide significant information about the object and more generally about the environment of the synthetic human body.

Once the various kinds of elements are defined, the modeled object shape is obtained by composition. Each element is linked to other elements at nodal points. In continuum mechanics, the equilibrium of a body presenting the same shape can be expressed by using the principle of stationarity of the total potential or the principle of virtual displacements. The equilibrium relation is applied to each element and the whole body is obtained by composing all elements.

There are several ways to exploit the intrinsic properties of the finite element method:

– The decomposition approach can be exploited for modeling penetrating shocks between two or more deformable objects. Each object is subdivided into many deformable subobjects which are able themselves to interact with each other in their turn because each of them brought with it its own properties.
– The composition approach can be used for modeling contacts without penetration between two or more objects. In this case, objects can be considered as subobjects evolving independently until a contact is detected and a global object is composed after contact. This process works if we take into account the contact forces, that prevent overlapping, into the problem [Bohm 1987].

12.5 Fourth Step: Task Planning

Task planning is a major problem in robotics and artificial intelligence. The problem complexity is directly dependent on the generality of the actor micro world. Given a task description, the problem consists in decomposing the task into a sequence of elementary movements (see Fig.12.4).

In order to generate these movements, the system should possess the following information:

– Description of the scene (topology, position, and orientation of the objects)
– Database of the rules governing the micro world (e.g., it is necessary to stand up before walking)
– Actor behavior (which shall modify the way of doing the movement; it corresponds to style parameters)
– Library of elementary movements which may be done by the actor (actor skills)

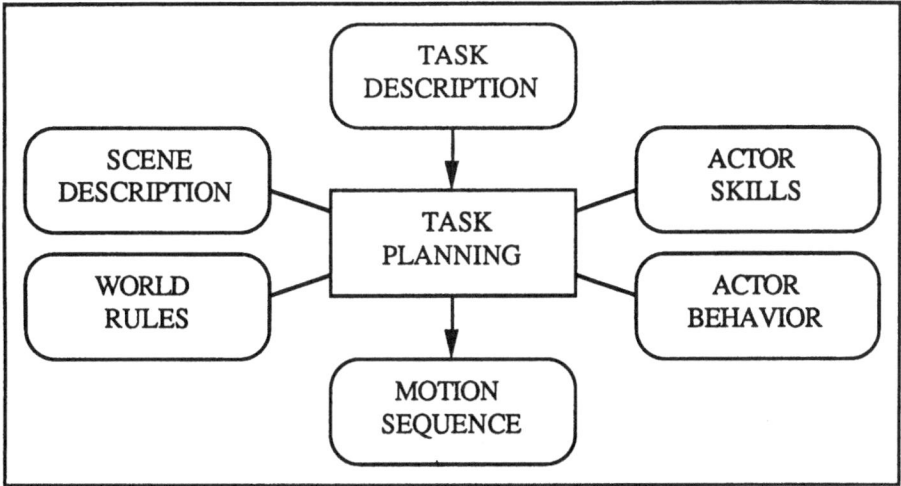

Fig. 12.4. Task planning

For example, the task "answer the phone" may be decomposed into the following sequence of elementary actions:

- Stand up from his chair.
- Determine a trajectory that avoids obstacles in the actor motion.
- Walk according to the trajectory.
- Determine a trajectory that avoids obstacles for object grasping.
- Grasp the telephone.
- Answer.

There are three ways of specifying tasks in a task-level system:

1. By example
2. By a sequence of model states
3. By a sequence of commands

The specification by example means for the operator "to perform the task at least once in order to explain it to the system." This is suitable in robotics, because the task may be physically specified by manually guiding the robot. This is of course impracticable in animation.

In the second type of method, the task is considered as a sequence of model states; each state is given by the configuration of all the objects in the environment. The configuration may be described by a set of spatial relationships. But what is the level of these relationships? High-level relationships correspond, for example, to indicating that at a given time an object A must be at a certain height and in front of another object B. The problem in this case is that the set of relationships should be converted into a set of equations and inequations which may be very difficult to solve. Moreover, a set of configurations may overspecify a state. Low-level relationships may correspond to the coordinates of the objects at a certain time—a simple keyframe description. Several methods for obtaining configuration constraints from symbolic spatial relationships have been proposed [Popplestone et al. 1980; Taylor 1976; Lozano-Perez 1976]. Goal-directed animation and motion specification methods using rule-based motion analysis have been proposed [Ridsdale et al. 1986; Ridsdale and Calvert 1990; Calvert 1989; Thalmann and Magnenat-Thalmann 1986; Doi et al. 1988].

The specification by a sequence of commands or a natural language interface is the most suitable and popular [Drewery and Tsotsos 1986; Badler 1989; Badler and Webber 1989; Kalita and Badler 1989; Esakov et al. 1989]. As stated by Zeltzer [1985], the animator can only specify the broad outlines of a particular movement and the animation system fills in the details. A nonexpert user may be satisfied with the default movements, as generated by a task specification like WALK FROM A TO B. However, a high-end user may want nearly total control over every nuance of an actor's movement to make a sequence as expressive as possible. This means that the animator does need to access different levels of the control hierarchy in order to generate new motor skills and to tweak the existing skills.

Note that the transformation from a high-level specification to a sequence of elementary motions is very similar to the problem of compiling. As in the processing of programming languages, three cases are possible: translation into a low-level code (classical compilers), translation into another programming language (preprocessor), and interpretation. In each case, the correspondence between the task specification and the motion to be generated is very complex. Consider three very essential tasks for a synthetic actor: grasping (Fig.12.5), walking (Fig.12.6) and talking (Fig.12.7).

Fig. 12.5. Animation sequence: flower grasping (designer: Lucie Marchand; © Nadia Magnenat-Thalmann and Daniel Thalmann 1988)

Fig. 12.6. Walking (from the film *Eglantine*, © Nadia Magnenat-Thalmann and Daniel Thalmann 1987)

Fig. 12.7. Talking (from the film *Rendez-vous à Montréal*, © Nadia Magnenat-Thalmann and Daniel Thalmann 1987)

Walking

To generate the motion corresponding to the task "WALK from A to B," it is necessary to take into account the possible obstacles and the nature of the terrain, and then evaluate the trajectories which consist of a sequence of positions, velocities, and accelerations. Given such a trajectory, as well as the forces to be exerted at end effectors, it is possible to determine the torques to be exerted at the joints by inverse dynamics and finally the values of joint angles may be derived for any time. In summary, the task-level system should integrate the following elements: obstacle avoidance, locomotion on rough terrains, trajectory planning, kinematics, and dynamics.

Grasping

To generate the motion corresponding to the task "PICK UP the object A and PUT it on the object B," the planner must choose where to grasp A so that no collisions will result when grasping or moving them. Then, grasp configurations should be chosen so that the grasped object is stable in the hand (or at least seems to be stable); moreover, contact between the hand and the object should be as natural as possible. Once the object is grasped, the system should generate the motions that will achieve the desired goal of the operation. A free motion should be synthesized; during this motion the principal goal is to reach the destination without collision, which implies obstacle avoidance. In this complex process, joint evolution is determined by kinematics and dynamics equations. In summary, the task-level system should integrate the following elements: path planning, obstacle avoidance, stability and contact determination, kinematics, and dynamics.

Talking

To generate the motion corresponding to the task "SAY THE SENTENCE How are you?," the system must analyze the sentence and separate it into phonemes, and then facial expressions corresponding to these phonemes must be selected. These expressions are themselves expressed as face deformations caused by muscles: jaw opening, eye opening, face folds, etc. Once the expressions have been selected, the system should indicate to the computer at which times the expressions must be activated and generate the frames according to a law (spline for example). In summary, the task-level system should integrate the following elements: phonemes detection, selection of facial expression, handling of facial parameters, and animation generation.

Energy, Spacetime, Kinematic, and Dynamic Constraints

In task-level animation, the animator specifies what the synthetic actor has to do, for instance, "jump from here to there." Witkin and Kass [1988] propose a new method, called **Spacetime Constraints**, for creating this animation. The requirements contained in the description, together with Newton's laws, comprise a problem of constrained optimization. The solution to this problem is a physically valid motion satisfying the constraints. More generally, an approach to imposing and solving geometric constraints on parameterized models was introduced by Witkin et al.

[1987]. Constraints are expressed as energy functions, and the energy gradient is followed through the model's parameter space. Using dynamic constraints, Barzel and Barr [1988] build objects by specifying geometric constraints; the models assemble themselves as the elements move to satisfy the constraints. Girard [1989] proposes an algorithm for optimizing limb movement in terms of both kinematics and dynamics-based variables and constraints. The algorithm makes use of dynamic programming to solve for a minimum-cost speed distribution along a parametric splined patch.

12.6 Fifth Step: Behavioral Animation

Behavioral animation [Reynolds 1987] corresponds to modeling the behavior of characters, from path planning to complex emotional interactions between characters. The animator is responsible for the design of these behaviors; his job is somewhat like that of a theatrical director: the character's performance is the indirect result of the director's instructions to the actor. Due to the personality of the character, his reactions may sometimes cause surprises. In an ideal implementation of a behavioral animation, it is almost impossible (as in a theatrical scene) to play the same scene twice exactly the same way. You cannot walk precisely the same way from the same bar to home twice.

Reynolds introduced a distributed behavioral model to simulate flocks of birds, herds of land animals, and schools of fish. The simulated flock is an elaboration of a particle system with the simulated birds being the particles. A flock is assumed to be the result of the interaction between the behaviors of individual birds. Working independently, the birds try both to stick together and avoid collisions with one another and with other objects in their environment. In a module of behavioral animation, the positions, velocities, and orientations of the actors are known from the system at any time. The animator may control several global parameters, e.g., weight of the obstacle avoidance component, weight of the convergence to the goal, weight of the centering of the group, weight of the velocity equality, maximum velocity, maximum acceleration, and minimum distance between actors. Girard and Amkraut [1990] also created a bird motion in the film Eurhythmy with FLOCK, an animation system which controls the motion of large populations using vector forcefields.

Haumann and Parent [1988] describe behavioral simulation as a means to obtain global motion by simulating simple rules of behavior between locally related actors. They developed a test-bed used to create a library of physically behaving actors which can realistically reproduce the motion of flexible objects [Haumann 1987].

Lethebridge and Ware [1989] propose a simple heuristically-based method for expressive stimulus-response animation. They model stimulus-response relationships using "behavior functions" created from simple mathematical primitives in a heuristic manner. Wilhelms (1990) describes a network approach for quickly developing behavioral animations. The purpose of her system is to devise a useful tool for animating and exploring behavior, instead of simulating biological circuits.

Renault et al. [1990] propose an innovative way of animating synthetic actors based on the concept of synthetic vision. The first aim was simple and fuzzy: to create an animation involving a synthetic actor automatically moving in a corridor avoiding other synthetic actors. To simulate this behavior, each synthetic actor uses a synthetic vision as its perception of the world and so as the unique input to its behavioral model. This model is based on the concept of Displacement Local Automata (DLA), which is similar to the concept of a script for natural language processing. A DLA is an algorithm that can deal with a specific environment. Two DLAs are described in detail called *follow-the-corridor* and *avoid-the-obstacle*. Vision simulation is the heart of their system. This vision has the advantage to avoid all problems of pattern recognition involved in robotic vision. In input, we have a database containing the description of 3D objects: the environment, the camera characterized by its eye and interest point. In output, the vision is built as a 2D array of pixels. Each pixel contains the distance between the eye and the point of the object for which this is the projection. The implementation is based on the IRIS 4D architecture; it extensively uses the Graphics Engine with z-buffer and double frame buffer. The projection which is used is a perspective projection with a view angle of 90°. The front buffer is used to display the projection of objects which allows the animator to know what the synthetic actor sees. In the backbuffer, for each pixel, the object identifier is stored. This vision-based model is being combined with a walking model [Boulic et al. 1990] to generate behavioral animation of synthetic actors walking in an environment. Such a project requires adapting the DLA's for avoiding obstacles to walking characters. A different behavior should be given to each synthetic actor giving them personality. The walking model is built from experimental data based on a wide range of normalized velocities. The model is structured in two levels. At a first level, global spatial and temporal characteristics (normalized length and step duration) are generated. At the second level, a set of parameterized trajectories produce both the position of the body in the space and the internal body configuration in particular the pelvis and the legs. This is performed for a standard structure and an average configuration of the human body. The experimental context corresponding to the model is extended by allowing a continuous variation of global spatial and temporal parameters according to the motion rendition expected by the animator. The model is based on a simple kinematic approach designed to keep the intrinsic dynamic characteristics of the experimental model. Such an approach also allows personification of the walking action in an interactive real-time context in most cases.

13. Case Studies of Computer-generated Films

13.1 The Film *Dream Flight*

The film *Dream Flight*, directed by both authors and Philippe Bergeron, was the first widely known fictional 3D animated film made using a computer. The film was a great success: it won the first prize at the Computer Graphics '82 Film Festival in London, and several other awards including Murcia Festival, Columbus Festival, and Yorkton festival. *Dream Flight* was also selected in traditional animation festivals like "Journées d'Animation d'Annecy", "Festival des Films du Monde de Montréal," and the TV Festival in Caracas. *Dream Flight* was shown (in whole or in part) on various TV channels in Canada, USA, France, Switzerland, and the United Kingdom.

An outline of the different stages of the production of a film scene, such as those in *Dream Flight*, is shown in Fig.13.1.

Scenario and Storyboard

Dream Flight is a fictional film with a simple scenario. A futuristic version of *The Little Prince*, it begins with the opening line, "Once upon a time, a small being lived on a distant planet. He was lonely and dreamed of seeing new world."

It is night. Hipi is sad, and throws stones into a small pond in the middle of a forest. A bird flying over the pond arouses in Hipi a desire to be free.

Inspired by the bird, Hipi flies towards new horizons—flying through space, travelling past strange objects towards Earth. He takes us through Europe, past the Eiffel Tower, and plunges into the Atlantic among yellow fish and seaweed, until a violent storm illuminates the surface of the water.

Then he arrives in New York. We see the Statue of Liberty, the streets of Manhattan, the city constructed entirely in glass. Hipi stops in the middle of Central Park where four human beings appear before him. After a minute of hesitation, Hipi extends his hand as a sign of friendship. One of the men advances his arm but stops and turns away suddenly. Frustrated, Hipi becomes very angry. Everything explodes. Rocks fall on New York, and the city collapses with the sound of thunder and a flash of lightning.

The towers of the World Trade Center emerge from a small pond. Hipi, sitting by the side of the pond, throws a pebble into the water, as at the beginning of the film, and the towers disappear.

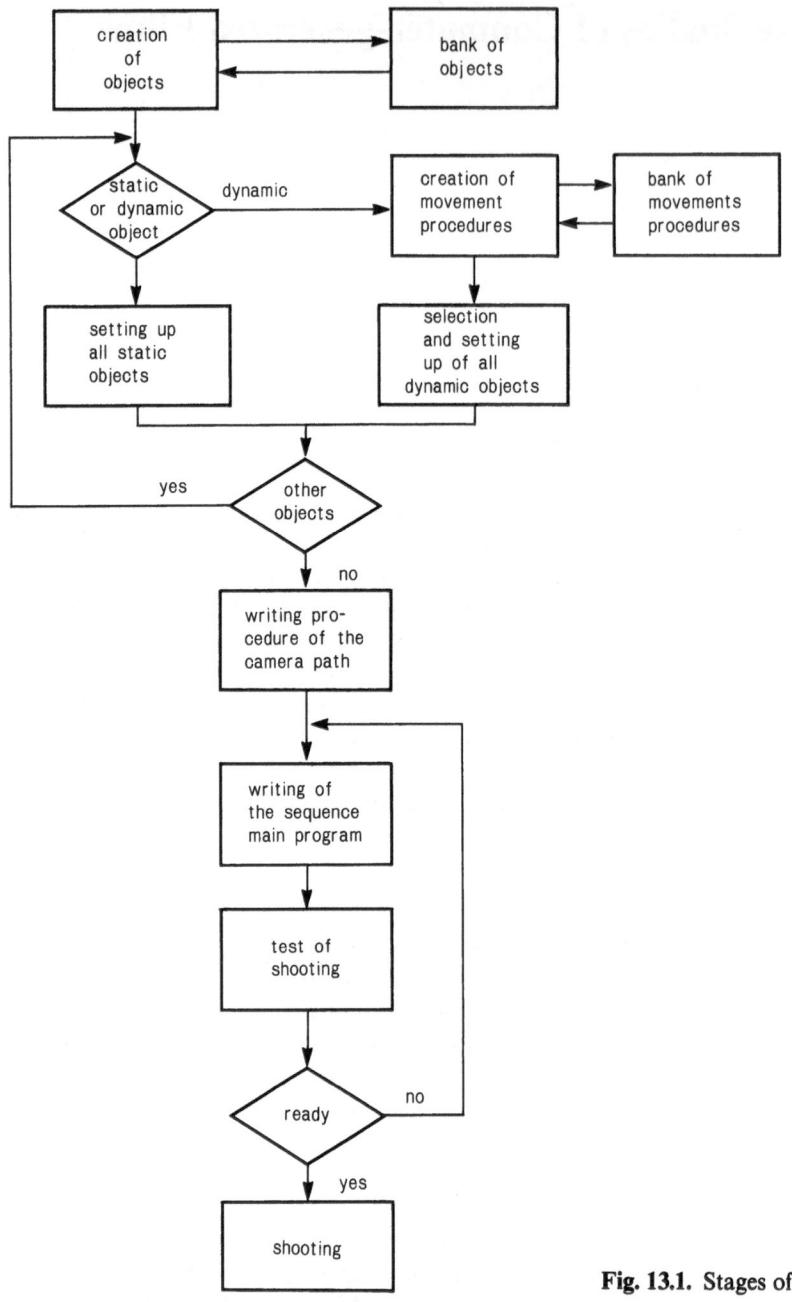

Fig. 13.1. Stages of production

Hipi's voyage was a dream, transformed into a nightmare by human rejection. The rocks that fell on New York were thrown by Hipi, who saw the entire scene in the pond. The bird passes again, and Hipi flies towards the horizon.

After devising a scenario, the next step was to establish the storyboard. For *Dream Flight*, the storyboard consisted of about 100 sketches with associated information. Figure 13.2 shows an excerpt of the storyboard.

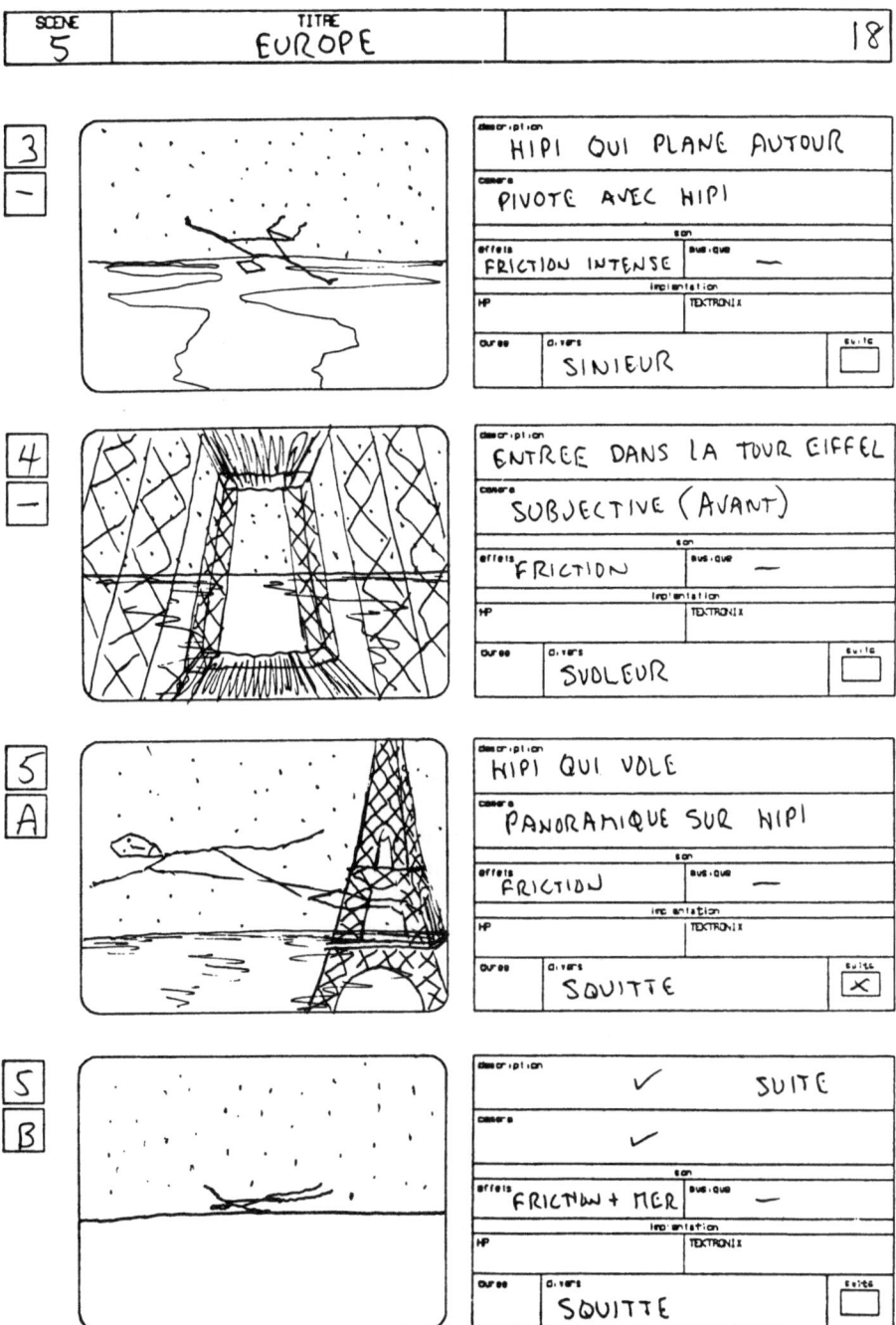

Fig. 13.2. Excerpts of the storyboard of *Dream Flight* (Directors: P. Bergeron, N. Magnenat-Thalmann, D. Thalmann)

Fig. 13.3. Sitting in the forest

Decor Creation

A decor can be considered a list of static objects. These objects can be built up using one of the methods described in Sect. 6.4. In *Dream Flight*, various decors are used, including trees, buildings, a bridge, and the Statue of Liberty.

Trees are defined by the position and the height of the main trunk. Branches are only present in the upper two thirds of the trunk and their length is considered constant. The lower, primary branches are oriented in the four major directions. Other branches are uniformly distributed in the vertical direction, but are randomly distributed around the trunk. The angle of the branch relative to the ground is dependent on the height of the branch.

Trees are described by three-dimensional graphical types:

   type TREE = *figure(var* BRANCHES: TEXT; NBRANCHES: INTEGER;
                          POSITION: VECTOR; HEIGHT, LENGTH: REAL);

where BRANCHES is a file of kinds of branches, NBRANCHES is the number of branches, POSITION is the position of the trunk, HEIGHT is the height of the trunk, and LENGTH the length of the branches.

Figure 13.3 shows a frame of *Dream Flight* with several trees.

The Verrazano-Narrows Bridge (Fig.13.4) and the Eiffel Tower (Fig.8.1) were produced by digitizing one part and by building the object by programming.

The Statue of Liberty (Fig.13.5) was separated into two parts: the base, which was partly digitized and then rebuilt by programming using symmetry operations (Fig.13.6), and the statue itself, which was digitized with a reconstruction method similar to that described in Sect. 6.4. Figure 13.7 shows four different views of the

Fig. 13.4. The Verrazano-Narrows Bridge

Statue of Liberty (including the head, which was digitized using the same method). The torch was not built according to this principle.

A **bird** is represented by an abstract graphical type:

> *type* BIRD = *figure*(FRAME : INTEGER; H : HALFBODY; W : WING;
>   C, D : VECTOR);

where H is the right halfbody, W the right wing, C the rotation center of the right wing, and D the direction of that rotation. As the right wing always starts in the maximal vertical position, it is only necessary to determine the angle of rotation downwards. This angle depends on the frame. For this we used a rotation with the Catmull acceleration/deceleration law.

Figure 13.8 shows an excerpt of the code which is executed when a variable of BIRD type is created. In this code, CYCLE is the number of frames required to make one wing flap up and down; FRAME is the current frame number; BETA is the rotation angle of the wing; ANGLEMAX is the maximum angle, and FRAC the phase fraction. For example, a bird is created and drawn according to the following sequence:

```
procedure DRAWBIRD(FRAME : INTEGER);
var FIRSTBIRD : BIRD;
begin
  create FIRSTBIRD(FRAME, RIGHTBODY, RIGHTWING, C, D);
  TRANSLATION(FIRSTBIRD, ⟨⟨0, 0, FRAME * BIRDSTEP⟩⟩,
              FIRSTBIRD);
  draw FIRSTBIRD;
  delete FIRSTBIRD;
end;
```

Fig. 13.5. Arrival in New York

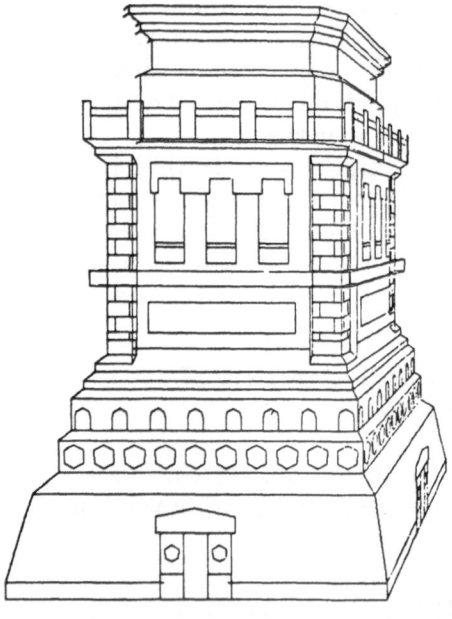

Fig. 13.6. Base of the Statue of Liberty

Fig. 13.7. Four views of the Statue of Liberty

13.2 The Film *Rendez-vous à Montréal*

Rendez-vous à Montréal is a seven-minute film which brings Marilyn Monroe and Humphrey Bogart back to life, as shown in Fig.13.9. It was produced for the celebration of 100 years of engineering in Canada. The film was made using the HUMAN FACTORY system, which allows users to recreate any human being in any setting by giving certain commands to the computer.

The film scenario is as follows: there are these two great legendary stars who are dead—but they're living in some kind of other world beyond the grave, and they long to return to earth. So first, Bogart appears and calls Marilyn and begs her to come to earth. Of course, Humphrey is a real macho guy, and he only has to call Marilyn for her to come. They decide to meet in Montreal near the Place Jacques-Cartier. So they meet inside a famous building. When Marilyn materializes in the building, she's not made of flesh and bones, but of scales, then stone and then gold. Humphrey gets rather impatient to see her in the flesh. But it takes a kiss—like Prince Charming—to bring her alive completely (Fig.13.9). And then the whole romantic episode begins. It is also the end of the film. For the spectator, the illusion is over. He/she feels frustrated and asks for more. This is the proof they live the illusion completely, and that is what we tried to prove.

```
type
   BIRD = figure(FRAME:INTEGER; H:HALFBODY; W:WING; C,D:VECTOR);
         const
            ACCDEC = 4;
         var
            RELATIVE:0..CYCLE;
            FRACTION,BETA:REAL;
            W2:WING;
            RIGHTPART,LEFTPART:FIG;
         begin
            RELATIVE := FRAME mod CYCLE;
            if RELATIVE > CYCLE div 2 then
               RELATIVE := CYCLE-RELATIVE;
            FRACTION := (RELATIVE*2)/CYCLE;
            BETA := LAW(ACCDEC,ANGLEMAX,FRACTION);
            ROTATION(W,C,BETA,D,W2);
            UNION(H,W2,RIGHTPART);
            delete H,W2;
            SYMYZ(RIGHTPART,LEFTPART);
            include RIGHTPART,LEFTPART
         end;
```

Fig. 13.8. The BIRD type

The film premiered in May 1987 at the Canadian Engineering Centennial Convention, which was attended by about 3000 delegates, and excerpts were shown on six TV channels the same week. Outside Canada, the first show was at CG International '87, Karuizawa, Japan and large excerpts were shown on the NHK channel 9 news. Since this time, the film has been selected at several festivals including the Banff festival and the Hiroshima festival. It was shown all through the summer of 1987 at EXPOTECH in Montreal, the largest scientific exhibition ever held in Canada.

Creating Synthetic Cinema Stars: a Challenge

It was a big challenge to synthesize Marilyn and Humphrey because everybody knows them. Today, it is still not possible to completely render an actor from an image synthesis point of view, but what has been important to us was the fact that everybody immediately recognized Marilyn and Humphrey. Although they appear in some way Barbie-like, we have been able to reconstitute their personality.

Fig. 13.9. Glass grasping (from the film *Rendez-vous à Montréal,* © Nadia Magnenat-Thalmann and Daniel Thalmann 1987)

Modeling the Actors

At the beginning, the computer needs to know the shapes of the characters and even the detail of their hands, for example. So a sculptor first sculpted Marilyn's and Humphrey's hands; orthogonal photos were taken, and then the information was entered into the computer, which, of course, cannot see, but reconstitutes the 3D information. The surface of the hand is divided into facets and then the vertices of the facets are entered into the computer—this is the classical digitizing process. In the same way, we had to create Humphrey's thumb and Marilyn's thumb so that their hands correspond to the personalities of the characters, as shown in Fig. 13.10. The heads and shoulders of Marilyn and Humphrey were digitized in the same way from plaster models.

The HUMAN FACTORY System

The main purpose of the HUMAN FACTORY system is the direction of synthetic actors in their environment. In this system, which is typically a fourth generation language, synthetic actors are controlled by animators and designers without any programming knowledge. Not only has the user a high-level interface with menus and commands, but also he/she may add his/her own commands and menus to the system. THE HUMAN FACTORY system is structured into several modules. The

Fig. 13.10. Hands (from the film *Rendez-vous à Montréal,* © Nadia Magnenat-Thalmann and Daniel Thalmann 1987)

complete organization is shown in Fig.13.11. Task level aspects are also introduced and there are further investigations to transform HUMAN FACTORY into a fifth generation system for the animation of synthetic actors.

13.3 The Film *Eglantine*

Eglantine is a robot (Fig. 13.12) who dreams of becoming human. After travelling in an imaginary world, she has become a woman (Fig. 13.13), she stretches, gets up, and climbs the stairs. The character has been constructed from a set of serial cross sections, like tracing the contours from a topographic map. One of the major difficulties in the animation process has been the modeling of the walking and climbing sequence.

13.4 The Film *Galaxy Sweetheart*

Galaxy Sweetheart is a demo reel to show the creation and dynamic transformation of synthetic actors. An extraterrestrial tries to create a woman using a computer. Several methods of transforming and building characters are involved that will be described below. After many interactive trials, our 3D character living in a galaxy finally succeeds in creating the woman he likes.

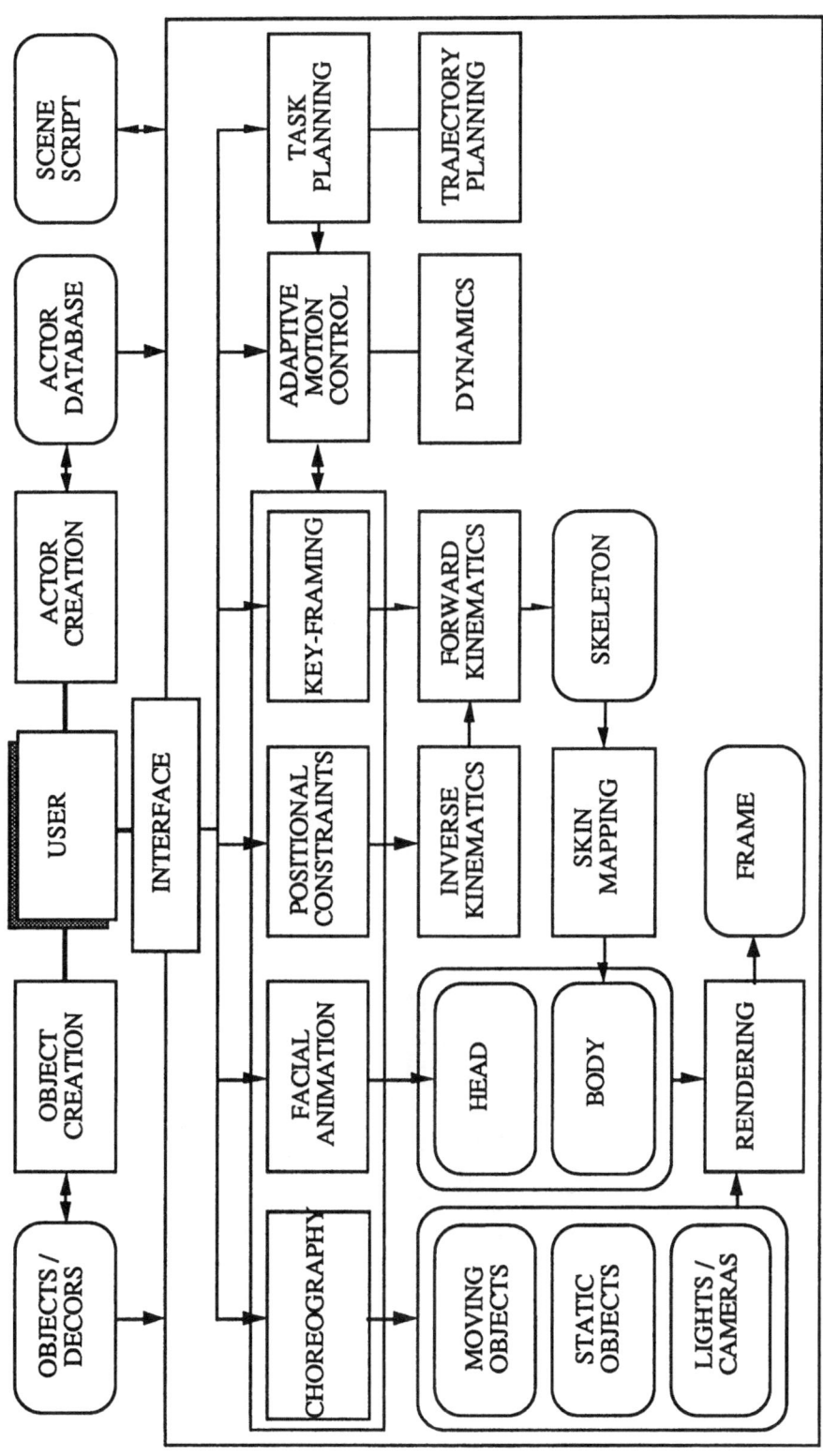

Fig. 13.11. The architecture of the HUMAN FACTORY system

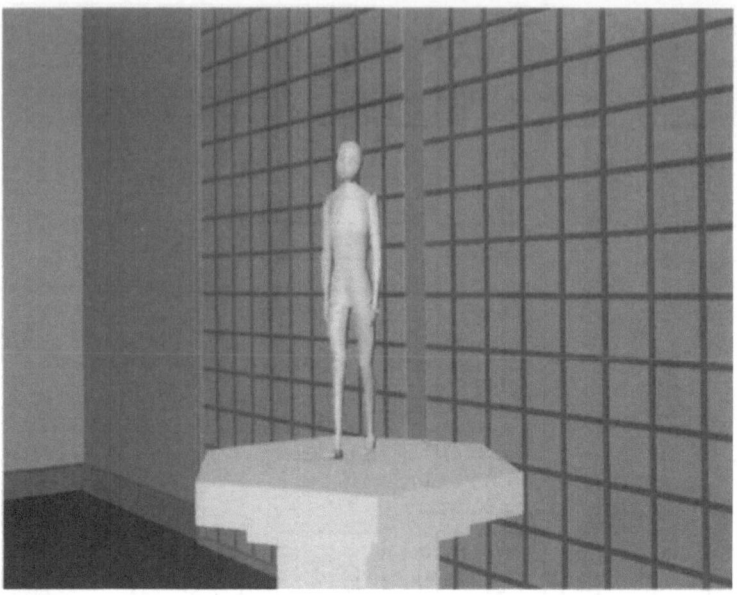

Fig. 13.12. Robot (from the film *Eglantine*, © Nadia Magnenat-Thalmann and Daniel Thalmann 1987)

Fig. 13.13. Eglantine stretching (from the film *Eglantine*, © Nadia Magnenat-Thalmann and Daniel Thalmann 1987)

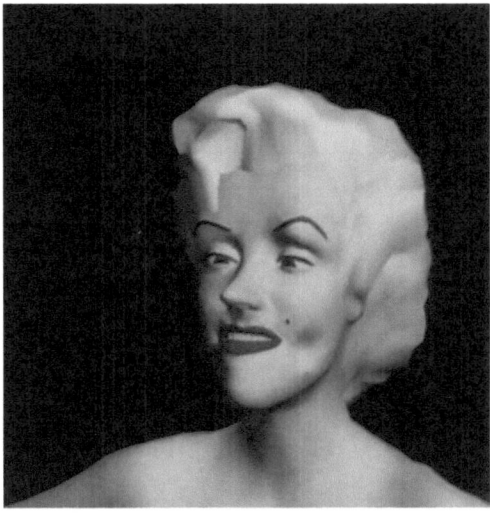

Fig. 13.14. Local deformations (from the film *Galaxy Sweetheart*, © Nadia Magnenat-Thalmann and Daniel Thalmann 1988)

Creation of a Synthetic Actor by Composition of Different Parts

This approach [Magnenat-Thalmann and Thalmann 1988] is based on the composition of irregular surfaces stored in a database in one coherent figure. This implies the use of elements common to both figures to allow them to be assembled.

Modification of an Existing Synthetic Actor Using Local Transformations

A local transformation [Magnenat-Thalmann et al. 1988b, 1989] is a transformation applied to a part of a figure and not the whole as a global transformation. Generally a local transformation consists of two steps. First, a region is determined by a selection operation; examples of selections are selection by vertices, selection inside a volume, selection using color, and selection based on set-theory operations applied to selected regions. Then, transformations are applied to regions, e.g., attraction by a vertex, general translation, or scale according to a plane. Figure 13.14 shows how a face may be deformed using such local transformations.

Generation of New Synthetic Actors Obtained by Interpolation Between Two Existing Actors

This method [Magnenat-Thalmann et al. 1989] consists of generating an in-between human face from two given human faces. The technique consists of extracting profiles of a digitized object from selected planes and generating a grid which corresponds to the original object. A correspondence is established between the profiles, then a correspondence between the parallel sections is found using a similar method; the correspondence between points is straightforward. Finally, an in-between human face is obtained just by linear interpolation.

References

Titles that are preceded with an asterisk (*) are not referred to in the text.

*Ackland B, Weste N (1980) Real time animation playback on a frame store display system. *Proc SIGGRAPH '80, Computer Graphics* 14(3):182–188

Akima H (1970) A new method of interpolation and smooth curve fitting based on local procedures. *J ACM* 17(4):589–602

Alexander S, Huggins WH (1967) *User's manual on PMACRO*. Johns Hopkins University

Andrews GR, Schneider FB (1983) Concepts and notations for concurrent programming. *ACM Computing Surveys* 15(1):3–43

Appel A (1967) The notion of quantitative invisibility and the machine rendering of solids. *Proc ACM National Conf*, pp387–393

Appel A (1968) Some techniques for shading machine rendering of solids. *SJCC*, AFIPS 32:37–45

*Armbrust R (1983) The simulation of space. *Computer Pictures* 1(1):24–27

Armstrong WW (1979) Recursive solution to the equations of motion of an N-link manipulator. *Proc 5th World Congress Theory Mach.Mechanisms*, Vol 2, pp1343–1346

Armstrong WW, Green M, Lake R (1987) Near real-time control of human figure models. *IEEE Comput Graphics Applications* 7(6):28–38

Armstrong WW, Green MW (1985a) Dynamics for animation of characters with deformable surfaces. In: N.Magnenat-Thalmann, D.Thalmann (eds) *Computer-generated images*, Springer, pp209–229

Armstrong WW, Green MW (1985b) The dynamics of articulated rigid bodies for purposes of animation. *The Visual Computer* 1(4):231–240

Arnaldi B, Dumont G, Hégron H (1989) Dynamics and unification of animation control. *The Visual Computer*. 5(1–2):22–31

Arnaldi B, Dumont G, Hégron G, Magnenat-Thalmann N, Thalmann D (1989) Animation control with dynamics. In: *State-of-the-art in computer animation*. Springer, Tokyo, pp113–124

*Arya K (1986) A functional approach to animation. *Computer Graphics Forum*, 5(4):297–312

Atherton P, Weiler K, Greenberg D (1978) Polygon shadow generation. *Proc SIGGRAPH '78, Computer Graphics* 12(3):275–281

*Badler NI (1975) *Temporal scene analysis: conceptual descriptions of objects movements*. Ph.D. dissertation, University of Toronto, Canada

Badler NI (1982) Human body models and animation. *IEEE Computer Graphics and Applications* 2(9):6–7

*Badler NI (1986a) Motion graphics, description and control. In: Badler NI, Tsotsos JK (eds) *Motion: representation and perception*. North Holland, pp295–302

Badler NI (1986b) Design of a human movement representation incorporating dynamics. In: Enderle G, Grave M, Lillehagen F (eds) *Advances in computer graphics I*. Springer, Heidelberg, pp499–512

Badler NI (1986c) Animating human figures: perspectives and directions. *Proc Graphics Interface '86*, pp115–120

Badler NI (1989) Artificial intelligence, natural language, and simulation for human animation. In: Magnenat-Thalmann N, Thalmann D (eds) *State-of-the-art in computer animation*. Springer, Tokyo, pp19–32

Badler NI, Morris MA (1982) Modeling flexible articulated objects. *Proc Computer Graphics '82*, Online Conf, pp305–314

Badler NI, Smoliar SW (1979) Digital representations of human movement. *Computing Surveys* 11(1):19–38

Badler NI, Webber BL (1989) Task-driven animation using a natural language interface, Proc. mechanics, control and animation of articulated figures, Massachusetts Institute of Technology (to be published in a book, Morgan Kaufmann, USA)

Badler NI, O'Rourke J, Toltzis (1979) A spherical representation of a human body for visualizing movement. *Proc IEEE 67*(10):1397–1403

Badler NI, O'Rourke J, Kaufman B (1980) Special problems in human movement simulation. *Proc SIGGRAPH '80*, Computer Graphics 14(3):189–197

Badler NI, Korein JD, Korein JU, Radack GM, Brotman LS (1985) Positioning and animating figures in a task-oriented environment. *The Visual Computer*. 1(4):212–220

Badler NI, et al. (1986) Multi-dimensional input techniques and articulated figure positioning by multiple constraints. *1986 Workshop on Interactive 3D Graphics*. Chapel Hill, North Carolina

Badler NI, Manoochehri KH, Walters G (1987) Articulated figure positioning by multiple constraints. *IEEE Comput Graphics Applications*. 7(6):39–51

* Baecker RM (1969a) *Interactive computer-mediated animation*. Ph.D. dissertation, Massachusetts Institute of Technology, Project Mac-Tr-61

Baecker RM (1969b) Picture-driven animation. *Proc Spring Joint Computer Conference*, AFIPS Press, 34:273–288

* Baecker R (1970) Current issues in interactive computer-mediated animation. *Proc 9th Annual Meeting UAIDE*, pp273–288

Baecker RM (1976) A conversational extensible system for the animation of shaded images. *Proc SIGGRAPH '76. Computer Graphics* 10(2):32–39

Ballard DH (1981) Strip trees, a hierarchical representation for curves. *Communications of the ACM* 24(5):310–321

Baraff D (1989) Analytical methods for dynamic simulation of non-penetrating rigid bodies. *Proc SIGGRAPH '89, Computer Graphics*. 23(3):223–232

* Barr A (1989) Teleogical modeling. Proc mechanics, control and animation of articulated figures, Massachusetts Institute of Technology (to be published in a book, Morgan Kaufmann, USA)

Barr AM (1981) Superquadrics and angle-preserving transformations. *IEEE Computer Graphics and Applications* 1(1):11–23

Barsky BA (1981) *The beta-spline: a local representation based on shape parameters and fundamental geometric measures*. Ph.D. thesis, University of Utah

Barsky BA (1984) A description and evaluation of various 3-D models. *IEEE Comput Graphics Applications* 4(1):38–52

Barsky BA (1985) *Computer graphics and geometric modelling using beta-splines*. Springer, Tokyo Berlin Heidelberg New York

Barzel R, Barr AH (1988) A modeling system based on dynamic constraints. *Proc SIGGRAPH '88, Computer Graphics*. 22(4):179–188

Batson RM, Edwards E, Eliason EM (1975) Computer-generated shaded relief images. *Research U.S. Geological* 3(4):401–408

* Baudelaire P, Gangnet M (1985) Computer-assisted animation—an overview. In: Enderle G, Grave M, Lillehagen F (eds) *Advances in computer graphics I*. Springer, Heidelberg, pp469–498

* Begley S (1982) The creative computers. *Newsweek*, July 12, pp44–47

* Bergeron P. (1983) A structured motion specification in 3D computer animation. *Proc Graphics Interface '83*, pp215–222

*Bergeron P (1985) Techniques for animating characters. SIGGRAPH '85 Tutorial Notes

*Beshers CM, Feiner SK (1988) Real-time 4D animation on a 3D graphics workstation. *Proc Graphics Interface '88*, pp1–7

Bézier PE (1972) *Numerical control–mathematics and applications*. Wiley, London

Blinn J (1977) Models of light reflection for computer synthesized pictures. *Proc SIGGRAPH '77*, 11(2):192–198

Blinn JF (1978) Simulation of wrinkled surfaces. *Proc SIGGRAPH '77, Computer Graphics* 12(3):286–292

Blinn JF (1982a) A generalization of algebraic surface drawing. *ACM Transactions on Graphics* 1(3):235–256

Blinn JF (1982b) Light reflection functions for simulation of clouds and dusty surfaces. *Proc SIGGRAPH '82, Computer Graphics* 16(3):21–29

Blinn JF, Newell ME (1976) Texture and reflection in computer generated images. *Communications of the ACM* 19(10):542–547

Bloomenthal J (1983) Edge inference with applications to anti-aliasing. *Proc SIGGRAPH '83, Computer Graphics* 17(3):157–162

Bohm J (1987) A comparison of different contact algorithms with applications. *Comput Struct* 26(1–2):207–221

Boisvert D, Magnenat-Thalmann N, Thalmann D (1989) An integrated view of synthetic actors. In: Earnshaw E, Wyvill B (eds) *New advances in computer graphics*. Springer, Tokyo, pp277–288

Bolduc F, Lejeune A, Magnenat-Thalmann N (1987) Image synthesis and 3D computer animation; a new approach for strategic analysis. *The Visual Computer* 3(1):51–56

Booth KS, MacKay S (1982) Techniques for frame buffer animation. *Proc Graphics Interface '82*, pp213–219

*Booth S, Kochanek DH, Wein M (1983) Computers animate film and video. *IEEE Spectrum*, pp44–51

*Borrell J (1981) The magic of computer animation. *Computer Graphics World* 10:25–33

Bosche C (1967) Computer-generated random dot images. *Design and Planning* 2:87–92

Bouknight WJ, Kelley K (1970) An algorithm for producing half-tone computer graphics presentations with shadows and moveable light sources. *SJCC*, AFIPS, 36:1–10

Boulic R, Magnenat-Thalmann N, Thalmann D (1990) Human free-walking model for a real-time interactive design of gaits. In: Magnenat-Thalmann N, Thalmann D (eds) *Computer Animation '90*. Springer, Tokyo, pp61–79

*Brady M (1982) Trajectory planning. In: Brady M (ed) *Robot motion: planning and control*. MIT Press, Cambridge, Mass., USA

Breen DE (1989) Choreographing goal-oriented motion using cost functions. In: Magnenat-Thalmann N, Thalmann D (eds) *State-of-the-art in computer animation*. Springer, Tokyo, pp141–152

Breen D, Getto P, Apodaca A, Schmidt D, Sarachan B (1987) The Clockworks; an object-oriented computer animation system. *Proc Eurographics '87, North Holland*, pp275–282

*Breen DE, Kühn V (1989) Message-based object-oriented interaction modeling. *Proc. Eurographics '89*, North Holland, pp489–502

Breen DE, Wozny MJ (1989) Message-based choreography for computer animation. In: Magnenat-Thalmann N, Thalmann D (eds) *State-of-the-art in computer animation*. Springer, Tokyo, pp69–82

Brinch Hansen P (1975) The programming language concurrent PASCAL. *IEEE Trans Software Engineering*, SE-1, 2:199–206

Brossard A, Camarero R, Thalmann D (1985) *Espaces de texture*. MIRALab, University of Montreal

Brotman LS, Netravali AN (1988) Motion interpolation by optimal control. *Proc SIGGRAPH '88, Computer Graphics* 22(4):179–188

Bruderlin A, Calvert T (1989) Goal-directed dynamic simulation of human walking. *Proc SIGGRAPH '89, Computer Graphics* 23(3):233–242

Burtnyk N, Wein M (1971a) Computer-generated key-frame animation. *J Soc Motion Picture and Television Engineers* 80:149–153

Burtnyk N, Wein M (1971b) A computer animation system for the animator. *Proc UAIDE 10th Annual Meeting*, pp3–5 to 3–24

Burtnyk N, Wein M (1974) Towards a computer animating production tool. *Proc Eurocomp Congress*, Online, Brunel, England, pp174–185

Burtnyk N, Wein M (1976) Interactive skeleton techniques for enhancing motion dynamics in key frame animation. *Comm ACM* 19(10):564–569

*Burtnyk N, Pulfer JK, Wein M (1971) Computer graphics and film animation. *INFOR*, pp1–11

*Buxton W (1982) Computer assisted filmmaking. *American Cinematographer* 63(8)

*Cachola DG, Schrack GF (1986) Modeling and animating three-dimensional articulate figures. *Proc Graphics Interface '86*, pp152–157

Calvert T (1988) The challenge of human figure animation. *Proc Graphics Interface '88*, pp203–210

Calvert T (1989) Composition of realistic animation sequences for multiple human figures Proc mechanics, control and animation of articulated figures, Massachusetts Institute of Technology (to be published in a book, Morgan Kaufmann, USA)

Calvert TW, Chapman J (1978) Notation of movement with computer assistance. *Proc ACM Annual Conf.* 2:731–736

Calvert TW, Chapman J, Patla A (1980) The integration of subjective and objective data in animation of human movement. *Proc SIGGRAPH '80, Computer Graphics* 14(3):198–203

Calvert TW, Chapman J, Patla A (1982a) Aspects of the kinematic simulation of human movement. *IEEE Computer Graphics and Applications* 2(9):41–50

Calvert TW, Chapman J, Patla A (1982b) The simulation of human movement. *Proc Graphics Interface '82*, pp227–234

*Calvert TW, Welman C, Gaudet S, Lee C (1989) Composition of multiple figure sequences for dance and animation. In: Earnshaw E, Wyvill B (eds) *New advances in computer graphics*. Springer, Tokyo, pp245–256

Carlson WE (1982) An algorithm and data structure for 3D object synthesis using surface patch intersections. *Proc SIGGRAPH '82, Computer Graphics* 16(3):255–263

*Carr JW, et al. (1970) Interactive movie making. *Proc 9th UAIDE Annual Meeting*, pp381–397

Catmull E (1972) A system for computer generated movies. *Proc ACM Annual Conference*, pp422–431

Catmull E (1974) *A subdivision algorithm for computer display of curved surfaces*. Ph.D. thesis, University of Utah

Catmull E (1975) Computer display of curved surfaces. *Proc IEEE Conf on Computer Graphics, Pattern Recognition and Data Structures*, also in: *Tutorial on interactive computer graphics*, IEEE Press, pp309–315

Catmull E (1978a) A hidden-surface algorithm with anti-aliasing. *Proc SIGGRAPH '78, Computer Graphics* 12(3):6–11

Catmull E (1978b) The problems of computer-assisted animation. *Computer Graphics* 12(3):348–353

Catmull E (1979) New frontiers in computer animation. *American Cinematographer*, October Issue

Catmull E (1984) An analytic visible surface algorithm for independent pixel processing. *Proc SIGGRAPH '84, Computer Graphics* 18(3):109–115

CGW (1982) Digital paint systems survey. *Computer Graphics World* 5(4):62–65

Chadwick J, Parent R (1988) Critter construction: developing characters for computer animation. *Proc Pixim 88*, pp283–305

Chadwick J, Haumann DR, Parent RE (1989) Layered construction for deformable animated characters. *Proc SIGGRAPH '89, Computer Graphics* 23(3):234–243

*Chen PC (1990) Applications of scientific visualization to meteorological data analysis and animation. In: Magnenat-Thalmann N, Thalmann D (eds) *Computer Animation '90*. Springer, Tokyo, pp31–38

*Chérif N (1990) GEMSA: computer-aided movement generation for scene animation, In: Magnenat-Thalmann N, Thalmann D (eds) *Computer Animation '90*, Springer, Tokyo,

pp119–128

Chmilar M, Wyvill B (1989) A software architecture for integrated modelling and animation. In: Earnshaw E, Wyvill B (eds) *New advances in computer graphics*. Springer, Tokyo, pp257–276

*Christopher R (1982) Digital animation does Dallas. *Videography*, February Issue, pp37–42

Chua TS, Wong WH, Chu KC (1988) Design and implementation of the animation language SOLAR. In: Magnenat-Thalmann N, Thalmann D (eds) *New trends in computer graphics*. Springer, Heidelberg, pp15–26

Chuang R, Entis G (1983) 3D shaded computer animation—step by step. *IEEE Computer Graphics and Applications* 3(9):18–25

Citron J, Whitney J (1968) CAMP computer assisted movie production. *FJCC, AFIPS Conference Proceedings* 33(2):1299–1305

Clark JH (1976) Hierarchical geometric models for visible surface algorithms. *Communications of the ACM* 19(10):547–554

Cleary J, Wyvill BM, Birtwistle GM, Vatti R (1986) Multiprocessor ray tracing. *Comput Graphics Forum* 5(1):3–12

Cohen MF (1989) Gracefulness and style in motion control. Proc Mechanics, Control and Animation of Articulated Figures, Massachusetts Institute of Technology (to be published in a book, Morgan Kaufmann, USA)

Cohen MF, Greenberg DP (1985) The hemi-cube: a radiosity solution for complex environments. *Proc SIGGRAPH '85, Computer Graphics* 19(3):31–40

Cohen MF, Greenberg DP (1986) An efficient radiosity approach for realistic image synthesis. *IEEE Comput Graphics Applications* 6(3):26–35

Cook RL, Torrance KE (1982) A reflection model for computer graphics. *ACM Trans Graphics* 1(1):7–24

Coons SA (1964) *Surfaces for computer-aided design of space figures*. Massachusetts Institute of Technology, ESL 9442-M-139

Coons SA (1974) Surface patches and B-spline curves. In: Barnhill, Riesenfeld (eds), *Computer aided geometric design*, Academic Press

Crow FC (1977a) The aliasing problem in computer-generated shaded images. *Communications of the ACM* 20(11):799–805

Crow FC (1977b) Shadow algorithms for computer graphics. *Proc SIGGRAPH '77, Computer Graphics* 11(2):242–248

Crow FC (1978a) Shaded computer graphics in the entertainment industry. *Computer*, IEEE Press, 11(3):11–23

Crow FC (1978b) The use of grayscale for improved raster display of vectors and characters. *Proc SIGGRAPH '78, Computer Graphics* 12(3):1–5

Crow FC (1981) A comparison of anti-aliasing techniques. *IEEE Computer Graphics and Applications* 1(1):40–48

Csuri C (1970) Real-time film animation. *Proc 9th UAIDE Annual Meeting*, pp289–305

Csuri C (1974) Real-time computer animation. *Proc IFIP Congress '74*, North-Holland, pp707–711

*Csuri C (1974) Computer graphics and art. *Proc IEEE* 62(4):503–515

Csuri C (1975) Computer animation. *Proc SIGGRAPH '75*, pp92–101

*Csuri C, Shaffer J (1968) Art, computers and mathematics. *Proc Fall Joint Computer Conf*, AFIPS, pp1293–1298

Csuri C, Hackathorn R, Parent R, Carlson W, Howard M (1979) Towards an interactive high visual complexity animation system. *Proc SIGGRAPH '79, Computer Graphics* 13(2):289–299

Dahl M, Nygaard (1968) *The SIMULA 67 common base language*. Norwegian Computing Centre

DeFanti T (1976) The digital component of the circle graphics habitat. *Proc National Computer Conference '76*, pp195–203

DeFanti T (1980) Language control structures for easy electronic visualization. *BYTE*, November Issue, pp90–106

*Denber MJ, Turner PM (1986) A differential compiler for computer animation. *Proc

SIGGRAPH '86, Computer Graphics 20(4):21–27

* Deyo R, Briggs JA, Doenges P (1988) Getting graphics in gear: graphics and dynamics in driving simulation. *Proc SIGGRAPH '88, Computer Graphics* 22(4):179–188

Dietrich F (1983) A micro computer system for real-time animation. *The Artist Designer and Computer Graphics*, Tutorial SIGGRAPH '83, 18:43–47

Doi A, Aono M, Urano N, Uno S (1988) AVENUE: an integrated 3D animation system. In: Magnenat-Thalmann N, Thalmann D (eds) *New trends in computer graphics.* Springer, Heidelberg, pp27–43

Dooley M (1982) Anthropometric modeling programs—a survey. *IEEE Computer Graphics and Applications* 2(9):17–25

Drewery K, Tsotsos J (1986) Goal-directed animation using english motion commands. *Proc Graphics Interface '86*, pp131–135

* Duff DS (1976) *Simulation and animation.* M.Sc. thesis, University of Toronto, Canada

Duff T (1979) Smoothly shaded renderings of polyhedral objects on raster displays. *Proc SIGGRAPH '79, Computer Graphics* 13(2):270–275

Duff T (1983) Computer graphics in the biggest box office hit: *Return of the Jedi. Proc Computer Graphics '83*, Online Conf., pp283–289

* Duncan W Jr (1982) Computer animation at Information International. *Tutorial notes on 3D computer animation*, SIGGRAPH '82

Dungan W, Stenger A, Sutty G (1978) Texture tile consideration for raster graphics. *Proc SIGGRAPH '78, Computer Graphics* 12(3):130–134

Ekman P, Friesen W (1978) *Manual for the facial action coding system.* Consulting Psychologist Press, Palo Alto, USA

Encarnacao J (1970) Survey of and new solutions for the hidden-line problem. *Proc GC Symp Delft*

* Esakov J, Badler NI (1989) An architecture for high-level human task animation control. In: Fishwick PA, Modjeski RB (eds) *Knowledge based simulation: methodology and application.* Springer-Verlag

Esakov J, Badler NI, Jung M (1989) An investigation of language input and performance timing for task animation. *Proc Graphics Interface '89*

Eshkol N, Wachmann A (1958) *Movement notation.* Weidenfeld and Nicolson, London

Evans SM (1976) *User's guide for the programs of combiman.* Report AMRLTR-76-117, University of Dayton, Ohio

Featherstone R (1983) Position and velocity transformations between robot end-effector coordinates and joint angles. *Int J Robotics Res* 2(2):35–45

Feibush EA, Levoy M, Cook RL (1980) Synthetic texturing using digital filters. *Proc SIGGRAPH '80, Computer Graphics* 14(3):294–301

* Feiner S, Salesin D, Banchoff T (1982) Dial: a diagrammatic animation language. *IEEE Computer Graphics and Applications* 2(9):43–54

* Ferderber S (1983) The commercial production designer. *Millimeter*, February Issue, pp52–66

* Fetter WA (1964) *Computer graphics in communication*, McGraw-Hill, New York

Fetter WA (1981) Wide angle displays for tactical situations. *Proc US Army Third Computer Graphics Workshop*, pp99–103

Fetter WA (1982) A progression of human figures simulated by computer graphics. *IEEE Computer Graphics and Applications* 2(9):9–13

Fishkin KP, Barsky B (1985) Algorithms for brush movements. *The Visual Computer* 1(4):221–230

Fiume E, Fournier A, Rudolph L (1983) A parallel scan conversion algorithm with anti-aliasing for a general-purpose ultracomputer. *Proc SIGGRAPH '83, Computer Graphics* 17(3):141–150

* Fiume E, Tsichritzis D, Dami L (1987) A temporal scripting language for object-oriented animation. *Proc Eurographics '87*, North Holland, pp283–294

* Foley JD, Van Dam A (1982) *Fundamentals of interactive computer graphics.* Addison-Wesley

* Foley TA, Lane DA, Nielson GM (1990) Towards animating ray-traced volume visualization. *The Journal of Visualization and Computer Animation,* 1(1)

Forest L, Magnenat-Thalmann N, Thalmann D (1986a) An integration of keyframe and algorithmic animation. In: Kunii TL (ed) *Advanced computer graphics.* Springer, Tokyo, pp263–274

Forest L, Rambaud D, Magnenat-Thalmann N, Thalmann D (1986b) Keyframe-based subactors. *Proc Graphics Interface '86,* Vancouver, Canada, pp213–216

Forsey D, Wilhelms J (1988) Techniques for interactive manipulation of articulated bodies using dynamics analysis, *Proc Graphics Interface '88,* pp8–15

Fortin D, Lamy JF, Thalmann D (1983) A multiple track animator system. *Proc. SIGGRAPH/SIGART Interdisciplinary Workshop on Motion: Representation and Perception,* Toronto, pp180–186

Fournier A, Fussell D, Carpenter L (1982) Computer rendering of stochastic models. *Communications of the ACM* 25(6):371–384

* Fox, Waite (1982) Computer animation with color registers. *BYTE,* pp194–214

* Frachia FD, Prusinkiewicz P, Martin J.M. de Boer JM (1990) Animation of the development of multicellular structures. In: Magnenat-Thalmann N, Thalmann D (eds) *Computer Animation '90.* Springer, Tokyo, pp3–19

* Friesen DP (1969) A professional animator looks at computer animation. *Proc 8th UAIDE Annual Meeting,* pp187–194

Fuchs H, Barros J (1979) Efficient generation of smooth line drawings on video displays. *Proc SIGGRAPH '79, Computer Graphics* 13(2):260–269

Futrelle RP (1974) GALATEA: Interactive graphics for the analysis of moving images. *Proc Information Processing 74,* North Holland, pp712–715

* Gagalowicz A, Ma SD (1988) Animation of stochastic model-based 3-D textures. *Proc Eurographics '88,* North Holland, pp313–326

Galimberti R, Montanari U (1969) An algorithm for hidden-line elimination. *Comm ACM* 12(4):206

* Gançarski P, Dufourd JF (1988) ASA + + : un système de production d'animations à scénarios interactifs. *Proc PIXIM '88,* pp263–282

* Geschwind DM (1982) The NOVA opering: a case study in digital computer animation. *Proc Computer Graphics '82,* Online Conf., pp325–335

Giloth C, Veeder J (1985) The paint problem. *IEEE Computer Graphics and Applications* 5(7):66–75

* Ginsberg CM, Maxwell D (1986) Graphical marionette. In: Badler NI, Tsotsos JK (eds) *Motion: representation and perception,* North Holland, pp303–317

Girard M (1987) Interactive design of 3D computer-animated legged animal motion. *IEEE Computer Graphics and Applications* 7(6):39–51

Girard M (1989) Constrained optimization of articulated animal movement in computer animation, Proc Mechanics, Control and Animation of Articulated Figures, Massachusetts Institute of Technology (to be published in a book, Morgan Kaufmann, USA)

Girard M, Maciejewski AA (1985) Computational modeling for the computer animation of legged figures. *Proc SIGGRAPH '85,* pp263–270

Girard M, Amkraut S (1990) Eurhythmy: concepts and process. *The Journal of Visualization and Computer Animation,* 1(1)

Goldberg A, Kay A (1976) *SMALLTALK-72 instruction manual.* Palo Alto, California, XEROX PARC

Goldberg A, Robson D (1983) *SMALLTALK-80, the language and its implementation.* Addison-Wesley

* Goldstein RA (1971) A system for computer animation of 3-D objects. *Proc 10th UAIDE Annual Meeting,* pp3–128 to 3–139

Goldstein RA, Nagel R (1971) 3-D visual simulation. *Simulation,* pp25–31

Gomez JE (1984) Twixt: a 3-D animation system. *Proc Eurographics '84,* North Holland, pp121–134

Goral CM, Torrance KE, Greenberg DP, Battaile B (1984) Modeling the interaction of light between diffuse surfaces. *Proc SIGGRAPH '84, Computer Graphics* 18(3):213–222

* Goss T (1983) Animation and the new machine. *Print,* March/April Issue, pp57–64

Gouraud H (1971) Continuous shading of curve surfaces. *IEEE Trans Computers* c-20(6): 623–629

Gourret JP, Magnenat-Thalmann N, Thalmann D (1989a) Simulation of object and human skin deformations in a grasping task. *Proc SIGGRAPH '89, Computer Graphics* 23(3):21–30

Gourret JP, Magnenat-Thalmann N, Thalmann D (1989b) The use of finite element theory for simulating object and human body deformations and contacts. *Proc Eurographics '89*, North Holland, Hamburg, pp477–488

* Green M (1981) A system for designing an animating objects with curved surfaces. *Proc Canadian Man-Computer Communications Society '81*, pp377–384

* Green M (1989) Using dynamics in computer animation: control and issues. Proc Mechanics, Control and Animation of Articulated Figures, Massachusetts Institute of Technology (to be published in a book, Morgan Kaufmann, USA)

Green M, Sun H (1988) A language and system for procedural modeling and motion. *IEEE Comput Graphics Applications* 8(6):52–64 (also in: *Proc Graphics Interface '88*, pp16–25)

Greenberg D, Marcus A, Schmidt AH, Gorter V (1982) *The computer image*. Addison-Wesley

* Greenberg JM (1985) Computer animation in distance teaching. Proc Graphics Interface '85, pp419–424 (also in: Magnenat-Thalmann N, Thalmann D (eds) *Computer-generated images*. Springer, Tokyo, pp260–266)

* Greenberg J (1987) Computer animation: direct to video. *Proc Computer Animation CG 87, Online*, pp39–49

Greif I, Hewitt C (1975) Actor semantics of PLANNER-73. *Proc ACM SIGPLAN SIGACT Conf*, pp67–77

Guenter B (1989) A system for simulating human facial expression. In: Magnenat-Thalmann N, Thalmann D (eds) *State-of-the-art in computer animation*. Springer, Tokyo, pp191–202

Gupta S, Sproull R (1981) Filtering edges for gray-scale displays. *Proc SIGGRAPH '81, Computer Graphics* 15(3):1–5

Guttag J (1977) Abstract data types and the development of data structures. *Communications of the ACM* 20(6):396–404

Hackathorn R (1977) ANIMA II:A 3-D color animation system. *Proc SIGGRAPH '77, Computer Graphics* 11(2):54–64

Hackathorn R, Parent R, Marshall B, Howard M (1981) An interactive microcomputer based 3-D animation system. *Proc Canadian Man-Computer Communications Society Conference '81*, pp181–191

* Haflinger DJ, Ressler PC (1971) Animation with IGS. *Proc 10th UAIDE Annual Meeting*, pp3–227 to 3–234

Hahn JK (1988) Realistic animation of rigid bodies. *Proc SIGGRAPH '88, Computer Graphics* 22(4):299–308

* Halas J (ed) (1974) *Computer animation*. Hastings House, New York

Halas J, Manvell R (1968) *The technique of film animation*. Hastings House, New York

Hall RA, Greenberg DP (1983) A testbed for realistic image synthesis. *IEEE Computer Graphics and Applications* 3(8):11–20

Hamilton Sir WR (1844) On quaternions or on a new system of imaginaries in algebra. *Philosophical Magazine* xxv, pp10–13

Hanrahan P (1983) Ray tracing algebraic surfaces. *Proc SIGGRAPH '83, Computer Graphics* 17(3):83–90

Hanrahan P, Sturman D (1985) Interactive animation of parametric models. *The Visual Computer* 1(4):260–266

Harada K, Nakamae E (1988) Locating sampling points for cubic splines. In: Magnenat-Thalmann N, Thalmann D (eds) *New trends in computer graphics*. Springer, Heidelberg, pp3–14

Harada K, Nakamae E (1989) Sampling point setting on cubic splines for computer animation. *The Visual Computer* 5(1–2):14–21

Haumann DR (1987) Modeling the physical behavior of flexible objects. SIGGRAPH '87 Course Notes on Topics in Physically Based Modeling

Haumann DR, Parent RE (1988) The behavioral test-bed: obtaining complex behavior from simple rules. *The Visual Computer* 4(6):332–347

Hedelman H (1984) A data flow approach to procedural modeling. *IEEE Comput Graphics Applications* 4(1):16–26

Hégron G, Arnaldi B, Dumont G (1988) Toward general animation control. In: Magnenat-Thalmann N, Thalmann D (eds) *New trends in computer graphics*. Springer, Heidelberg, pp54–63

* Hégron G, Palamidese P, Thalmann D (1989) Motion control in animation, simulation and visualization. *Computer Graphics Forum*, 8(4):347–352

Heise R, MacDonald BA (1989) Quaternions and motion interpolation: a tutorial. In: Earnshaw E, Wyvill B (eds) *New advances in computer graphics*. Springer, Tokyo, pp229–244

Herbison-Evans D (1978) NUDES 2: a numeric utility displaying ellipsoid solids, version 2. *Proc SIGGRAPH '78, Computer Graphics* 12(3):354–356

Herbison-Evans D (1980) Rapid raster ellipsoid shading. *Computer Graphics* 13(4):355–361

Herbison-Evans D (1982) Real-time animation of human figure drawings with hidden-lines omitted. *IEEE Computer Graphics and Applications* 2(9):27–33

* Herbison-Evans D (1983) Manipulating ellipsoids in animation. *Computer Graphics World* 7:78–82

Hewitt C (1971) *Description and theoretical analysis (using schemata) of PLANNER: a language for proving theorems and manipulating models for a robot*. Ph.D. dissertation, Massachusetts Institute of Technology

Hewitt C, Atkinson R (1977) Parallelism and synchronization in actor systems. *Proc ACM Symposium on Principles of Programming Languages*

Hewitt C, Smith B (1975) Towards a programming apprentice. *IEEE Trans Software Engineering*, SE-1(1):26–45

Hewitt C, Bishop P, Steiger R (1973) A universal modular actor formalism for artificial intelligence. *Proc Intern Joint Conf on Artificial Intelligence*, pp235–245

Hild H, Pins M (1989) A 3D error diffusion dither algorithm for half-tone animation on bitmap screens. In: Magnenat-Thalmann N, Thalmann D (eds) *State-of-the-art in computer animation*. Springer, Tokyo, pp181–190

Hill DR, Pearce A, Wyvill B (1988) Animating speech: an automated approach using speech synthesised by rules. *The Visual Computer* 3(5):277–289

Hollerbach JM, Sahar G (1983) Wrist-partitioned, inverse kinematic accelerations and manipulator dynamics. *Int. J Robotics Res* 2(4):61–76

Honey FJ (1971a) Artist oriented computer animation. *J Soc of Motion Picture and Television Engineers* 80(3):154

Honey FJ (1971b) Computer animated episodes by single axis rotations. *Proc 10th UAIDE Annual Meeting*, pp3–120 to 3–226

Hong MT, Magnenat-Thalmann N, Thalmann D (1988) A general algorithm for 3-D shape interpolation in a facet-based representation. *Proc Graphics Interface '88*, Edmonton, Canada, pp229–235

* Hopgood FRA (1969) GROATS: a graphic output system for atlas using the 4020. *Proc 9th UAIDE Annual Meeting*, pp401–410

* Hubschman H, Zucker SW (1982) Frame-to-frame coherence and the hidden surface computation: constraints for a convex world. *ACM Trans Graphics* 1(2):129–162

* Huggins WH, Entwisle DR (1969) Computer animation for the academic community. *SJCC, AFIPS Conference Proceedings* 34:623

* Hunter GM (1977) Computer animation survey. *Comput and Graphics*, Pergamon Press, 2:225–229

* Hurn B (1981) Computer animation for industrial training. *Computer Graphics World* 10:65–68

Isaacs PM (1989) Two tools for scientific visualization and computer animation. Proc Mechanics, Control and Animation of Articulated Figures. Massachusetts Institute of Technology (to be published in a book, Morgan Kaufmann, USA)

Isaacs PM, Cohen MF (1987) Controlling dynamic simulation with kinematic constraints, behavior functions and inverse dynamics. *Proc SIGGRAPH '87, Computer Graphics*.

21(4):215–224

Isaacs PM, Cohen MF (1988) Mixed methods for complex kinematic constraints in dynamic figure animation. *The Visual Computer* 4(6):296–305

*Iversen WR (1982) Processor animates 3-D surface images. *Electronics*, pp149–150

John NW, Willis PJ (1989a) The controller animation system. *Comput Graphics Forum* 8(2):133–138

John NW, Willis PJ (1989b) Some methods to choreograph and implement motion in computer animation. In: Magnenat-Thalmann N, Thalmann D (eds) *State-of-the-art in computer animation*, Springer, Tokyo, pp125–140

Judice JN, Jarvis JF, Ninke W (1974) Using ordered dither to display continuous tone pictures on an AC plasma panel. *Proc Society for Information Display*, pp161–169

Julesz B (1966) *Computers, patterns and depth perception.* Bell Laboratories Record 44(8): 261–267

Kahn KM (1976) *An actor-based computer animation language.* MIT AI Working Paper No 120

Kajiya JT (1982) Ray tracing parametric patches. *Proc SIGGRAPH '82, Computer Graphics* 16(3):245–254

Kajiya JT (1983) New techniques for ray tracing procedurally defined objects. *Proc SIG-GRAPH '83, Computer Graphics* 17(3):91–99

Kalita J, Badler NI (1989) A semantic analysis of action verbs based on physical primitives. Proc Mechanics, Control and Animation of Articulated Figures. Massachusetts Institute of Technology (to be published in a book, Morgan Kaufmann, USA)

*Kallis SA (1971) Computer animation techniques. *J SMPTE* 80(3):145–148

*Kawaguchi Y (1981) *Digital image* (in Japanese). ASCII Publishing

Kay A (1969) *The reactive engine.* Ph.D. thesis, University of Utah

Kay DS Greenberg D (1979) Transparency for computer synthesized images. *Proc SIG-GRAPH '79, Computer Graphics* 13(2):158–164

*King A, Stapleton M (1989) Computer animation: a personal view. In: Landsdown J, Earnshaw E (eds) *Computers in art, design and animation.* Springer, New York, pp246–252

*Kinnucan P (1982) Solid modelers make the scene. *High Technology* 2(4):38–44

Kitching A (1973) Computer animation—some new ANTICS. *Br Kinematography Sound Television J* 55(12):372–386

Knowlton KC (1964) A computer technique for producing animated movies. *Proc SJCC AFIPS Conference* 25:67–87

Knowlton KC (1965) Computer-produced movies. *Science* 150:1116–1120

*Knowlton K (1968) Computer-animated movies. *Emerging Concepts in Computer Graphics*, Benjamin, New York, pp243–370

Knowlton KC (1970) EXPLOR-A generator of images. *Proc 9th UAIDE Annual Meeting*, pp543–583

*Knowlton K (1972) Collaborations with artists: a programmer's reflections. *Proc IFIP Working Conf on Graphic Languages*, North-Holland, pp399–418

Knowlton K, Cherry L (1977) Atoms, a 3D opaque molecule system. *Comput Chem* 1(3):161–166

Kochanek D, Bartels R (1984) Interpolating splines with local tension, continuity and bias tension. *Proc SIGGRAPH '84*, pp33–41

Komatsu K (1988) Human skin model capable of natural shape variation. *The Visual Computer* 3(5):265–271

Korein JU (1985) A geometric investigation of reach, MIT Press, Mass., USA

Korein JU, Badler NI (1982) Techniques for generating the goal-directed motion of articulated structures. *IEEE Comput Graphics Applications*, Nov 1982, pp71–81

Korein J, Badler N (1983) Temporal anti-aliasing in computer generated animation. *Proc SIGGRAPH '83, Computer Graphics* 17(3):377–388

Kroyer B (1986) Animating with a hierarchy. *Seminar on Advanced Computer Animation, SIGGRAPH '86*

*Kunii TL, Gotoda H (1990) Modeling and animation of garment wrinkle formation process. In: Magnenat-Thalmann N, Thalmann D (eds) *Computer Animation '90*. Springer, Tokyo,

pp131–147

Laban R (1966) *Choreutics*. Ullman L (ed) MacDonald and Evans, London

Lane JM, Carpenter LC, Whitted T, Blinn JF (1980) Scan line methods for displaying parametrically defined surfaces. *Communications of the ACM* 23(1):23–34

Lansdown RJ (1982) Computer aided animation: a concise review. *Proc Computer Graphics '82*, Online Conf, pp279–290

* Lansdown J (1983) The economics of computer-aided animation. *Proc Computer Graphics '83*, Online Conf, pp267–275

Lasseter J (1987) Principles of traditional animation applied to 3D computer animation. *Proc SIGGRAPH '87, Computer Graphics* 21(4):35–44

* Laybourne K (1979) *The animation book*. Crown

Lee MW, Kunii TL (1989) Animation design: a database-oriented animation design method with a video image analysis capability. In: Magnenat-Thalmann N, Thalmann D (eds) *State-of-the-art in computer animation*. Springer, Tokyo, pp97–112

* Lee MW, Kunii TL, Duerst MJ (1990) Motion comparison in computer animation. In: Magnenat-Thalmann N, Thalmann D (eds) *Computer Animation '90*. Springer, Tokyo, pp191–206

Leister W, Müller H, Stösser A, Neidecker B (1988) "Occursus cum novo," computer animation by raytracing in a network. In: Magnenat-Thalmann N, Thalmann D (eds) *New trends in computer graphics*. Springer, Heidelberg, pp83–92

Lethridge TC, Ware C (1989) A simple heuristically-based method for expressive stimulus-response animation. *Computers and Graphics*, 13(3):297–304

* Levine SR (1975) Computer animation at Lawrence Livermore laboratory. *Proc SIGGRAPH '75*, pp81–84

* Levitan EL (1977) *Electronic imaging techniques*. Van Nostrand

* Levoy M (1977) A color animation system based on the multiplane technique. *Proc. SIGGRAPH '77, Computer Graphics* 11(2):65–71

* Lewell J (1981) The computer paintings of David Em. *Business Screen*, October Issue, pp38–40

* Lewell J (1983) The pioneers: John Whitney Sr. *Computer Pictures* 1(3):22–24

Lewis JP, Parke FI (1987) Automated lip-synch and speech synthesis for character animation. *Proc CHI '87 and Graphics Interface '87*, Toronto, pp143–147

* Lieberman LI (1971) Compufilms: a computer animation process. *Simulation* 16(1):33–36

Lipscomb JS (1981) Reversed apparent movement and erratic motion with many refreshes per update. *Computer Graphics* 14(4):113–118

Liskov B, Zilles S (1974) Programming with abstract data types. *Proc SIGPLAN Symposium on Very High Level Languages*, pp50–59

* Lopes PF, Gomes MR (1990) Computer pinscreen simulation. In: Magnenat-Thalmann N, Thalmann D (eds) *Computer Animation '90*. Springer, Tokyo, pp165–176

Low KH, Dubey RN (1986) A comparative study of generalized coordinates for solving the inverse-kinematics problem of 6R robot manipulator. *Int J Robotics Res* 5(4):69–88

Lozano-Perez (1976) The design of a mechanical assembly system. Artificial Intelligence Laboratory, Massachusetts Institute of Technology, AI TR 397

Lozano-Perez (1982) Task planning. In: Brady M (ed) *Robot motion: planning and control*. MIT Press, Cambridge, Mass., USA

Lozano-Perez T, Wesley MA (1979) An algorithm for planning collision-free paths among polyhedral obstacles. *Commun ACM* 22(10):560–570

Maciejewski AA, Klein CA (1985) Obstacle avoidance for kinematics redundant manipulators in dynamically varying environments. *Int J Robotics Res*, Fall issue

Magnenat-Thalmann N (1989) The problematics of facial animation. In: *State-of-the-art in computer animation*. Springer, Tokyo, pp47–55

* Magnenat-Thalmann N (1990) New trends in the direction of synthetic actors. *Proc. Computer Graphics International '90*. Springer, Tokyo

* Magnenat-Thalmann N, Thalmann D (1983a) 3D computer animation films using a programming language and interactive systems. *Proc Computer Graphics '83*, Online Conf, pp247–257

Magnenat-Thalmann N, Thalmann D (1983b) The use of 3D high-level graphical types in the MIRA animation system. *IEEE Computer Graphics and Applications* 3(9):9–16

Magnenat-Thalmann N, Thalmann D (1984a) CINEMIRA: a 3D computer animation language based on actor and camera data types. Technical Report, University of Montreal

Magnenat-Thalmann N, Thalmann D (1984b) 3D shaded director-oriented computer animation. *Proc Graphics Interface '84*, Ottawa, pp1–7

Magnenat-Thalmann N, Thalmann D (1985a) 3D Computer animation: more an evolution problem than a motion problem. *IEEE Comput Graphics Applications* 5(10):47–57

Magnenat-Thalmann N, Thalmann D (1985b) An indexed bibliography on computer animation. *IEEE Comput Graphics Applications* 5(7):76–86

Magnenat-Thalmann N, Thalmann D (1985c) Controlling evolution and motion using the CINEMIRA-2 animation sublanguage. In: *Computer-generated images*. Springer, Tokyo, pp249–259

Magnenat-Thalmann N, Thalmann D (1985d) Subactor data types as hierarchical procedural models for computer animation. *Proc Eurographics '85*, Nice, pp121–128

Magnenat-Thalmann N, Thalmann D (1985e) A new tool for business graphics: the animated data system. *Proc Trends and Applications*, Washington, USA, pp116–122

* Magnenat-Thalmann N, Thalmann D (1986a) Building complex bodies: combining computer animation with CAD. *Computers in Mechanical Engineering (CIME)* 4(6):26–33

Magnenat-Thalmann N, Thalmann D (1986b) Special cinematographic effects using multiple virtual movie cameras. *IEEE Comput Graphics Applications* 6(4):43–50 (also in: Kunii TL (ed) *Computer graphics, visual technology and art*. Springer, Tokyo, pp271–283)

Magnenat-Thalmann N, Thalmann D (1986c) Three-dimensional computer animation based on simultaneous differential equations. *Proc Conf Continuous Simulation Languages*, Society for Computer Simulation, San Diego, pp73–77

Magnenat-Thalmann N, Thalmann D (1987a) Mechanics and robotics for animating synthetic actors. SIGGRAPH '88 Course Notes on Synthetic Actors: The impact of artificial intelligence and robotics on animation, pp85–98

* Magnenat-Thalmann N, Thalmann D (1987b) Procedural animation blocks in discrete simulation. *Simulation* 49:102–108

Magnenat-Thalmann N, Thalmann D (1987c) The direction of synthetic actors in the film *Rendez-vous à Montréal*. *IEEE Comput Graphics Applications* 7(12):9–19

Magnenat-Thalmann N, Thalmann D (1988) Construction and animation of a synthetic actress. *Proc Eurographics '88*, North Holland, pp55–66

Magnenat-Thalmann N, Thalmann D (eds) (1989a) *State-of-the-art in computer animation*. Springer, Tokyo

Magnenat-Thalmann N, Thalmann D (1989b) Creation and deformation of surfaces for the animation of human bodies. Proc Mechanics, Control and Animation of Articulated Figures. Massachusetts Institute of Technology (to be published in a book, Morgan Kaufmann, USA)

Magnenat-Thalmann N, Thalmann D (1989c) Motion control of synthetic actors: an integrated view of human animation. Proc Mechanics, Control and Animation of Articulated Figures, Massachusetts Institute of Technology

Magnenat-Thalmann N, Thalmann D (1989d) Synthetic actors: the simulation of human motion. *Comput Bull*, British Computer Society, Series IV, Vol. 1, part 1, pp12–14

Magnenat-Thalmann N, Thalmann D (1989e) The problematics of human prototyping and animation. *Comput Graphics Forum*, North Holland, 8(2):115–123

Magnenat-Thalmann N, Thalmann D, Larouche A, Lorrain L (1982) GRAFEDIT: an interactive general-purpose graphics editor. *Computers and Graphics* 6(1):41–46

Magnenat-Thalmann N, Chourot N, Thalmann D (1984a) Color gradation, shading and texture using a limited terminal. *Computer Graphics Forum, the EUROGRAPHICS journal*, March Issue

* Magnenat-Thalmann N, Thalmann D, Fortin M, Langlois L (1984b) MIRA-SHADING: a language for the synthesis and the animation of realistic images. *Frontiers in Computer Graphics*, Springer, Tokyo Berlin Heidelberg New York, pp101–113

Magnenat-Thalmann N, Thalmann D, Fortin M (1985) MIRANIM: An Extensible Director-

Oriented System for the Animation of Realistic Images. *IEEE Computer Graphics and Applications*, 5(3):61–73

Magnenat-Thalmann N, Thalmann D, Béland S (1986) The integration of particle and polygon rendering using an A-buffer algorithm. *Proc Eurographics '86*, Lisbon, pp161–169

Magnenat-Thalmann N, Laperrière R, Thalmann D (1988a) Joint-dependent local deformations for hand animation and object grasping. *Proc Graphics Interface '88*, pp26–33

Magnenat-Thalmann N, Minh TM, de Angelis M, Thalmann D (1988b) Human prototyping. In: Magnenat-Thalmann N, Thalmann D (eds) *New trends in computer graphics*. Springer, Heidelberg, pp74–82

Magnenat-Thalmann N, Primeau E, Thalmann D (1988c) Abstract muscle action procedures for human face animation. *The Visual Computer* 3(5):290–297

Magnenat-Thalmann N, Thalmann D, Hong MT, de Angelis M (1989) Design, transformation and animation of human faces. *The Visual Computer* 5(1–2):32–39

*Mahieddine M, Lafon JC (1990) An object-oriented approach for modelling animated entities. In: Magnenat-Thalmann N, Thalmann D (eds) *Computer Animation '90*. Springer, Tokyo, pp177–187

*Maiocchi R, Pernici B (1990) Directing an animated scene with autonomous actors. In: Magnenat-Thalmann N, Thalmann D (eds) *Computer Animation '90*. Springer, Tokyo, pp41–60

Mallgren WR (1982) Formal specification of graphic data types. *ACM Trans Programming Languages and Systems* 4(4):687–710

Malowany AS, Kashef B (1984) A color real-time animation system. *Proc Graphics Interface '84*, pp43–50

Mandelbrot BB (1975) Stochastic models for the earth's relief, the shape and fractal dimension of coastlines, and the number area rule for islands. *Proc Natl Acad Sci USA* 72(10):2825–2828

Mandelbrot BB (1977) *Fractals: form, chance and dimension*. Freeman, San Francisco

Mandelbrot BB (1982) *The fractal geometry of nature*. Freeman, San Francisco

Mandelbrot BB, Van Ness JW (1968) Fractional Brownian motions, fractional noises and applications. *SIAM Review* 10(4):422–437

*Marino G, Morasso P, Zaccaria R (1985) NEM: a language for animation of actors and objects. *Proc Eurographics '85*, North Holland, pp129–142

*Marion A, Fleischer K, Vickers M (1984) Towards expressive animation for interactive characters. *Proc Graphics Interface '84*, pp17–20

Marshall R, Wilson R, Carlson W (1980) Procedure models for generating three-dimensional terrain. *Proc SIGGRAPH '80, Computer Graphics* 14(4):154–159

Max NL (1979) Atom LLL:—atoms with shading and highlights. *Computer Graphics* 13(2):165–173

Max N (1989) Polygon-based post-process motion blur. In: Magnenat-Thalmann N, Thalmann D (eds) *State-of-the-art in computer animation*. Springer, Tokyo, pp 169–180

*Max N, Blunden J (1980) Optical printing in computer animation. *Proc SIGGRAPH '80, Computer Graphics* 14(3):171–177

*Max N, Hayashi N, Wakabayashi T (1990) Computer simulation and animation of muscle cross-bridge Motion. *The Journal of Visualization and Computer Animation*, 1(1)

Max NL, Lerner DM (1985) A two-and-a-half-D motion-blur algorithm. *Proc SIGGRAPH '85, Computer Graphics* 19(3):85–93

*McCarthy M (1982) Animation's new protege. *Video Systems*, pp40–46

McGhee, Iswandhi GI (1979) Adaptive locomotion of a multilegged robot over rough terrain. *IEEE Trans Syst Man Cybern*, April, pp176–182

Mezei L, Zivian A (1971) ARTA: an interactive animation system. *Proc Information Processing 71*, North-Holland, pp429–434

Miller G (1988) The motion dynamics of snakes and worms. *Proc SIGGRAPH '88, Computer Graphics* 22(4):169–173

Miller G (1989) Goal-directed animation of tubular articulated figures or how snakes play golf. Proc Mechanics, Control and Animation of Articulated Figures, Massachusetts Institute of Technology (to be published in a book, Morgan Kaufmann, USA)

* Miskowich D (1982) Digital technology and motion pictures. *Computer Graphics World* 7:50–62

* Mittelman P (1983) Computer graphics at MAGI. *Proc Computer Graphics '83*, Online Conf, pp291–301

Miura T, Iwata J, Tsuda J (1967) An application of hybrid curve generation—cartoon animation by electronic computers. *Proc Spring Joint Computer Conference*, p141

Moore M, Wilhelms J (1988) Collision detection and response for computer animation. *Proc SIGGRAPH '88, Computer Graphics* 22(4):289–298

Morasso P (1983) Three dimensional arm trajectories. *Biological Cybernetics*

* Mudur SP, Singh JH (1978) A notation for computer animation. *IEEE Trans on Systems, Man and Cybernetics*, SMC-8(4):308–311

Muir DW (1985) Computer animation in engineering. In: Kunii TL (ed) *Computer graphics, visual technology and art*. Springer, Tokyo, pp299–308

* Myers AJ (1976) A digital video information storage and retrieval system. *Proc SIGGRAPH '76, Computer Graphics* 10(2):45–50

* Nahas M, Huitric H, Rioux M, Domey J (1990) Registered 3D-texture imaging. In: Magnenat-Thalmann N, Thalmann D (eds) *Computer Animation '90*. Springer, Tokyo, pp81–91

Nahas M, Huitric H, Saintourens M (1988) Animation of a B-spline figure. *The Visual Computer* 3(5):272–276

* Neelamkavil F, Beare L (1988) Techniques for animation on microcomputers. *Computer Graphics Forum*, 7(1):21–27

* Negroponte N, Pangaro P (1976) Experiments with computer animation. *Computer Graphics* 10(2):40–44

Newell ME (1975) *The utilization of procedure models in computer synthetized images*. PhD dissertation, University of Utah

Newell ME, Newell RG, Sancha TL (1972) A new approach to the shaded picture problem. *Proc ACM National Conf* pp443

* Newman WM, sproull RF (1973) *Principles of interactive computer graphics*. McGraw-Hill

Nishimura H, Ohno H, Kawata T, Shirakawa I, Omuira K (1983) LINKS-1:A parallel pipelined multimicrocomputer system for image creation. *Proc 10th Symp Computer Architecture, SIGARCH '83*, pp387–394

Nishita T, Nakamae E (1974) An algorithm for half-toned representation of three-dimensional objects. *Information Processing Society of Japan*, vol 14

Nolan J, Yarbrough L (1968) An on-line computer drawing and animation system. *Proc IFIP Congress 1968*, North-Holland, Amsterdam, p605

Noll AM (1965a) Stereographic projections by digital computers. *Computers and Automation* 14:32–34

* Noll AM (1965b) Computer generated three-dimensional movies. *Computers and Automation*, November Issue, p20

Noll AM (1967) Computers and the visual arts. *Design and Planning* 2:65–80

Noma T, Kunii TL (1985) ANIMENGINE: An engineering animation system. *IEEE Comput Graphics Applications* 5(10):24–33 (also in: Magnenat-Thalmann N, Thalmann D (eds) *Computer-generated images*. Springer, pp 189–202, and in: Proc Graphics Interface '85, pp83–90)

Norton A (1982) Generation and display of geometric fractals in 3-D. *Proc SIGGRAPH '82, Computer Graphics* 16(3):61–67

* Odgers CR (1982) Criteria for choosing a camera for use in a video digitizing system. *Tutorial Notes on Computer Animation, SIGGRAPH '82*, pp108–119

* Odgers CR (1983) Fundamentals of video recording for computer animation. *Tutorial Notes on Computer Animation SIGGRAPH '83*, pp175–186

Oppenheim AV, Schafer RW (1975) *Digital signal processing*. Prentice-Hall, Englewood Cliffs

O'Rourke J, Badler NI (1979) Decomposition of three-dimensional objects into spheres. *IEEE Trans Pattern Analysis and Machine Intelligence*, RAMI-1:295–306

Ostby EF (1989) Simplified control of complex animation. In: Magnenat-Thalmann N, Thalmann D (eds) *State-of-the-art in computer animation*. Springer, Tokyo, pp59–68

Papathomas TV, Julesz B (1987) Animation with fractals from variations on the Mandelbrot

Set. The *Visual Computer* 3(1):23–26

Papert S (1970) Teaching children thinking. *Proc IFIP World Conference on Computer Education*, New York, ppI/73-I/78

Parke FI (1972) Animation of faces. *Proc ACM Annual Conference*, vol 1

Parke FI (1974) *A parametric model for human faces*. PhD dissertation, University of Utah

* Parke FI (1975) A model for human faces that allows speech synchronized animation. *Computers and Graphics* 1(1):1–4

* Parke FI (1980) Adaptation of scan and slit-scan techniques to computer animation. *Proc. SIGGRAPH '80, Computer Graphics* 14(3):178–181

Parke FI (1982) Parameterized models for facial animation. *IEEE Computer Graphics and Applications* 2(9):61–68

* Pattanaik SN (1989) A stylized model for animating Beharata Natyam, an Indian classical dance form. In: Landsdown J, Earnshaw E (eds) *Computers in art, design and animation*. Springer, New York, pp264–273

* Patterson R (1982) The making of *TRON*. *American Cinematographer* 63(8)

Peachey DR (1985) Solid texturing of complex surfaces. *Proc SIGGRAPH '85, Computer Graphics* 19(3):279–286

Pearce A, Wyvill B, Wyvill G, Hill D (1986) Speech and expression: a computer solution to face animation. *Proc Graphics Interface '86*, pp136–140

* Pentland A, Williams J (1989) Good vibrations: modal dynamics for graphics and animation. *Proc SIGGRAPH '89, Computer Graphics* 23(3):215–222

Perlin K (1985) An image synthesizer. *Proc SIGGRAPH '85, Computer Graphics* 19(3):287–296

Phong BT (1975) Illumination for computer generated pictures. *Communications of the ACM* 18(6):311–317

Piller E (1980) Real-time raster scan unit with improved picture quality. *Computer Graphics* 14(1–2):35–38

Pintado X, Fiume E (1988) Grafields: field-directed dynamic splines for interactive motion control. *Proc Eurographics '88*, North Holland, pp43–54

* Plant G (1987) The role of the designer in 3D computer animation. *Proc Computer Animation CG 87, Online*, pp51–59

Platt JC, Barr AH (1988) Constraint method for flexible models. *Proc SIGGRAPH '88*, pp279–288

Platt S, Badler N (1981) Animating facial expressions. *Proc SIGGRAPH '81, Computer Graphics* 15(3):245–252

Pletincks D (1988) The use of quaternions for animation, modelling and rendering. In: Magnenat-Thalmann N, Thalmann D (eds) *New trends in computer graphics*. Springer, Heidelberg, pp44–53

Pletincks D (1989) Quaternions calculus as a basic tool in computer graphics. *The Visual Computer* 5(1–2):2–13

Plunkett DJ, Bailey MJ (1985) The vectorization of a ray-tracing algorithm for improved execution speed. *IEEE Comput Graphics Applications* 5(8):52–60

Popplestone RJ, Ambler AP, Bellos IM (1980) An interpreter for a language for describing assemblies. *Artif Intell* 14:79–107

Porter T (1978) Spherical shading. *Proc SIGGRAPH '78, Computer Graphics* 12(3):282–285

* Potel MJ (1977) Real-time playback in animation systems. *Proc. SIGGRAPH '77, Computer Graphics* 11(2):72–77

Potmesil M, Chakravarty I (1982) Synthetic image generation with a lens and aperture camera model. *ACM Trans Graphics* 1(2):85–108

Potmesil M, Chakravarty I (1983) Modeling motion blur in computer-generated images. *Proc SIGGRAPH '83, Computer Graphics* 17(3):389–399

* Potmesil M, Heffert EM (1987) FRAMES: Software tools for modeling, rendering and animation of 3D scenes. *Proc SIGGRAPH '87, Computer Graphics* 21(4):85–94

Potter TE, Willmert KD (1975) Three-dimensional human display model. *Computer Graphics* 9(1):102–110

* Potts J (1983) Animating the indescribable. *Government Data Systems*, May/June Issue,

pp10–13

Reeves WT (1980) *Quantitative representations of complex dynamic shape for motion analysis.* PhD thesis, University of Toronto, Canada

Reeves WT (1981) In-betweening for computer animation utilizing moving point constaints. *Proc SIGGRAPH '81*, ACM, pp263–269

Reeves WT (1983) Particle systems—a technique for modeling a class of fuzzy objects. *Proc SIGGRAPH '1983, Computer Graphics* 17(3): 359–376

Reeves WT, EF Ostby EF, Leffler S (1990) The Menv modelling and animation environment. *The Journal of Visualization and Computer Animation*, 1(1)

Renault O, Magnenat-Thalmann N, Thalmann D (1990) A vision-based approach to behavioral animation. *The Journal of Visualization and Computer Animation*, 1(1)

* Ressler SP (1982) An object editor for a real time animation processor. *Proc Graphics Interface '82*, pp221–226

Reynolds CW (1978) *Computer animation in the world of actors and scripts.* SM thesis, Architecture Machine Group, Massachusetts Institute of Technology

Reynolds CW (1982) Computer animation with scripts and actors. *Proc SIGGRAPH '82, Computer Graphics* 16(3): 289–296

Reynolds C (1987) Flocks, herds, and schools: a distributed behavioral model. *Proc SIG-GRAPH '87, Computer Graphics* 21(4): 25–34 (also published in: *Proc Computer Animation CG 87, Online*, pp71–87)

* Ribble EA (1982) *Synthesis of human skeletal motion and the design of a special-purpose processor for real-time animation of human and animal figure motion.* MSc thesis, The Ohio State University

Riesenfeld RF, Cohen E, Fish RD, Thomas SW, Cobb ES, Barsky BA, Schweizer DL, Lane JM (1981) Using the oslo algorithm as a basis for CAD/CAM geometric modelling. *Proc NCGA '81*, National Computer Graphics Association, pp345–356

Ridsdale G, Calvert T (1990) Animating microworlds from scripts and relational constraints. In: Magnenat-Thalmann N, Thalmann D (eds) *Computer Animation '90.* Springer, Tokyo, pp107–118

Ridsdale G, Hewitt S, Clavert TW (1986) The interactive specification of human animation. *Proc Graphics Interface '86*, pp121–130

Romney GW (1970) Computer assisted assembly and rendering of solids. Computer Science Department, University of Utah, TR-4-20

Roth SD (1982) Ray casting for modeling solids. *Computer Graphics and Image Processing* 18: 109–144

Rubin S, Whitted T (1980) A three-dimensional representation for fast rendering of complex scenes. *Proc SIGGRAPH '80, Computer Graphics* 14(3): 110–116

* Russett R, Starr C (1976) *Experimental animation.* Van Nostrand Reinhold, New York

Schachter BJ (1980a) Long crested wave models. *Computer Graphics and Image Processing* 12: 187–201

Schachter BJ (1980b) Real time display of texture. *Proc 5th International Conference on Pattern Recognition*, pp789–791

Schachter BJ (1981) Computer image generation for flight simulation. *IEEE Computer Graphics and Applications* 1(4): 29–68

Schachter BJ (1983) Generation of special effects. In: *Computer image generation*, Wiley, New York, pp155–172

Schlag JF (1986) Eliminating the dichotomy between scripting and interaction. *Proc Graphics Interface '86*, pp202–206

Schmacker RA, Brand B, Gilliland M, Sharp W (1969) *Study for applying computer-generated images to visual simulation.* AFHRL-TR-69-14, US Air Force Human Resources Lab.

Schröder P, Zeltzer D (1988) Pathplanning inside Bolio. In: Thalmann D (ed) *Synthetic actors: the impact of artificial intelligence and robotics and animation.* Course Notes SIGGRAPH '88, pp194–207

Schweitzer D (1983) Artificial texturing: an aid to surface visualization. *Proc SIGGRAPH '83, Computer Graphics* 17(3): 23–29

Schweitzer D, Cobb ES (1982) Scanline rendering of parametric surfaces. *Proc SIGGRAPH*

'82, *Computer Graphics* 16(3):265–271

* Selbie S (1989) An introduction to the use of dynamic simulation for the animation of human movement. In: Magnenat-Thalmann N, Thalmann D (eds) *State-of-the-art in computer animation.* Springer, Tokyo, pp33–46

* Serra L, Chua TS (1990) A Frame-based 3D graphics system for kinematic animation with constraints. *Proc. Computer Graphics International '90.* Springer, Tokyo

* Shinagawa Y, Kunii TL, Nomura Y, Okuno T, Young Y (1990) Automating view function generation for walk-through animation. In: Magnenat-Thalmann N, Thalmann D (eds) *Computer Animation '90.* Springer, Tokyo, pp227–237

Shoemake K (1985) Animating rotation with quaternion curves. *Proc SIGGRAPH '85, Computer Graphics* 19(3):245–254

Shoup RG (1973) Some quantization effects in digitally generated pictures. *Proc Soc Information Display Intern. Symposium,* p58

Shoup RG (1979) Colour table animation. *Proc SIGGRAPH '79, Computer Graphics* 13(2):8–13

* Shoup RG (1979) SUPERPAINT: the digital animator. *Datamation,* May issue, pp150–156

* Siegel HB (1987) An overview of computer animation and modelling. *Proc Computer Animation CG 87, Online,* pp27–37

Sims K (1987) *Locomotion of jointed figures over complex terrains.* MS thesis, Massachusetts Institute of Technology Media Lab

Sims K, Zeltzer D (1988) A figure editor and gait controller for task level animation. In: Thalmann D (ed) *Synthetic actors: The impact of artificial intelligence and Robotics on Animation.* Course Notes SIGGRAPH '88, pp164–182

Sinden FW (1967) Synthetic cinematography. *Perspective* 7, 4:279–289

Smith AR (1978) *PAINT.* Technical Memo No 7, New York Institute of Technology

Smith AR (1979) Tint fill. *Proc SIGGRAPH '79, Computer Graphics* 13(2):276–283

Smith AR (1983) Digital filmmaking. *Abacus* 1(1):28–45

Smoliar SW, Tracton W (1978) A lexical analysis of labanotation with an associated data structure. *Proc ACM Annual Conf* 2:727–730

Smoliar SW, Weber L (1977) Using the computer for a semantic representation of labanotation. *Computing and the Humanities,* Univ. Waterloo Press, pp253–261

* Sorensen P (1981) Computer imaging—an apple for the dreamsmiths. *Cinefex* 6, October issue

* Sorensen P (1982) Tronic imagery. *Cinefex* 8, April issue

* Sorensen P (1983) Movies, computers and the future. *American Cinematographer,* January issue

Spencer-Smith T, Wyvill G (1989) Four-dimensional splines for motion control in computer animation. In: Magnenat-Thalmann N, Thalmann D (eds) *State-if-the-art in computer animation.* Springer, Tokyo, pp153–168

* Spina L (1982) Paint-by-pixels: computer power comes to TV artists. *Millimeter Magazine* 10(2)

Steketee SN, Badler NI (1985) Parametric keyframe interpolation incorporating kinetic adjustment and phrasing control. *Proc SIGGRAPH '85,* pp255–262

Stern G (1979) Softcel: an application of raster scan graphics to conventional cel animation. *Proc SIGGRAPH '79, Computer Graphics* 13(3):284–288

Stern G (1983a) Bbop: a system for 3D key frame figure animation. *SIGGRAPH '83 Tutorial,* pp240–243

Stern G (1983b) Bbop—A program for 3-dimensional animation. Proc Nicograph '83, pp403–404

* Stevenson R (1973) *The animated film.* AS Barnes, New York

Stösser A, Schmitt A, Neidecker B, Müller H, Maus T, Leister W (1988) Occursus cum novo—tools for efficient photo-realistic animation. *Proc EUROGRAPHICS '88,* North Holland, pp31–42

* Sturman D (1984) Interactive keyframe animation of 3-D articulated models. *Proc Graphics Interface '84,* pp35–40

* Sturman D (1986) A discussion on the development of motion control systems. In: SIG-

GRAPH course on computer animation: 3D motion specification and control

* Styne BA (1990) Command history in a reversible painting system. In: Magnenat-Thalmann N, Thalmann D (eds) *Computer Animation '90.* Springer, Tokyo, pp149–164

Sugimoto K, Duffy J (1981) Determination of extreme distances of a robot hand. *J Mech Design* 103

* Susman G (1989) The making of pencil test. In: Magnenat-Thalmann N, Thalmann D (eds) *State-of-the-art in computer animation.* Springer, Tokyo, pp203–214

Sutherland I (1963) *SKETCHPAD: a man-machine graphical communication system.* Ph.D. thesis, Massachusetts Institute of Technology

Sutherland IE, Sproull RF, Schumacker RA (1974) A characterization of ten hidden-surface algorithms. *Computing Surveys* 6(1):1–55

Szabo NS (1978) Digital image anomalies: static and dynamic. *Proc Symposium Society of Photo-Optical Instrumentation Engineers,* vol 162: Visual simulation and realism, pp11–15

* Takashima Y, Shimazu H, Tomono M (1987) Story driven animation. *Proc Computer Human Interface and Graphics Interface '87*

Talbot PA, Carr III JW, Coulter RC Jr, Hwang RC (1971) Animator: an on-line two-dimensional film animation system. *Communications of the ACM* 14(4):251–259

* Taylor R (1983) Designing for the feature film. *Tutorial notes on the Artist/Designer and Computer Graphics, SIGGRAPH '83,* pp31

Taylor RH (1976) The synthesis of manipulator control programs from task-level specifications. Artificial Intelligence Laboratory, Stanford University, AIM-282

Terzopoulos D, Fleischer K (1988a) Deformable models. *The Visual Computer* 4(6):306–331

Terzopoulos D, Fleischer K (1988b) Modeling inelastic deformation: viscoelasticity, plasticity, fracture. *Proc SIGGRAPH '88, Computer Graphics* 22(4):269–278

Terzopoulos D, Platt J, Barr A, Fleischer K (1987) Elastically deformable models. *Proc SIGGRAPH '87, Computer Graphics* 21(4):205–214

Thalmann D (1989) Motion control: from keyframe to task-level animation. In: *State-of-the-art in computer animation.* Springer, Tokyo, pp3–17

Thalmann D, Magnenat-Thalmann N (1979) Design and implementation of abstract graphical data types. *Proc 3rd Intern Computer Software and Applications Conf (COMPSAC '79),* Chicago, IEEE Press, pp519–524

Thalmann D, Magnenat-Thalmann N (1983) Actor and camera data types in computer animation. *Proc Graphics Interface '83,* pp203–210

Thalmann D, Magnenat-Thalmann N (1986) Artificial intelligence in three-dimensional computer animation. *Comput Graphics Forum* 5(4):341–348

Thalmann D, Magnenat-Thalmann N, Bergeron P (1982) *Dream Flight:* a fictional film produced by 3D computer animation. *Proc Computer Graphics '82,* Online Conf, pp353–368

Thalmann D, Ratib O, Magnenat-Thalmann N, Righetti A (1985) A model for the three-dimensional reconstruction and animation of the heart. *The Visual Computer* 1(4):241–248

* Thornton R (1983) Computer assisted animation at NYIT. *Proc Computer Graphics '83,* Online Conf, pp277–282

Torrance KE, Sparrow EM (1967), Theory for off-specular reflection from roughened surfaces. *J Opt Soc Am* 57(9):1105–1114

* Tost D, Brunet P (1990) A definition of frame-to-frame coherence. In: Magnenat-Thalmann N, Thalmann D (eds) *Computer Animation '90.* Springer, Tokyo, pp207–225

Tost D, Pueyo X (1988) Human body animation: a survey. *The Visual Computer* 3(5):254–264

Turkowski K (1982) Anti-aliasing through the use of coordinate transformations. *ACM Trans Graphics* 1(3):215–234

Turner R, Gobbetti E, Balaguer F, Mangili A, Thalmann D, Magnenat-Thalmann N (1990) An object-oriented methodology using dynamic variables for animation and scientific visualization. *Proc. Computer Graphics International '90.* Springer, Tokyo

Van Baerle S (1986) Character animation: combining computer graphics and traditional animation. In: SIGGRAPH course on computer animation: 3D motion specification and control

Verbeck CP, Greenberg DP (1984) A comprehensive light-source description for computer graphics. *IEEE Comput Graphics Applications* 4(7):66–75

Walker RJ (1950) *Algebraic curves.* Springer, Berlin Heidelberg New York (Reprint 1980)

* Wallace BA (1981) Merging and transformation of raster images for cartoon animation. *Proc SIGGRAPH '81, Computer Graphics* 15(3):253–262

Warn DR (1983) Lighting controls for synthetic images. *Proc SIGGRAPH '83, Computer Graphics* 17(3):13–21

Warnock J (1969) *A hidden-surface algorithm for computer-generated half-tone pictures.* Univ. Utah Computer Sci Dept, TR4-15, NTIS AD-753 671

* Waters K (1986) Expressive three-dimensional faces. *Proc Computer Graphics '86,* Online

Waters K (1987a) A muscle model for animating three-dimensional facial expression. *Proc SIGGRAPH '87,* 21(4):17–24

Waters K (1987b) Animating human heads. *Proc Comput Animation CG 87,* Online, pp89–97

Waters K (1989) Towards autonomous control for three-dimensional facial animation. In: Landsdown J, Earnshaw E (eds) *Computers in art, design and animation.* Springer, New York, pp253–263

Watkins GS (1970) *A real-time visible surface algorithm.* Univ. Utah Computer Sci Dept, UTEC-CSc-70-101, NTIS AD-762004

* Weber J, Fluekiger P, Field MJ (1990) Computer-animated chemical models. In: Magnenat-Thalmann N, Thalmann D (eds) *Computer Animation '90.* Springer, Tokyo, pp21–29

Weber L, Smoliar SW, Badler NI (1978) An architecture for the simulation of human movement. *Proc ACM National Conference,* pp737–745

Weiler K, Atherton P (1977) Hidden surface removal using polygon area sorting. *Proc SIGGRAPH '77, Computer Graphics* 11(2):214–222

* Wein M, Burtnyk N (1972) A computer facility for film animation and music. *Proc CIPS '72,* pp212, 201–212, 205

* Wein M, Burtnyk N (1976) Computer animation. In: *Encyclopedia of computer science and technology,* vol 5, Marcel Dekker, pp397–436

* Weinberg R, Sorensen V (1988) Computer animation for the OMNIMAX film seasons. *Proc Pixim '88,* pp307–311

* Weiner DD, Anderson SE (1968) A computer animation movie language for educational motion pictures. *Proc FJCC,* pp1318

* Weinstock N (1983) New technologies for the realization of ideas. *Millimeter,* February issue, pp71–76

* Wesley Bethel E, Uselton SP (1989) Shape distortion in computer-assisted keyframe animation. In: Magnenat-Thalmann N, Thalmann D (eds) *State-of-the-art in computer animation.* Springer, Tokyo, pp215–224

* Whitney JH (1971) A computer art for the video picture wall. *Proc IFIP Congress 1971,* North-Holland, Amsterdam, pp1382–1386

* Whitney J (1980) *Digital harmony.* Byte Books, McGraw-Hill, Peterborough, NH, USA

Whitted T (1980) An improved illumination model for shaded display. *Communications of the ACM* 23(6):343–349

Whitted T (1983) Anti-aliased line drawing using brush extrusion. *Proc SIGGRAPH '83, Computer Graphics* 17(3):151–156

Wilhelms J (1986) Virya—a motion control editor for kinematic and dynamic animation. *Proc Graphics Interface '86,* pp141–146

Wilhelms J (1987a) Towards automatic motion control. *IEEE Comput Graphics Applications* 7(4):11–22

Wilhelms J (1987b) Using dynamic analysis for realistic animation of articulated bodies. *IEEE Comput Graphics Applications* 7(6):12–27

Wilhelms J (1989) Dynamic experiences. Proc Mechanics, Control and Animation of Articulated Figures. Massachusetts Institute of Technology (to be published in a book, Morgan Kaufmann, USA)

Wilhelms J (1990) Behavioral animation using an interactive network. In: Magnenat-Thalmann N, Thalmann D (eds) *Computer Animation '90.* Springer, Tokyo, pp95–106

Wilhelms J, Barsky B (1985) Using dynamic analysis to animate articulated bodies such as humans and robots. In: Magnenat-Thalmann N, Thalmann D (eds) *Computer-generated images.* Springer, pp209–229

Wilhelms J, Moore M, Skinner R (1988) Dynamic animation: interaction and control. *The Visual Computer* 4(6):283–295

*Williams L (1978) Casting curved shadows on curved surfaces. *Proc SIGGRAPH '78, Computer Graphics* 12(3):270–274

*Williams L (1983) Overview of 3D animation. *Tutorial Notes on Computer Animation SIGGRAPH '83*, pp212–219

* Willmert KD (1978) Graphic display of human motion. *Proc ACM '78 Conf*, pp715–719

Wirth N (1983) *Programming in MODULA-2*, 2nd edn. Springer, Berlin Heidelberg New York Tokyo

Withrow C (1970) *A dynamic model for computer-aided choreography.* Computer Science Department, University of Utah, No 70–103

Witkin A, Kass M (1988) Spacetime constraints. *Proc SIGGRAPH '88, Computer Graphics* 22(4):159–168

Witkin A, Fleischer K, Barr A (1987) Energy constraints on parameterized models. *Proc SIGGRAPH '87, Computer Graphics* 21(4):225–232

Wyvill B, Wyvill G (1989) Using soft objects in computer-generated character animation. In: Landsdown J, Earnshaw E (eds) *Computers in art, design and animation.* Springer, New York, pp283–297

Wyvill B, McPheeters C, Novacek M (1985) High level descriptions for 3D stochastic models. In:Magnenat-Thalmann N, Thalmann D (eds) *Computer-generated images.* Springer, To-kyo, pp26–34

Wyvill B, McPheeters C, Wyvill G (1986) Animating soft objects. *The Visual Computer* 4(6):235–242

Wyvill B, Chmilar M, Herr C (1988) A simple model of human animation. In: Thalmann D (ed) *Synthetic actors: the impact of artificial intelligence and robotics on animation.* Course Notes SIGGRAPH '88, pp164–182, pp99–110

Yaeger L, Upson C, Myers R (1986) Combining physical and visual simulation—creation of the planet Jupiter for the film "2010." *Proc SIGGRAPH '86, Computer Graphics* 20(4):85–94

Yau JFS, Duff ND (1988) 3D Facial animation using image samples. In: Magnenat-Thal-mann N, Thalmann D (eds) *New trends in computer graphics.* Springer, Heidelberg, pp64–73

* Zajac EE (1965) Computer animation: a new scientific and educational tool. *J SMPTE* 74:1006–1008

Zajac EE (1966) Film animation by computer. *New Scientist* 29:346–349

Zeltzer D (1982a) Motor control techniques for figure animation. *IEEE Computer Graphics and Applications* 2(9):53–59

* Zeltzer D (1982b) Representation of complex animated figures. *Proc Graphics Interface '82*, pp205–211

* Zeltzer D (1983) Knowledge-based animation. *Proc SIGGRAPH/SIGART Workshop on Motion*, pp187–192

Zeltzer D (1985) Towards an integrated view of 3D computer animation. *The Visual Computer* 1(4):249–259 (also in: Magnenat-Thalmann N, Thalmann D (eds) *Computer-generated images.* Springer, Tokyo, pp230–248)

Zeltzer D (1987) Motor problem solving for three-dimensional computer animation. *Proc L'Imaginaire Numérique*

Zeltzer D (1989) Direct manipulation of virtual worlds. Proc Mechanics, Control and Animation of Articulated Figures. Massachusetts Institute of Technology (to be published in a book, Morgan Kaufmann, USA)

* Zeltzer D, Csuri C (1981) Goal-directed movement simulation. *Proc Canadian Man-Compu-ter Communications Society '81*, pp271–280

* Zeltzer D, Pieper S, Sturman D (1989) An integrated graphical simulation platform. *Proc Graphics Interface '89*

* Zimmerlin R, Stanley J, Stone W (1978) A sensor simulation and animation system. *Proc SIGGRAPH '78, Computer Graphics* 12(3):105–110

Appendix: Computer-generated Films

1961
TWO-GYRO GRAVITY-GRADIENT ATTITUDE CONTROL SYSTEM—
E.E. Zajak, 4 min

1962
*AND-HANDS—*S. Van Der Beek, Univ. Texas, 2 min

1964
*A COMPUTER TECHNIQUE FOR THE PRODUCTION OF ANIMATED MOVIES—*K. Knowlton, Bell Labs, 17 min
*POEMFIELD—*S. Van Der Beek, K, Knowlton, Bell Labs, 5 min

1966
*L6: BELL TELEPHONE LABORATORIES LOW-LEVEL LINKED LIST LANGUAGE—*K. Knowlton, Bell Labs, 16 min
*AN EXAMPLE OF L6 PROGRAMMING—*K. Knowlton, Bell Labs, 32 min
*FORCE, MASS AND MOTION—*F.W. Sinden, 10 min
*SST COCKPIT VISIBILITY SIMULATION—*W. Fetter, 8 min
*LAPIS—*J. Whitney, L.A. Studio, 10 min

1967
*MAN AND HIS WORLD—*S. Van Der Beek and K. Knowlton, 1 min
DYNAMIC FIELD DISTRIBUTIONS IN GUNN-EFFECT DEVICES—
D.E. McCumber, 12 min
*STUDIES WITH RANDOM TEXTURE—*B. Julesz and C. Bosche, 4 min

1968
*POEMFIELD 2—*S. Van Der Beek and K. Knowlton, 8 min
*EXPERIMENTS IN MOTION GRAPHICS—*J. Whitney and J. Citron, 12 min
*PER-MU-TA-TIONS—*J. Whitney and J. Citron, 7 min
*4-DIMENSIONAL HYPERCUBE—*A.M. Noll, 3 min
*4-D HYPERMOVIE—*A.M. Noll, 5 min
*COMPUTER-GENERATED BALLET—*A.M. Noll, 3 min
*SIMULATED BASILAR MEMBRANE MOTION—*R.C. Lummis and
A.M. Noll, 5 min

A PAIR OF PARADOXES—R.N. Shepard and E.E. Zajak, 2 min
BINARY BIT PATTERNS—M. Whitney and J. Whitney, 3 min
MEASURE FOR MEASURE—NYIT, 14 min

1969

TRANSFORMS—S. Van Der Beek and R. Baecker, 4 min
SORCERER'S APPRENTICE—W. Fetter, 4 min
THE SECOND MAN—W. Fetter, 10 min
GENESYS—R. Baecker, E. Martin and L. Smith, MIT, 25 min
STRUCTURE OF PROTEINS—J. de Rosnay, D. Barry, 9 min
DYNAMICS SYMBOLS—W. Huggins and P. Beck, 3 min

1970

UFO'S—K. Knowlton and L. Schwartz, Bell Labs, 3 min
PIXILLATION—K. Knowlton and L. Schwartz, Bell Labs, 4 min
A RELATIVISTIC RIDE—J. Schwartz and E. Taylor, 4 min
REAL TIME—Ohio State University, 10 min
INTEGRATION OVER A SOLID OF REVOLUTION—S. Anderson
THE GAME OF CHESS—S. Anderson, 10 min
MATRIX—J. Whitney and J. Citron, 6 min

1971

ART FROM COMPUTERS—L. Mezei, 8 min
MATRIX II—J. Whitney and J. Citron, 6 min
PATCHWORK 71—K. Wilson, 30 min
CAESAR—Computer Image Corp.,
METADATA—P. Foldes, National Film Board Canada, 9 min
NRC SAMPLER—National Research Council Canada, 9 min
SPACE SHUTTLE FLIGHT SIMULATION—LBJ Space Center, 6 min
OLYMPIAD—K. Knowlton and L. Schwartz, Bell Labs, 3 min

1972

ABSTRACTIONS ON A BEDSHEET—B. Etra, 7 min
VIEW OF THE ROAD—W. Fetter, 10 min
SPACE FILLING CURVES—N. Max, 25 min
1984—General Electric, 25 min
MATRIX III—J. Whitney and J. Citron, 7 min
AFFINITIES—L. Schwartz and K. Knowlton, 4 min
ENIGM—L. Schwartz and K. Knowlton, 4 min
GOOGOLPLEX—L. Schwartz and K. Knowlton, 5 min
APOTHEOSIS—L. Schwartz and K. Knowlton, 4 min
MUTATIONS—L. Schwartz and K. Knowlton, 7 min
I HAD AN IDEA—G. Demos, 10 min
PHOSPHENES—F. Foster and R. Speer, 5 min
MORNING ELEVATOR—A. Layzer and J. Miller, 4 min
MAN-COMPUTER SYNERGISTICS—J.B. Schneider et al., 23 min
CGI FOR REAL-TIME VISUAL SIMULATION—General Electric, 11 min

GRASS—T. DeFanti, Ohio State University, 10 min
ROBOTICS—R. MacGhee, Ohio State University, 7 min
HAND–FACE—E. Catmull, Univ. Utah, 5 min
FLEXIPEDE—T. Pritchett, Atlas Lab., 1 min

1973
JEKYLLUM—J. Baudot and C. Schneegans, Univ. Montreal, 4 min
IKE'S WOMEN-TINA—J. Biehl and J. Aken, 3 min
SONG OF URANUS—B. George and R. Siegel, 4 min
COYOTE AND SKUNK—Computer Image Corp., 7 min
ALGOL THE DEMON STAR—M.L. Meeks and S. Martin, 7 min
SIRIUS AND THE WHITE DWART—M.L. Meeks and S. Martin, 8 min
THE MOTION OF STARS—M.L. Meeks and S. Martin, 8 min
PAPILLONS—L. Schwartz and K. Knowlton, 4 min
INNOCENCE—L. Schwartz and K. Knowlton, 2 min
THE GAME OF LIFE—S. Anderson, 12 min
REGULAR HOMOTOPICS IN THE PLANE—N. Max, 29 min
HARMONIC PHASORS II—W. Huggins, 17 min
LIMITED VISIBILITY LANDINGS—General Electric, 4 min
METAMORPHOSIS—K. Knowlton and L. Schwartz, 10 min

1974
FIRST FIG—L. Cuba and G. Imhoff, 6 min
HUNGER—P. Foldes, National Film Board Canada, 12 min
THE TAINTED SKY—K. Wilson, 8 min
RON HAYS MUSIC-IMAGE PRESENTATION—R. Hays, 50 min
SHAPES—G. Demos, 7 min
ABC—C. Playfair et al., 2 min
PLANETARY MOTION AND KEPLER'S LAWS—M.L. Meeks and S.
  Martin, 9 min
STAR CLUSTERS—M.L. Meeks and S. Martin, 7 min
TALKING FACE—F.I. Parke, Univ. Utah, 5 min
ANIMATION COURSE FILM—University of Utah, 15 min

1975
THREE VIEWS OF WATER—D. Sandin, 6 min
THE ANTICS SHOWREEL—A. Kitching and C. Emmett, 5 min
MS MUFFETT—L. Katz, B. Etra and L. Etra, 3 min

1976
THE PRISM SHOWREEL—Imperial College, 4 min
NCC-GRASS POOP TAPE—D. Sandin, T. DeFanti and P. Morton, 15 min
NYIT SAMPLES—NYIT, 10 min
YIN HSIEN—M. Whitney, L.A. Studio, 9 min
TURNING A SPHERE INSIDE OUT—N. Max, 23 min
WIPEPOEM—P. Scala, Syracuse Univ., 6 min
SCOPE II—P. Scala, Syracuse Univ., 5 min

1977

*CELL DIVISION IN THE CARTILAGE PLATE DURING BONE
   GROWTH*—N. Kembler, Univ. London, 7 min
THE INTERACTION OF D + + HD—K. Birkinshaw, Univ. London, 7 min
THE STAR WARS COMPUTER ANIMATION—L. Cuba, Univ. Illinois, 10
   min
ANIMA II—Ohio State Univ., 20 min
VISULINK—Advanced Products Operations, 4 min
NEW DEVELOPMENTS IN DAY-NIGHT CGI—Evans and Sutherland, 7 min
FINITE ELEMENTS—A. Kitching and C. Emmett, Atlas lab, 10 min
TAYLOR POLYNOMIALS—J. Gilbert and J. Richmond, BBC, 3 min

1978

SPACE SHUTTLE FLIGHT SIMULATION—R. Weinberg and J. Smith, LBJ
   Space Center, 7 min
LIMIT SURFACES AND SPACE FILLING CURVES—N. Max, Topology
   Films Project, 10 min
CHEMICAL CONFORMATION—T. Pritchett, P. Chandler and B. Whatley,
   Atlas Lab, 3 min
DRIVING THROUGH A JUNCTION—G. Lupton, CAD Centre, 1 min
WIRE TREES WITH 4 VECTORS—Univ. Illinois, 4 min
REFERENCE CARRIER—P. Morton, Univ. Illinois, 2 min
LOOP CYCLE—P. Morton and J. Veeder, Univ. Illinois, 2 min
DATA BURSTS: THIRD MOVE +—Univ. Illinois, 3 min
SPIRAL 3—T. DeFanti et al., Univ. Illinois, 10 min
CRYSTAL GROWTH—K. Knowlton, G. Gilmer and M. Shugard, Bell Labs,
   10 min

1979

EUCLIDEAN ILLUSIONS—S. Van Der Beek and R. Weinberg, NASA, 11 min
VOYAGER 1 ENCOUNTERS JUPITER—J. Blinn and C.E. Kohlhase, 3 min
VOYAGER 2 ENCOUNTERS JUPITER—J. Blinn and C.E. Kohlhase, 6 min
PIONEER 11 SATURN ENCOUNTER—J. Blinn et al., 2 min
THEMES TV TITLE SEQUENCE—T. Pritchett, Atlas Lab, 1 min
THE ALIEN—J. Lansdown, Systems Simulation, 2 min
THE STRUCTURE AND FUNCTION OF HAEMOGLOBIN—D. Clarke,
   Univ. London, 5 min
VAPOR TRAILS—S. Pettigrew, 5 min
CASE WESTERN SAMPLER—F.I. Parke, Case Western Univ., 5 min
BAOBAB—K. Knowlton and E. Ghent, 20 min
VISUAL LEARNING—T. Linehan and C. Csuri, Ohio State Univ., 8 min
SUNSTONE—E. Emshwiller, NYIT, 3 min
TOPES—Bell Labs
NEWSHOLE—University of Toronto
VIDEOCEL—Computer Creations Inc.

1980

INFORMATION INTERNATIONAL DEMO REEL—Information
International Inc.
DNA WITH ETHIDIUM—N. Max, Lawrence Livermore Lab
THE COMPLEAT ANGLER—T. Whitted, Bell Labs
PEAK—N. Snitly

1981

DOXORUBICIN-DNA—N. Max, Lawrence Livermore Lab
DIGITAL EFFECTS DEMO REEL—Digital Effects Inc.
MAGI–SYNTHAVISION DEMO REEL—MAGI Inc.
SPATIAL DATA MANAGEMENT SYSTEM—C. Herot et al.
PANTOMATION—T. DeWitt et al.
ARTIFACTS—The Vasulkas
CTS FLIGHT SIMULATOR—Evans and Sutherland
TIME RIDER—JVC Japan
IMAGINATION—Acme Cartoon Company Inc.
VIDSIZER—D. Franzblau
ZGRASS PAINT DEMO—C. Giloth, Real Time Design Inc.
ABEL DEMO REEL—W. Kovacs et al., Robert Abel and associates
*OHIO STATE COMPUTER GRAPHICS RESEARCH GROUP TERRAIN
MODEL*—C. Csuri et al., Ohio State University
COMPUTER-ASSISTED DANCE NOTATION—T. Calvert et al., Simon
Fraser University
THE GRIP-75 MAN-MACHINE INTERFACE—Computer Science
Department, University of North Carolina
ARABESQUE—J. Whitney, UCLA, 5 min
ABEL SAMPLER—Robert Abel and associates, 5 min
SUBWAY—Digital Effects, 4 min
SORTING OUT SORTING—R. Baecker and D. Sherman, University of
Toronto, 30 min

1982

EVANS AND SUTHERLAND DEMO '82—Evans and Sutherland
CARLA'S ISLAND—N. Max, Lawrence Livermore Lab
ZGRASS DEMO—Real Time Design Inc.
ABEL '82 DEMO—Robert Abel and Associates
GALILEO—J. Blinn et al., Jet Propulsion Lab., NASA
DISSPLA ANIMATION—ISSCO
TRIPLE-I DIGITAL SCENE SIMULATION REEL—Information
International Inc.
ACME CARTOON COMPANY SAMPLES '82—ACME Company
CLOCK—R. Balabuck, 1 min
TRON (partial)—Walt Disney Productions, Animation by Robert Abel and
Associates, Digital Effects, Information International Inc., MAGI–Synthavision

STAR TREK II (partial)—Paramount Pictures Animation by Lucasfilm Ltd
DIGITAL EFFECTS '82 DEMO REEL—Digital Effects, 7 min
FOUR SEASONS OF JAPAN—M. Yoshinari, NHK, 5 min
EXPO'85—M. Yoshinari, NHK, 30 sec
CUCUMBER STUDIOS DEMO REEL—Cucumber studios
T-POT AND FACES—S. Colson
DIGITAL PICTURES DEMO REEL—Digital Pictures
VIDEO GRAPHICS DEMO—Molinaire
IMATIQUE SHOWREEL—Image West
NOVA OPENING—D. Geschwind, NYIT
ILLUSION 2—C. Stanbury
MAGI-SYNTHAVISION SHOWREEL—MAGI-Synthavision
DILEMNA—J. Halas
SYMMETRY TEST 11A—P.A. Newell, 4 min
GRUNMAN NON-EDGE CIG—Grunman Aerospace, 4 min
HUMANONON—M. Francois, 4 min
VOL LIBRE—L. Carpenter, Lucasfilm, 2 min
DREAM FLIGHT—P. Bergeron, N. Magnenat-Thalmann and D. Thalmann
    Hautes Etudes Commerciales et Université de Montréal, 13 min
THE CUBE CUBE—M. Gerhard, Lawrence Livermore Lab, 2 min
SPACE OPERATIONS SIMULATOR—P. Galicki, 8 min
DANCING IMAGES—A.R. Marion, Atari Research, 18 min

1983
GROWTH MYSTERIOUS GALAXY—Osaka University, 5 min
COMPUTER CREATION DEMO TAPE—Computer Creation Inc., 8 min
NIPPON UNIVAC KAISHA DEMO REEL—Nippon Univac Kaisha Ltd., 3
    min
UNIVERSITY OF NORTH CAROLINA 1983 SAMPLER—University of
    North Carolina, 5 min
INTERIOR LIGHT AND SHADOW—Hiroshima University, 5 min
JULIA—H.O. Peitgen, 1 min
RETURN OF THE JEDI (partial)—Lucasfilm Ltd, 6 min
ACT III—VCA Teletronics, 6 min
CRANSTON-CSURI PRODUCTIONS DEMO REEL—Cranston-Csuri
    Productions Inc., 8 min
COMPOSITE NEWS—N. Burson, 8 min
LASER PRESENTATION—S. Heminover, 7 min
MOVIE MAKER DEMO TAPE—Interactive Picture Systems, 4 min
CALYPSO CAMEO—V. Sorenson and T. DeWitt, 2 min
PACIFIC DATA IMAGES DEMO REEL—Pacific Data Images Inc., 4 min
INERTIAL CONFINEMENT FUSION—N. Max, Lawrence Livermore Lab., 3 min
RAY TRACINGS—Raster Technologies, 1 min
ABEL AND ASSOCIATES RECENT WORK—Robert Abel and associates, 6 min
SNOW WHITE AND THE SEVEN PIXELS—D. Em, 2 min
NYIT CGL SAMPLER—New York Institute of Technology, 11 min
BLINN DEMO—J. Blinn, 4 min

TRANSLATION—R. Moran, Graphic Communications, 3 min
MANDALA 1983—Seibu Promotional Network, 2 min
SUZUKI GR650 "TEMPER"—R. and B. Efx, 1 min
SUPERMAN III, LET THE GAMES BEGIN—Atari, 2 min
MARKS AND MARKS SAMPLE REEL—Marks and Marks, 2 min
ONLY EYES—M. Rawlings, 3 min
BO GEHRING DEMO TAPE—Bo Gehring associates, 8 min
OMNIBUS VIDEO DEMONSTRATION TAPE: HI LITES—Omnibus
  Computer Graphics, 1 min
NUKE THE DUKE—C. Kesler, 5 min
EXERCISES IN DIGITAL HARMONY—J. Whitney, UCLA, 7 min
BLOOMING STARS—E. Genda, Japan, 7 min
OUA OUA/DIGITAL DANCER—E. Tannenbaum, 7 min
OHIO STATE UNIVERSITY SAMPLE REEL—Ohio State University, 3 min
ORIGAMI—NHK, Japan, 5 min
SYSTEMS SIMULATION DEMO REEL—T. Pritchett and J. Lansdown,
  Systems Simulation Ltd., 3 min
PANOPTICA PREVIEWS '83—Vertigo Graphics, 20 sec
AURORA SYSTEMS DEMO 1983—Aurora Systems, 4 min
ECONOMARS EARTH TOURS—Lawrence Livermoore Lab., 7 min
VERTIGO GRAPHICS DEMO TAPE—Vertigo Graphics, 3 min
ANTI-FRICTION DRIVE—R. Abel and associates, 4 min
WHEN MANDRILLS RULED THE HEAVENS—Sandia National Lab., 2 min
DIGITAL EFFECTS DEMO REEL—Digital Effects Inc., 7 min
MOBILE IMAGE DEMO REEL—Mobile Image, 5 min
NADIA'S CRIME—J. Gurrin, 6 min
VIDCOLOR DEMONSTRATION—Mobile Image, HRS Industries and Hal
  Roach Studios, 3 min
MENULAY—B. Buxton et al., 10 min
TELIDON ANIMATION—E. Gordon, 5 min
TACTICAL EDGE—Evans and Sutherland, 10 min
NEVER BEFORE—Robert Abel and associates
COMPUTER GRAPHICS SHOWREEL—Ellis and Barton Productions
BMW TECHNOLOGY—Steiner Films, Germany
NORWICH UNION-FAMILY MAN—Lodge–Cheesman Productions, U.K.
SHARP-VOYAGE IN PERFECTION—Sogitec Audiovisual, France
CHANNEL 4-LOOK FORWARD—Electronic Art, U.K.
TVS-THE REAL WORK—Moving Picture Company, U.K.
SMITHS INDUSTRIES INDUSTRIAL TITLE SEQUENCE—Digital
  Productions
COLLECTION COMPOSITES—Pearce Studios, U.K.
JAPAN COMPUTER GRAPHICS LAB DEMO—Japan Computer Graphics
  Lab, 3 min
PIXEL PLAY—Nakajima, Japan
SPN—Seibu Production Network
BENESH NOTATION—Singh
SMALLTALK—Xerox Corp.

LISA—Apple Computers, 3 min
SHRIOGUMI DEMO—Shirogumi, Japan, 2 min

1984
ABEL AND ASSOCIATES DEMO—Robert Abel and associates, Holywood, 5 min
THE ADVENTURES OF ANDRE AND WALLY B.—Lucasfilm Ltd, 2 min
BEETHOVEN'S SIXTH IN CIG—G. Gardner, Grumman Aerospace Corp., 5 min
THE BICYCLE COMPANY—John Cavala, 1 min
BIO-SENSOR—Osaka University, 3 min
BROADWAY VIDEO 84 SPECIAL EFFECTS—Broadway video, 2 min
COMPOSITE NEWS (2nd edition)—Nancy Burson, 5 min
CRANSTON CSURI PRODUCTIONS DEMO REEL—Cranston Csuri Productions, 6 min
THE CUBE'S TRANSFORMATION—R. Resch, 5 min
DIGITAL EFFECTS: OUR FAVORITES—Digital Effects, 5 min
DIGITAL FANTASY—Visible Language Workshop, 1 min
DIGITAL PICTURES SHOW REEL—Digital Pictures Ltd, 3 min
DREAM HOUSE—S. Pryor, 3 min
EIDOS SHOW REEL—Eidos, 4 min
FIRST FLIGHT—MAGI Synthavision, 4 min
FLY LORENZ—H. Jurgens, 4 min
GRAPHICS AT GLOBO—TV GLOBO, 7 min
GROWTH II: MORPHOGENESIS—Y. Kawaguchi, 6 min
I, ROBOT—Atari Inc., 2 min
JCGL DEMO—Japan Computer Graphics Lab, 5 min
JOBLOVE–KAY SAMPLE REEL—Joblove–Kay Inc., 2 min
THE LAST STARFIGHTER (preview)—Digital Productions, 3 min
THE LAST SUPPER AT THE COMPUTER—Eidos, 1 min
LINK FLIGHT SIMULATION DEMO—The Singer Company, 2 min
MAGI DEMO REEL—MAGI synthavision, 6 min
LA MAISON VOLE—Institut National de l'Audiovisuel, 3 min
MARTIAN MAGNOLIA—J. Mareda, 2 min
THE MECHANICAL UNIVERSE—JPL Computer Graphics Lab., 7 min
MIRA '84 DEMO REEL—N. Magnenat-Thalmann and D. Thalmann, 5 min
MOVIE MAKER DEMO REEL—Interactive Picture Systems Inc., 1 min
NYIT COMPUTER GRAPHICS LAB.—New York Institute of Technology, 10 min
OHIO STATE UNIVERSITY DEMO REEL—Ohio State University, 8 min
OMNIBUS PRESENTATION—Omnibus Computer Graphics Inc., 3 min
PACIFIC DATA IMAGES DEMO—Pacific Data Images, 6 min
PORTAL—D. Ackerman, 5 min
PUZZLE—G. Lorig, 1 min
RAY TRACING—M. Sweeney, D. Forsey, 4 min
SEASONS—Videograf, 1 min
SKIN MATRIX £—E. Emshwiller, 7 min

SNOOT AND MUTTLY—Susan Van Baerle and Douglas Kingsbury, Ohio State University
SOUND INTO GRAPHICS—Univ. Illinois and Univ. Utah, 2 min
STAR RIDER—Computer Creations, 5 min
STILL LIFE—E. Nakamae, 5 min
THE SUDANESE MOEBIUS BAND—D. Asimov, 1 min
TANTRA '84—Ko Nakajaima, 4 min
TERMS OF ENTRAPMENT—Research Institute of Scripps Clinic, 2 min
TRASH—Susan Van Baerle and Douglas Kingsbury, Ohio State University
VERTIGO PRESENTATION—Vertigo Computer Imagery Inc., 3 min
VIDEO WALLPAPER I—VCA Teletronics, 3 min
VISUAL IMAGE PRESENTATION—Acme Graphics, 3 min
WAG THE FLAG—Southern Software, 5 min
WE ARE BORN OF STARS (preliminary version)—Toyo LINKS Corporation, 1 min
WHISPERS IN A PLANE OF LIGHT—Viper Optics, 10 min
WONDER WORKS—Omnibus Computer Graphics, 30 sec
9600 BAUDS—H. Huitric and M. Nahas, 5 min

1985
ALBERT—Synthetic Video, USA, 2 min
ANY FLO—Michel Bret, France, 5 min
BOOK FOUR TITLES—London Weekend Television, UK, 30 min
BOSCH FGS4000 DEMO TAPE—Robert Bosch, USA
CALCULATED MOVEMENTS—L. Cuba, USA
CFD WORKSTATION—NASA Ames, USA
COMPUTER COWBOY—Artronics Inc.
CRANSTON-CSURI 1985 DEMO REEL—Cranston-Csuri Productions, USA
DAY-DREAMS—Digital Effects, USA, 6 min
DEMO 85—Telegraph, France, 5 min
DEMO INA 85—INA, France, 2 min
DEMO TAPE—J.F. Colonna, France, 10 min
DIGITAL ART SHOW REEL—Digital Art, Belgium, 4 min
DIGITAL EFFECTS DEMO REEL—Digital Effects, USA
DIGITAL PRODUCTIONS DEMO REEL—Digital Productions, USA
ENSAD—P. Hénon, France, 4 min
EURYTHMY—Susan Amkraut and Michael Girard, Ohio State University, USA
FEAST OF LIGHTS—E. Nakamae, University of Hiroshima, Japan
FLOW FANTASIA '85—T. Sasaki, Japan
FRACTAL GENERATION,—Lathrop
GASTRONOMICA—Illegal Command, France, 7 min
GED—Science, Chute
GI 10000 REAL TIME VISUAL SYSTEM—Sogitec electronique, France, 1 min
GM SATURN ROBOTIC ASSEMBLY—Z-axis
GRASP LAB-VOXEL DEMO—University of Pennsylvania, USA
GROWTH III: ORIGIN—Yoichiro Kawaguchi, Japan

HAVE A KOCH—D. Kirk, Apollo Computers, USA

INTELLIGENT LIGHT 1985 DEMO REEL—Intelligent Light Inc., USA

INTERPOLATING SPLINES—Doris Kochanek, Canada

JCGL DEMO 85—Japan Computer Graphics Lab, 4 min

JEUX DE BILLES—INA, France, 25 min

LIMBO LAND—Reitzer

LUMINAR—Sanborn and Wrinkler

MAGI DEMO REEL '85—MAGI, USA

MIRA DEMO '85—N. Magnenat-Thalmann and D. Thalmann, MIRALab, Canada, 3 min

MIRROR WITH A MEMORY—J. Gardiner, MIT, USA, 7 min

MOLECULAR DYNAMICS—M. Lerner and N. Max, Lawrence Livermore Lab., USA

MR. YORICK SKULL—Liebman

MT FUJI—Nikatsu Video, Japan, 45 min

NURSERY SONG—Technofront, USA

OMNIBUS DEMO REEL 1985—OMNIBUS, Canada

PDI ASSORTMENTS—Pacific Data Images, USA

PIXELS AT AN EXHIBITION—Bacon

PRECISION BATHROOM—Weil and Helman

QUEST-A LONG RAY'S JOURNEY INTO LIGHT—M. Sciulli, Apollo Computer, 2 min 30s

RALPH THE PUNK—Athanas and Horn

ROBERT ABEL AND ASSOCIATES DEMO REEL—Robert Abel and Associates, USA

SIGGRAPH '85 ADVANCED COMPUTER ANIMATION COURSE NOTES—J. Rosebush and P. Bergeron, USA

SILICON GRAPHICS DEMO—Silicon Graphics Inc., USA

SOGITEC DEMO REEL '85—SOGITEC, France

T'AI CHI CHUAN—P. Karas, Digital Effects, USA, 3 min

TARA—G. Leitner, Columbia University, USA. 2 min

TELEPRESENCE TECHNOLOGY—Rappaport, USA

TERMS OF ENTRAPMENT—Olson, USA

THE LAST STARTFIGHTER EXCERPTS—Digital Productions, USA

THE MAKING OF BRILLIANCE—Robert Abel and Associates, USA

TONY DE PELTRIE—P. Lachapelle et al., University of Montreal, Canada, 5 min

TORI IN THE HAPERSPHERE—Margolis

TREES—California Institute of Technology, USA

TUBER'S TWO STEP—Chris Wedge, USA

UNC'85 INTERACTIVE GRAPHICS SAMPLER—University of North Carolina—USA

VIDEOPLACE SAMPLER—Krueger

1986

4K TAPE—Jane Veeder, USA

A VISITOR ON A FOGGY NIGHT—E. Nakamae, Hiroshima University, Japan

ABEL SIGGRAPH PRESENTATION REEL—Abel Image Research, USA
ACME DEMO REEL '86—Imagica Computer Graphics Center, USA
ANIMATION ASSORTMENT—New York Institute of Technology, USA
CALTECH 1986 DEMO REEL—Al Barr et al., California Institute of
  Technology, USA
COMPUTER GRAPHICS FOR YOUNG SHERLOCK HOLMES—Pixar,
  USA
CRANSTON-CSURI 1986 DEMO REEL—Cranston–Csuri Productions, USA
DEMO REEL SOGITEC 1986—Sogitec, France
DETAILS COUNT—General Electric Corporation, USA
DOGUMASTER—Tokyo Kogahuin College of Art, Japan
DYNAMICS OF $E^{i\theta} X(1 - X)$—A. Norton, IBM T.J. Watson Research Center,
  USA
ECOLOGY: OCEAN—Y. Kawaguchi, Nippon Electronics College, Japan
ELECTRIC IMAGE SHOWREEL '86—Electric Image Ltd, UK
FGS-4000 1986 DEMO TAPE—Robert Bosch Corporation, USA
HARD WOMAN—Digital Productions, USA
HOT AIR—J. Mareda, Sandia National laboratories, USA
HUMAN VECTORS—Dov Jacobson, USA
IMAGE NOUVEAU—Digital Productions, USA
INTERIORS—San Francisco Production Group, USA
JCGL DEMO REEL '86—Japan Computer Graphics Lab, Japan
KNOT REEL—Andrew Witkin, Schlumberger Palo Alto Research, USA
LENSES OVER ROLLING CHROME—Joe L. Clark Jr, Video Post & Transfer,
  USA
LIFE ON TITAN—Melvin L. Prueitt, Los Alamos National Laboratory, USA
LIGHT BEAMS—Nelson Max, Lawrence Livermore Lab, USA
LOXO Jr—Pixar, USA
METAFABLE—Ohio State University, USA
METAMORPHOSIS ANALYSIS & ILLUSIONS—Computer Animation Lab.,
  Germany
MOTION STUDIES—Michael Girard, Ohio State University, USA
NEW THREADS—Jerry Weill, AT&T Bell Labs, USA
OBELISK—Victor Company, Japan
OMNIBUS SIGGRAPH '86—J. Kleiser, Omnibus Computer Graphics, USA
PACIFIC DATA IMAGES 1986—Pacific Data Images, USA
PIXAR DEMO REEL—Pixar, USA
R-GREENBERG ASSOC. GROUP REEL—R–Greenberg Associates, USA
SERENITY—Omnibus Computer Graphics, Canada
SIMULATION EXCELLENCE—Evans and Sutherland Computer Corporation,
  USA
SOFT II—Brian and Geoff Wyvill, University of Calgary, Canada
SPEEDER—Art Center College of Design, Pasadena, USA
SUPER RESOLUTION—MIT Media Labs, USA
THE ARTIST AS PERFORMER—Marilyn Abers, The Media Staff, USA
THE BLUE CHAIR & GHOTTI—Anne Seidman, Ohio State University, USA
THE CARON'S WORLD—NHK Science and Technology, Japan
THE FANTASTIC ANIMATION MACHINE—The Fantastic Animation
  Machine, USA

THE MECHANICAL UNIVERSE...BEYOND—JPL Computer Graphics Lab., USA

TOYO LINKS DEMO REEL '86—Toyo Links Corporation, Japan

TWO-BIT PIXEL FULL COLOR ENCODING—Tom DeFanti, University of Illinois at Chicago, USA

VERTIGO DEMO REEL—Vertigo, Canada

VISION OBIOUS—Ruedy Leeman, Ohio State University, USA

WOOD TURNING—Terry Thrift, Imagenesis, USA

Z—Tanya Weinberger, Telesis Productions, USA

1987

1987 CORPORATE MONTAGE DEMO REEL—Animatrix Inc., USA, 2 min

AGUSTA, A-129 REAL-TIME SIMULATION—General Electric Company, USA, 4 min

BALLOON GUY—Chris Wedge, Ohio State University, USA, 1 min 40 s

BLACK TRINITRON—Steiner Film, Germany, 30 s

BLUEPRINT, ENGINE, RAPID PROTOTYPING—Robert Abel and Associates, USA, 1 min 40 s

BOOM BOOM BOOM—Visuals, AT&T Bell Labs, USA

BUD LIGHT VIDEO WARS—Optimus Inc., USA, 40 s

C.G. TOWN—Eihachiro Nakamae, Hiroshima University, Japan, 1 min 40 s

COMPUTER ANIMATIONS JAZZ UP THE ARABIC LANGUAGE—The Dovetail Group Inc., USA, 1 min 12 s

COMPUTER GRAPHICS AND ANIMATION GROUP—MIT Media Lab, USA, 1 min 30 s

DANCE OF THE STUMBLERS—Steve Segal, USA, 2 min 30 s

DEJA VU—4D Art and Design, USA, 2 min

DEMO REEL II, 1987—Synthetic Video, USA, 3 min

DYNAMIC SIMULATIONS OF FLEXIBLE OBJECTS—Ohio State University, USA, 1 min 30 s

ECOLOGY II: FLOAT—Yoichiro Kawaguchi, Nippon Electronics College, Japan, 4 min

EGLANTINE—Nadia Magnenat Thalmann and Daniel Thalmann, MIRALab, Canada, 3 min

FABRICATED RHYTHM—Jerry Weill, AT&T Bell Labs, USA, 1 min

FAIR PLAY—Michael Sciulli, Apollo Computer, USA, 3 min

FGS-4000 DEMO TAPE—Broadcast Television System, Inc., USA, 6 min 30 s

FINALE L.A.-THE MOVIE—Jet Propulsion Lab., USA

INSTABILITIES IN SUPERSONIC FLOWS—National Center for Supercomputer Applications, USA, 1 min

JCGL DEMO FOR SIGGRAPH '87—Japan Computer Graphics Lab., Japan, 3 min 30 s

JO, BEAUBOURG AND CIO—Thomson Digital Images, France, 1 min 40 s

LIFT OFF—NASA-Johnson Space Center, USA, 1 min 20 s

MENTAL IMAGES—Mental Images GmbH and Co, Germany, 2 min

MOLECULAR DYNAMICS OF SOLUTIONS—IBM Corporation, USA, 2 min

MUSIQUE NON-STOP—New York Institute of Technology, USA, 4 min
OILSPOT AND LIPSTICK—Walt Disney Pictures, USA, 2 min 30 s
PAINDORA'S CHAIN—Alan Barr, California Institute of Technology, USA,
  1 min 20 s
PDI PARTY MIX—Pacific Data Images, USA, 2 min 15 s
PEPPY—Toyo Links, Japan, 1 min 40 s
POLIOVIRUS—Research Institute of Scripps Clinic, USA, 1 min 20 s
PRUDENTIAL MOON ROCK, PRUDENTIAL CANYON ROCK—Digital
  Productions –Abel– Omnibus, USA, 1 min 10 s
RED'S DREAM—Pixar, USA, 3 min 45 s
RENDEZ-VOUS À MONTRÉAL—Nadia Magnenat Thalmann and Daniel
  Thalmann, MIRALab, Canada, 7 min
RIGID-BODY DYNAMICS SIMULATIONS—Ohio State University, USA,
  2 min 30 s
SIGGRAPH '87—Cranston-Csuri productions, USA, 3 min
SIGGRAPH '87 FILM AND VIDEO SHOW LOGO SEQUENCE—Ray
  Tracing Corporation and Motion Magic, USA
SIGGRAPH '87 OPENING SEQUENCE WITH BEN BOVA—Joan Collins
  and Associates, USA, 4 min
SIGN OF THE TIMES—MIX EFEX-Pacific Video, USA, 3 min
SOGITEC SHOW REEL—Sogitec, France, 5 min
SPACE STATION—Boeing Computer Services, USA, 1 min
STANLEY AND STELLA: BREAKING THE ICE—Craig Reynolds,
  Symbolics, USA, 3 min
SUN AND SHADE—Nelson Max, Lawrence Livermore National Lab., USA,
  40 s
SYNTEX OPENER LAZERUS—Joanne P. Culver, Berkeley, USA, 50 s
SYSTEME PARTICULIER—Studio Base 2, France, 1 min
TDI SCIENCE AND INDUSTRY—Thomson Digital Image, France, 4 min
TEST OF VOXEL-BASED GROWTH PROGRAM, SKIRT RESEARCH—
  New York Institute of Technology, USA, 1 min 30 s
*THE FANTASTIC ANIMATION MACHINE SIGGRAPH '87 SAMPLE
  REEL*—The Fantastic Animation Machine, USA, 2 min 30 s
THE QUANTUM MECHANICAL INVERSE—James Blinn, Jet Propulsion
  Laboratory, USA, 5 min 30 s
THEATRICAL MOTION PICTURE COMPUTER GRAPHICS—New York
  Institute of Technology, USA, 5 min 30 s
TOYO LINKS BROADCAST DEMO REEL 1987—Toyo Links Corporation,
  Japan, 2 min 50 s
TV-CF FOR KIRIN METS—Taiyo Kikaku Co., Japan, 1 min
VICTORY SAUSAGE—John Whitney Sr., USA, 2 min 40 s
XEROX CITY—Sirius Communications Company, USA, 1 min 30 s

1988

A CLOSE ENCOUNTER IN THE FOURTH DIMENSION—IBM T.J.
  Watson Research center, 2 min 46 s
ANIMATIC GENERIQUES—Animatica, Spain, 2 min 20 s

ARD FUSSBALLEUROPAMEISTERSCHAFT 88—Mental Images, Germany,
  21 s
AUTOMAPPE—Michel Bret, France, 4 min
THE ART DREAM—Center for Art and Animation, USA, 2 min 30 s
BEAT DEDICATION—Visible Language Workshop, MIT Media Lab, USA
BERLIN KULTURSTADTEUROPAS 88—Mental Images, Germany, 22 s
BMW Z1 "It seems to be a dream"—Steiner Films, Germany, 5 min
  16 s
BROKEN HEART—Joan Staveley, Ohio State University, USA, 2 min 31 s
BURNING LOVE—Pacific Data Images, USA
CORBEAU ET RENARD—Fantome, France, 1 min 50 s
COMMODORE AMIGA 500—Digital Pictures, UK, 50 s
COMPUPHOBIA OR TECHNOLOGICAL THREAT—Bill Kroyer, USA
COOTIE GETS SCARED—Computer Animation Group, MIT Media Lab,
  USA, 3 min 10 s
CT6 AUTOMOBILE—Evans and Sutherland, USA
DIGITAL PICTURES ADS—Digital Pictures, UK
DINOSAUR STUFF—Ohio State University, USA
ECLIPSE—ACCAD, Ohio State University, USA, 2 min
ELECTRIC IMAGE SHOWREEL '88—Electric Image Ltd, UK, 4 min
EMBRYO—Yoichiro Kawaguchi, Nippon Electronics College, Japan
FLYING LOGOS, INC.—Homer and Associates, USA, 2 min 12 s
FOOTSTEPS—Computer FX, UK
FORMATION OF VENUS PLASMA CLOUDS AND STREAMERS—
  National Center for Supercomputing Applications, USA
FUNCTION OF THE BRAIN CELLS—Atelier Bister Animation Art GmbH
GALAXY SWEETHEART—Nadia Magnenat Thalmann and Daniel Thalmann,
  MIRALab, Canada, 6 min
GALLIA—Art Synthèse, France, 2 min 20 s
GOING BANANAS—Alan Barr, California Institute of Technology, USA
GREAT TRAIN RUBBERY—Brian Wyvill, University of Calgary, Canada,
  3 min 24 s
HAIR—Jerry Weill, Optomystic, USA, 2 min 16 s
HUMAN HAIR IN THE BACKLIGHT—NTT Human Interface La, Japan,
  4 min 30 s
HYBRID VENUS—Pierre Friloux, USA, 3 min
JUMPIN' JACQUES SPLASH—Sogitec, France, 40 s
KEY CHANGE—Rod Bogart, University of Utah, USA
KRIPTO AND THE SUPREMES—Buffin Seydoux Computer Animation,
  France, 5 min
LA VIE DES BETES—Canal+, France, 3 min
LES ILES ONT UNE AME—Nadia Magnenat Thalmann and Daniel
  Thalmann, MIRALab, Canada, 45 s
LIEUX COMMUNS—Espace et Stratégie communication, France, 1 min 30 s
LINKS CORPORATION DEMO REEL FOR SIGGRAPH '88—Links
  Corporation, Japan
LOOKING IN—Craig Caldwell, USA, 1 min

MICKEY MOUTH—Harold Harris, Topix, Canada
NATURAL PHENOMENA—Gavin Miller, Alias Research, Canada
NCSA SCIENTIFIC VISUALIZATION 1988—National Center for
  Supercomputing Applications, USA, 4 min 15 s
NEWSNIGHT—BBC-Digital Pictures, UK, 16 s
OCCURSUS CUM NOVO—University of Karlsruhe, Germany, 5 min
OH ATSIMENU NAMELI—Leslie L. Wilson, USA
ON THE ROAD WITH DRIVING SIMULATION—Evans and Sutherland,
  USA, 1 min 16 s
ORGANIC ARCHITECTURE—Ned Greene, New York Institute of
  Technology, USA
PARTICLE DREAMS—Karl Sims, Whitney Demos Productions, USA, 6 min
PDI DEMO REEL—Pacific Data Images, USA, 7 min 48 s
PENCIL POLKA—Electric Picture Works, USA
PENCIL TEST—Galyn Susman, Apple Computer, 1 min 30 s
PIBOS—Tokyo Kogakuin College of Arts, Japan, 2 min 30 s
POLLY GONE—Shelley Lake, USA, 3 min
PYGMALION—Monique Nahas, Université Paris 7, France, 3 min
RADIO BREMEN—Mental Images, Germany, 1 min
SAMSUNG HUMAN TECH II—Rhythm and Hues, USA, 30 s
SCRUBBLING BUBBLES—Rueddy W. Leeman et al., USA
SEXTONE FOR PRESIDENT—Kleiser-Walczak Construction Co., USA, 30 s
SIO BENBOR—Fantome, France
SMARTIES 'BLUEPRINT'—Robinson Lambie-Nairn Ltd, UK
SOARON AND BLASTARR CHARACTER ANIMATION—ARCCA
  Animation Inc., Canada
SPACE STATION—Production Masters, Inc., USA, 2 min 10 s
SPACETIME CONSTRAINTS—Andrew Witkin, Schlumberger Palo Alto
  Research, USA
STYLO—Eurocitel, France
THE CONQUEST OF FORM—IBM UK Lab, UK, 6 min 30 s
THE SKY—Eihachiro Nakamae, Hiroshima University, 2 min 5 s
TIN TOY—Pixar, USA, 5 min 8 s
TREADMILL—Geoff Campbell, Canada, 1 min

1989
21ST AT 3RD BOOGIE WOOGIE—Christine Foltz, London, UK
A MOONLIT SPRING NIGHT AT MAMA TEMPLE—Naoko Motoyoski,
  Tokyo, Japan
A PUBLIC SERVICE ANNOUNCEMENT—University of Waterloo, Canada
A VIEW OF A ROOM—Ralph Gert, New York, USA
ALEA—MIT Media Lab, USA
ATTACK OF THE FLYING LOGOS—Gregory MacNicol, USA
AUSTRALIA POST—Zap Productions, Australia
BIRDBRAINSTORM—Peter Voci, New York Institute of Technology, USA
BREEZE—Xaos, USA
CASSINI AT SATURN—Thomas Casey, Productions Masters, USA

COLUMBUS ON THE EDGE—David Hatson, William Paterson College, USA
COMPLEXITY SIMPLE—Kajima Corporation, Japan
COMPOSITION IN RED, GREEN, BLUE—Edward Zajek, Syracuse
   University, USA
CONTINUUM 1. INITIATION—Post Perfect, New York, USA
CORE DUMP—John Fujii, Advanced Computing Center for the Arts and
   Design, USA
COUNTDOWN, SUNNICRUST OATS, TV8 STATION ID—John
   McCormack, Australia
CRACK FISH—Kevin B. Ray, Byte by Byte, USA
DEMO '89 ON SYNTHETIC ACTORS—N.Magnenat-Thalmann, University
   of Geneva, D. Thalmann, Swiss Federal Institute of Technology, Switzerland
DEMON REEL—Animatica, Spain
DIGITAL PICTURES ANIMATION—Julian Woodfield, Digital Pictures, UK
DIRTY POWER—Robert Lurye, Ohio State University, USA
DISPLACEMENT ANIMATION OF INTELLIGENT OBJECTS—Symbolics,
   USA
DON'T TOUCH ME—Kleiser-Walczac, USA
DYNAMIC SIMULATIONS—Paul Isaacs, New York Institute of Technology,
   USA
ECHOES OF THE SUN—Expo '90 Fujitsu Ltd, Japan
ESMERALDA—Jessica Kantor, Brooklyn, USA
EURHYTHMY—Susan Amkraut and Michael Girard, SCAN, The Netherlands
EVERYBODY HAS HIS GEM—Yuriko Amemiya, Tokyo, Japan
FAUX PAS—Softimage, Canada
FIRST CHOICE—Sonja Tessari, Canada
FIRST CONTACT—Robert Wolff, Apple Computer, USA
FISH—Jonathan Bock, Castaic, USA
FLORA—Yoichiro Kawaguchi, Nippon Electronic College, Japan
FOUNDRY—Mark Malmberg, XAOS, USA
FRANCE-1789—Ex Machina, France
FRONTS AND CENTERS—Thomas F. Banchoff, Brown University, USA
GAS TURBINE FLOWFIELD SIMULATION—NASA Ames Research Center,
   USA
GIBBON EVENT—Alan Ridenour, UCLA, USA
GRINNING EVIL DEATH—Bob Sabiston, MIT Media Lab., USA
GUNPLAY—Kevin B. Ray, Byte by Byte, USA
HARD TIME ON PLANET EARTH—ARCCA Animation, USA
HEMAN-THE POWER IS BACK—Chris Walker, USA
HER MAJESTY'S SECRET SERPENT—Gavin Miller, Apple Computer, USA
HONEY, I SHRUNK THE KIDS—Kroyer Films, USA
HUGHES SATELLITE SIMULATION—David Breen, Rensselaer Polytechnic
   Institute, USA
IMAGINA CLIP—CMP Gmbh and Co., Germany
IMAGINATION—Links Corporation, Japan
IN SEARCH OF NEW AXIS—Polygon Picture Inc., USA
IN TIME...IT HAPPENS—Jay Banchero, Bellevue, USA

INDUSTRIAL LIGHT AND MAGIC SIGGRAPH '89 REEL—Industrial Light and Magic, USA

INFORUM—Design–Effects, USA

KARKADOR—Peter Callas, Long Island, USA

KAWASAKI SAFETY INTELLIGENT PLAZA—Shinichi Kasahara, Kajima Corporation, Japan

KNICKKNACK—PIXAR, USA

L'ANNIVERSAIRE—National Film Board, Canada

LAMB AND COMPANY CHARACTER DEMO REEL—Lamb and Company, USA

LEELA—Chitra Shriram, Columbus, USA

LEONARDO'S DELUGE—Karl Sims, Optomystic, USA

LET IT RAIN—Leslie L. Wilson, Chico, USA

LINKS CORPORATION DEMO REEL—Shuji Asano, Links Corporation, Japan

LITTLE STORIES—Marilyn Wulff, Chicago, USA

LOCOMOTION—Pacific Data Images, USA

LORELEI—Thomas Casey, Productions Masters, USA

MACINSTEIN—Steve Eagle, USA

MARGAUX CARTOON—Electric Picture Works, USA

MARS-THE MOVIE—Jet Propulsion Laboratory, USA

MATHEMATICS!—James Blinn, Pasadena, USA

MCEWANS L.A. "LOW ALCOHOL"—David Botterell, Snapper Films, UK

MEDIEVAL GENOVA—E. Morten, Automa, Italy

MEGACYCLES—AT&T Bell Labs, USA

METROLIGHT STUDIOS SHOW REEL—Al DiNoble, USA

MULTIVISUALS 1989 DEMO REEL—Gregory Steven, Lowe, Australia

MUSIC FOR THE EYES—Marc Conahan, Camerawork, USA

NBC 1988 OLYMPIC GAMES—Filigree films Inc., USA

NEW EXPLORERS OPENING—Michael Cully, Post Effects, USA

NIGHT CAFÉ—Sharon Calahan, Cubicomp Canada Inc., Canada

NOVA CYGNY 1975—Space Telescope Science Institute, USA

NUMERICAL EXPERIMENTS ON THE INTERACTION OF DISK GALAXIES—NASA Ames Research Center, USA

ONCE A PAWN A FOGGY KNIGHT—David S. Ebert, Ohio State University, USA

ONE SPECIAL... COMING'RIGHT UP—Peter Oppenheimer, New York Institute of Technology, USA

PARFUMS DE VIE—Sogitec, France

PDI SELECTED CUTS—Pacific Data Images, USA

PEEDEE MEETS THE DRAGON—Jerry Weil, Optomystic, USA

PENCIL TEST—BEHIND THE SCENES—Ken Turkovsli, Apple Computer, USA

PEPSI PRESENTS: "WIRED"—David Botterell, Snapper Films, UK

PHILOMENE—Fantôme, France

PLASTIC LANDING—Fred Dech, Chicago, USA

PLUTO—Space Telescope Science Institute, USA

PREPARATION OF TF1 FEAST—Fantôme, France
PROVOCATIVE CHEESE AND SINGING BURGERS—Sonja Tessari, Canada
QWERTY—Anne van Ogtrop, Computer Image, USA
RADIO CHANNEL ID—Lorraine Nichols, Movietime Channel, USA
RANDOM HOUSE—Doug Johnson, Brooklyn, USA
RAYTRACING OF COMPUTED TOMOGRAMS—Cancer Research Center, Heidelberg, Germany
REDNOSE RABITT—Digital Art Production, Belgium
REVOLVE EVOLVE—ACCAD, USA
ROOTIN 'TOOTIN'—Computer FX, England
SCENES AT A STREET CORNER—Eichiro Nakamae, Hiroshima University, Japan
SCULLEY'S DREAM—David Smalley, Quaker Hill, USA
SDSC SCIENTIFIC VISUALIZATION—San Diego Supercomputer Center, USA
SEND IN THE CLOUDS—Geoffrey Y. Gardner, Grunman Data Systems, USA
SHOCKING DEFORMATIONS IN MICROSECONDS—G.W. Hannaway and Associates, USA
SIO BENBOR JUNIOR—Fantôme, France
SOAP OPERA—New York Institute of Technology, USA
SOFT LANDING—RGB Computer Graphics Service, Italy
SPACE STATION "FREEDOM"—Intelligent Light, USA
STUDY OF A NUMERICALLY MODELED SEVERE STORM—NCSA, USA
STUFF WE DID—Henry Seydoux, Paris, France
TEATIME IN OBJECT SPACE—G.W. Hannaway and Associates, USA
TEMPEST IN A TEAPOT—Tom Desmarais, Richland, USA
TEMPEST—Pete Liwinowicz, Apple Computer Inc., USA
THE HAMMER SEQUENCE—New York Institute of Technology, USA
THE LITTLE DEATH—Symbolics Inc., USA
THE MAKING OF WITHOUT BORDERS—Design–Effects, USA
THE SOUND OF ONE HAND CLAPPING—Ann Stroukoff, USA
THE UNIVERSE WITHIN—NHK, Japan
THE VIRTUAL LOBBY—John Rohlf, The University of North Carolina, USA
THROW IT IN THE HARBOUR—Computer Graphics Lab, Boston University, USA
TIPSY TURVY—IBM Research, Yorktown Heights, USA
TROUBLE IN THE BASEMENT—Doug Johnson, Brooklyn, USA
TRW ENGINEERING VISUALIZATION—TRW, USA
VEGETABLES—Lamb and Co, USA
VH1-TOPS-TV DINNER—Filigree Films, USA
VIDEOPERETTE—ExMachina, France
VIOMECHAWARS—High Tech Lab, Japan
VISUALIZATION OF SIMULATED TREATMENT OF AN OCULAR TUMOR—Wayne Little, Cornell University, USA

VOYAGER: JOURNEY TO THE OUTER PLANETS—Jet Propulsion Lab.,
  USA
WALDO C. GRAPHICS: BEHIND THE SCENES—Pacific Data Images,
  USA
WAX: OR THE INVENTION OF TELEVISION AMONG THE BEES—
  David Blair, New York, USA
ZIGGRAF—Jay Banchero, Bellevue, USA

Subject Index